ELEPHANT BOYS

DEDICATED TO AUNT ADA,
DOYENNE OF THE MCDONALD FAMILY.
SHE WAS AN ASTUTE BUSINESSWOMAN,
A STRONG PERSONALITY AND
A STOREHOUSE OF INFORMATION.

SANS MEMORY,
SANS HISTORY,
SANS ALL.

ELEPHANT BOYS

TALES OF LONDON AND
LOS ANGELES UNDERWORLDS

BOYS

BRIAN McDONALD

MAINSTREAM
PUBLISHING

EDINBURGH AND LONDON

Where appropriate some names have been changed. Efforts have been made to establish copyright holders; however, some were untraceable.

First published in Great Britain in 2000 by
MAINSTREAM PUBLISHING COMPANY (EDINBURGH) LTD
7 Albany Street
Edinburgh EH1 3UG

ISBN 1 84018 295 4

A catalogue record for this book is available from the British Library

Typeset in Stone and Neuland Black
Printed and bound in Great Britain by Creative Print and Design Wales

CONTENTS

INDEX OF MAPS AND TABLES

INTRODUCTION

Fascination with the underworld and its fringes is not new or uncommon. In olden times scribes recorded public rituals of sacrifice and murder; mighty kings and queens plotted and manoeuvred their adversaries into prison and the death chamber; heads were displayed on pikes or adorned fortress gates. In not so olden times crowds caroused at public executions, bellowing delight as some unfortunate wretch plummeted towards hell. In Indian Territory, which is now Oklahoma, Hanging Judge Parker's hangman, George Maledon, dropped as many as six in one go. Parker's court once presided over the execution of more than seventy offenders, as entranced spectators enjoyed a day's amusement.

In London, carts trundled to Tyburn Tree, carrying condemned prisoners with ropes around their necks ready for hoisting up on the scaffold. On their miserable ride they were pelted with food and stones by picnickers, right up to the point where the cart was drawn away. The drop was too short to break their necks, compelling them to gyrate in agony, some with relatives hanging on their legs to hasten the end – all to wildly cheering crowds of onlookers.

These same people read avidly of the tales of the James and Younger Brothers inventing bank robbery and looting trains, even though the banks they robbed had local people's money which could not be replaced by another branch of the bank as it would be today. Still they idolised these thieves and murderers. The romance of Butch Cassidy, the Sundance Kid and the mysterious Etta Place made a pleasurable movie. Britain's Dick Turpin has a popular image – the tricorn hat, the cloak draped around his upright manly figure as he sits tall in the saddle declaring 'Stand and deliver' – which is far removed from the murdering ruffian that he and the sullied heroes of the American West really were.

In America's depression-damaged 1930s the antics of Bonnie and Clyde, Pretty Boy Floyd and John Dillinger, as they defied the authorities, provided headline stories. Newspapers and radio programmes provided gangsters with a romantic camouflage by creating colourful nicknames . . . Scarface, Pretty Boy, Snake Eyes, Golf Bag, Machine Gun and Ma made better headlines. The notoriety of such personalised gangsters had to be curbed or authority would diminish its standing in the eyes of the public. FBI chief J. Edgar Hoover made a point of hunting down bank robbers and petty thieves while at the same time ignoring the sinister emerging gangster organisation generally described as the Mafia. There was scant publicity to be gained chasing shadows. Hoover purged his conscience by stating publicly that the Mafia did not exist.

Despite Hoover's selective myopia Hollywood has seen to it that we will always remember the celebrated gangsters of the past. They are almost always American, the usual exceptions being Robin Hood, Zorro, William Tell, Turpin and a handful of others mostly portrayed as heroes or freedom fighters.

In Britain we tend to dwell on Victorian villains, particularly Jack the Ripper and Charles Peace, or early-twentieth-century murderers such as Crippen. We then jump to the 1960s, with the Krays, sometimes the Richardsons, and certainly the Great Train Robbers – but many early decades are forgotten. Ask people to name gangsters from the 1920s and 1930s and the answers will almost certainly be Al Capone, Bonnie and Clyde and (most likely remembered by the older ones) John Dillinger. How many would mention the Sabinis, Cortesis, Brummagem Hammers or the Elephant Boys? How many recall the race gang wars which ran from as early as 1910 through to the 1950s? Old gangsters, like old soldiers, fade away. Some sooner than others.

Inner cities the world over have their gang cultures. It is not only in the streets of New York and Chicago, so well known because in America public profiles of the darker side of life are well documented and posted around the world to overwhelm the domestic varieties. It is also in every city or town that has a darkly lit street or an illegal drop-in where the Devil can do his work. In Britain, apart from a brief spell in the 1950s and '60s when gangs monopolised the Sunday papers, we have a reticent attitude to our shady side and tend to fade our scoundrels away a touch more quickly than the Americans.

I grew up around the Elephant and Castle. My dad and his numerous brothers and sisters lived in the area that is south London. From an early age I knew that the Elephant Boys were the top gang, not only in London and the Southeast, but in the whole country. Old-timers talked of the vast gang of organised shoplifters and its network of receivers. Women, as much as men, brought their booty from just over the river in the City of London and the West End to back parlours, under-the-counter shops, market stalls and pawnbrokers concealed in the close-mouthed community around the Elephant. Anything that could be pinched could be sold. This was a world where jobs were so scarce that starvation and ill health brought on by the dreadful living conditions threatened whole families with extinction. In this world there evolved a survival syndrome dedicated to looking after its own.

When 'boosting' declined as an industry at the onset of the First World War other activities had to be found to supplant thieving traditions. Among the new industries supported and controlled by the Elephant Gang were night-clubs, protection rackets, extortion, gambling, dog- and horseracing pitches, horse-thieving, car-thieving and beatings. Complementing these activities were receiving, safe-breaking, black-marketeering, smash-and-grab, burglary, hijacking, jump-up, robbery and wages grabs. Families developed their own specialities. Individuals loaned themselves out to organisations in London and beyond.

In all criminal fraternities there is the need for physical dexterity. Gangsters may be crafty, but not always tough, so the leadership goes to someone with the ability to control followers and select from them proficient right-hand men (and women) to specialise in brain or muscle. It dawned upon these leaders that to flourish they needed the respect of London's other gangs. In a series of battles the Elephant Boys established their fighting prowess across London. It began in the 1920s and was still experiencing repeat doses of violence in the 1940s and '50s. The huge gang provided toughs for other districts and many gangs paid tribute to the accepted masters – it was the only way they would be allowed to operate. In my youth the knowledge of chastening expeditions to the Angel, Brixton, Aldgate, Clapham, Mile End, Paddington, Camden Town, Stepney and Shepherd's Bush was cherished by young men who aspired to become one of the boys.

When I looked back at my family it struck me just how far spread in time they were for just a few generations. I was the youngest of three children. My father was third youngest of thirteen children from a family that had originated in Scotland and somehow come to be settled in the Lambeth area of south London. To put things into perspective: when my grandmother, Phoebe Morley, was born in 1849 it was a time when nearly 54,000 people died of cholera in London (more than 500 of them recently dying in two streets off the Waterloo Road). Waterloo Station had been built the previous year, clearing away some of the hovels located on and under the river Thames, and providing a train service for the deceased to be buried in the countryside where there was more room. Many denizens of the riverfront sleep in leafy Surrey cemeteries.

Grandma Mac, as Phoebe became known, was three when the Duke of Wellington was buried and seven when Stanley met Livingstone. Only a few hundred yards from where she was born in New Street, Lambeth (now Newburn Street) was the famous, or infamous, Vauxhall Gardens – gathering place for roisterers and rogues which was to close for ever on 25 July 1859. I wonder if she ever went there. While Grandma Mac was a girl, twelve in fact, Prince Albert died; and when Abraham Lincoln was assassinated in 1866 she was only sixteen. My great-grandfather fought in the Zulu War and my grandfather fought in the Boer War.

On 13 October 1867 Phoebe was married, aged eighteen, to William McDonald at Trinity Church, Lambeth, and went to live on Carlisle Street, Lambeth. The church was flattened by a bomb during the Second World War. They produced thirteen children: my uncles and aunts and my father, Arthur James McDonald (always called Jim). Some of these uncles also fought in the Boer War and all the surviving brothers fought in the First World War. Aunt Ada was a suffragette. Occasionally frustrating the forces of law and order were my uncle Wag and his brothers Bert, Walter (Wal), Tom and Jim, who flitted through the flimsy fringes of the racing underworld mixing with the terrors of south, east, north and west London. Two uncles transported their misdeeds to Hollywood.

The Shell Building now stands where my dad was born. A stone's throw away is the County Hall building and a little further in the opposite direction is the Oxo Tower. Concert halls now occupy the South Bank of the Thames where once wharves, mills, factories, timber yards and a shot tower employed the masses of working-class people who crowded into poor housing hugging the river bank. York Road, Lambeth, is still a thoroughfare from Waterloo Bridge to Westminster Bridge: travellers along it see only a busy main road passing behind Waterloo railway station and it is impossible now to imagine the lines of tenements and shacks inhabited by swarms of river rats, as they were sometimes called. The whole of the Lower Marsh area of Lambeth teemed with itinerant crafts- and tradespeople. Hawkers sold their wares in the street; libertines drunk themselves ill in gin palaces and listened to bawdy entertainment in the Canterbury Arms; tearaways fought in the streets and pubs; and even law-abiding citizens learned the rules of survival. Mostly they were poor, unemployed poor or employed poor – often there was little difference, but that difference meant providing just enough for the family to live on without appealing to charity in order to prevent illness and death from starvation.

The worst of the slums were torn down before the turn of the twentieth century, to be replaced by much-needed schools, hospitals and flats. One such block of improved housing was Princes Buildings, where my dad was born in 1887. The family moved all around Lambeth and Southwark, forming connections with Vauxhall, Waterloo, Kennington, Walworth, the Elephant and Castle and, later, the Borough.

Much of the basis of the legends has disappeared in the mists of time. Folklore is traditionally spread by word of mouth, sometimes embellished, but always with sufficient truth to verify its authenticity. Stories are often supported by random newspaper reports – frustratingly, without any regular pattern – but they are there if you search for them. My story centres on knowledge passed on by family members, friends and reported incidents. Through these sources I discovered my uncle Wag and added it to my

personal knowledge of the Elephant and Castle of my youth.

Added to the chat about the myth, tradition and reality of the Elephant Boys are my aunt Ada's striking recollections of my father's family. She took a central role in the family structure. To her came the postcards from abroad and the visits when other members of the family wanted solace or somewhere to sit tight; she had a sharp business brain and, like all manipulators, a magnificent memory and knowledge of her subject. She and my dad would tell tales which I at once sought to emulate. I needed to find out if I could be crafty or tough, or both, so I went to look . . .

ELEPHANT BOYS

PART ONE

1. IN OFF THE YELLOW

The Forty-nine Club off Soho's Brewer Street was a sparsely furnished, seedy drinking club, one of many such places seeking to provide cheap excitement on the edge of notorious central London. It attracted impressionable young men looking for entry into London's West End underworld. We had heard how the White brothers had been ousted as the premier West End gangsters in a two-day battle with Jack Spot and Scarface Jock Russo; and in these stark surroundings we were looking for the glamour of those off-centre Runyonesque characters who were our role models after the dust of the Second World War had settled.

Local gangs, especially those in southeast London, were well known to us. We knew their histories, their top men, and their prowess and ranking in the established hierarchy of villainy. From an early age we had mingled with every form of scoundrel and reprobate within walking distance of our 'patch' at the Borough. The culture of the Elephant and Castle Boys had been handed down through generations of families: the Reyburns, Brindles, Garretts, Carters, Callahans, Rosas, Richardsons and Roffs. All had close family ties and were also sets of brothers. Their pedigree had been certified in toe-to-toe stand-up fist fights and general rough-and-tumble pub and street battles. From their ranks, and those of singular tough guys like Boy Boy Stanford, Danny Irving, Bonker Hammond, Mad Frankie, Whippet, Waggy and Ossie, came the punchers, con men, thieves and razor slashers which made the Elephant and Castle the prime supply source of London's hard men.

THE BOROUGH

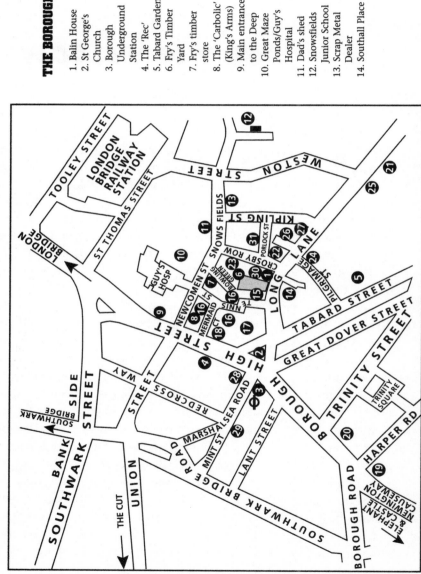

It was the Elephant Boys who provided the heavy mob which kept the West End gang lords in power. Over the years Billy Kimber, Darby Sabini, Jack Spot, Billy Howard, Billy Hill and Albert Dimes have harnessed the power of south Londoners to grab, and hold on to, control of the West End underworld. Outsiders like the Whites and later the Krays failed to get more than a toehold on London's juiciest spots. Losing the goodwill of the Elephant Boys was to be in serious trouble, as Jack Spot would one day find out.

The Elephant Gang was a loose-knit assembly. Most of them did not live at the Elephant and Castle, but were from the Walworth and Old Kent Roads, Kennington, Lambeth, Waterloo, Blackfriars, Peckham, Camberwell – and the Borough, where our little team came from. We styled ourselves the Balin Boys and were now ready for the big time.

The Forty-nine Club was a 'spieler' where dice games were played under the protection of established hard men. Touts rounded up lads like ourselves who then paid a few shillings to join the game. If we were lucky enough to win, we could walk away with our winnings without some tough trying to relieve us of them; or at the least we could get a head start.

That night in the summer of 1954 four of us, including Dave Morbin and myself, had been taken to the Forty-nine by Charlie Don – a big lad in his early twenties, who acted as doorman and bouncer for a succession of clubs and pubs. Charlie was a good-natured giant, over six feet tall with a good-looking ruddy face. He wore a light grey four-buttoned tailored suit in the fashionable Edwardian style. He was a 'puncher', a man who could be counted on to stand up and fight anyone, within reason: he knew his place well enough not to stand up to the likes of Charlie Richardson or Tony Reuter, but he had a reputation for being 'game'.

The dice school progressed in its usual way. Blue smoke, from cigarettes angled in the corners of mouths, curling past hooded lights; the clink and rustle of money; the whispers and yells of success and failure – all combined to produce an atmosphere guaranteed to quicken the blood of young men and lead them to rash judgements in the heat and excitement of concentrated gambling. Money changed hands mostly in small bets, but a lot of money could be won or lost in an evening. The croupier, provided by the club, took something out of the pot from every winning

run, or winners would 'see the croop' by tossing him a portion of their winnings. Curiously there never was a set amount. Players knew instinctively what to give and it worked very well. Occasional cheapskates were simply 'rowed out' of the games by not being invited back, a reputation nobody wanted. Drinks and sandwiches also brought in money.

To be successful a game had to be protected. We trusted Charlie – who had befriended us, even though we were younger than him and therefore of a different generation in the way of things – to take us to a safe place. We thought he must be the 'top man'. Then in walked Tommy Smithson.

Tommy was making a name for himself. He had been badly cut up by Billy Hill and Sonny Sullivan as a punishment for carrying a gun in his pocket when summoned to a meeting after beating up Sonny's brother Slip Sullivan. Tommy made his living by taking protection money from Maltese pimps and small spielers, especially in the East End where he fostered the up-and-coming Kray twins, setting them up in a club in Hackney which he regarded as his manor.

Charlie Don acknowledged him with a 'Hello Tommy' and whispered to us that it was Tommy Smithson, our first sight of West End villainy. Naturally we now assumed Tommy was the 'man'. Then he stepped into the gambling ring and stood on the croupier's hand. Charlie stepped forward only to be pushed off. It was immediately apparent that he was not in the same league as Smithson. A little fish had been gobbled up by a big fish.

Things then moved fast. An even bigger fish came through the wall of startled punters. Strong arms grabbed Smithson around the neck and shoulders, propelled him backwards to the door, spun him through the doorway and heaved him down the single flight of stairs which led to the street. Johnny Carter, a heavy from the Elephant (well, the Old Kent Road anyway), followed Smithson down the stairs, flung him through the door – which was shut at the time – and laid into him with fists and feet in the street outside.

We four followed close behind Charlie Don and witnessed Smithson getting a good kicking. His companion, who must have been keeping watch outside, made a half-hearted attempt to intervene. Sensing my moment for glory I jumped on his back while Dave Morbin gave him a couple of good thumps about the kidneys. We spiralled around but couldn't make him go down. I remember Charlie screaming 'Let me have him, let me have him' as he stepped forward and sent a couple of crashing blows into his face. Down he went, spark out, with me still clinging to him.

I disentangled myself from Charlie's handiwork and watched Smithson get up, bloody and staggering, as Carter walked alongside him and gave him some more. There was a measured professionalism about it. Deliberately aimed punches which, when I think back, remind me of a lumberjack felling a tree. Then we went back into the Forty-nine leaving the mess outside. Whatever prearranged signal had brought Carter forth I do not know. He appeared like a genie out of a bottle, chopped Smithson down, and returned to his post. He wrapped a handkerchief around a damaged hand, told Charlie to give us a drink and disappeared into a back room. The game resumed.

We felt we had arrived. Johnny Carter was known to us: his reputation had been gained by carving up some very hard men in battles over illegal bookie pitches and for a share of the lucrative protection rackets, soaking money from the scores of clubs, boozers and clip joints crammed into Soho's maze of narrow streets. He was a genuine razor man, an expert with a chiv. When released from a five-year stretch for following his craft he had been recruited at the prison gates by arch-villain Jack Spot and taken into membership of Spot's firm, dealing out broken arms and decorated faces to order. He was a vicious gangster – a fact softened for us by the callowness of youth.

Months later I was playing snooker in a club in Leicester Square when in walked Smithson. He was not a man to forget or forgive. I was seventeen, he was in his thirties, he came straight for me so I picked up the yellow ball and cracked him on the head. He went down and I went out, quickly. I'd hit him so hard my mate thought I'd killed him so I stayed at his place until I was sure Smithson was up and about. By this time I was well in with Johnny Carter and Jack Spot, which protected me from the few friends Smithson had. Mostly he was a loner acting the lone-wolf tough guy, but he was still dangerous for all that. I'm told Spot, who loathed Smithson, roared with laughter when someone told him 'Mac hit Smithson and Smithson hit the floor'. Corny, but true.

I saw him once more after that as I entered the Fifty-one Club off

ELEPHANT BOYS

Charing Cross Road. He was coming out and we passed in the doorway. He looked a wreck, his scars from previous battles were highly visible and clearly he was past his best. Whether he recognised me or not I do not know. I went in and he walked right past me. I believe the hairs bristled on the back of my neck.

He was still putting the frighteners on Maltese brothel-keepers eighteen months later. Somehow they tricked him into visiting a Maida Vale vice den where they held him down while Phil Ellul shot him to death. His funeral was a spectacular send-off by the boys. The Kray twins provided black limousines to help produce a procession to rival the departures of Chicago's finest, Billy Hill wept crocodile tears as he placed a wreath on the grave and a young man contributed a posy of yellow flowers fashioned in the shape of a billiard ball.

2. GENESIS

I remember sitting on a yellow brick wall scanning the acres of debris surrounding the council flats where I spent most of my early days. The flats still stand in Long Lane at about the merging of Southwark and Bermondsey, as they were in those days. We lived on the Southwark side in an area generally known as the Borough.

The yellow wall was built as a screen to shelter us from the ruins of the Second World War piled on our doorstep. The area was strewn with rubble from the remains of old brick buildings that had been bombed or pulled down to make way for council building. Most of the inhabitants of the flats had been bombed out of their previous homes. In common with them my mother, father, elder brother and myself had been bombed out of our house in Lant Street, Southwark – a turning off the Borough High Street – exactly two weeks after we had moved in.

Temporarily located in a rest centre in Laxton Street School in Long Lane, we soon moved into newly built Balin House. This stood beside what used to be the old Marshalsea prison, at that time a mortuary; part of its underground level had been exposed to the sky and had been sealed and turned into a vast water tank for use by firemen during the war. There were many such tanks. They existed for some time after the war had ended. For a dare we would sidle along the precariously narrow edge of the containing wall. Some actually swam in the tanks and there was at least one reported drowning.

Many fenced-in areas were now open after iron railings had been removed and melted down, with aluminium saucepans and other metal hardware contributed by hard-up housewives, to be regenerated as weapons and ammunition for the war effort.

ELEPHANT BOYS

I could stand in the centre of acres of debris, amid bricks, broken glass and splintered wood bestowed by Hitler's bombs. North, east, west and south were strewn with the rubble of broken homes and factories. The horizon was broken only by the grim face of Guy's Hospital, the ruins of a paint and ink factory and the protruding concrete reinforced roof of an air-raid shelter which pointed its sloping roof to the sky like an antenna probing for more of Hitler's bombers. A short way away the Blue Eyed Maid was just visible beyond more ruins and broken walls. Closer was the hole in the ground where once stood the bowels of the old Marshalsea – now sealed on all sides and filled with water to provide the reservoir for the fire brigade. The mortuary brooded close by.

Many pre-war slums had been wiped away. Into this desolation a block of flats, seventy in all, had been built and named Balin House. It was stocked with people from temporary rest centres whose homes had been blitzed off the face of southeast London. We moved into No. 60. In No. 70 lived the Rothery family; one of the Rotherys, Juney, would later marry Great Train Robber Buster Edwards.

The block stood on the edge of desolation. Out of the surrounding ruins small boys with freckled faces and unruly mops of hair bobbed in and out of makeshift camps, secret mines and quarries. Here and there were small camp-fires surrounded by clusters of kids, bursting out of their patched make-do-and-mend clothing, probing the wreckage in the hope of securing some precious commodity.

Part of the grounds of the Marshalsea had been turned into garden allotments and I remember a skull being dug up along with other human bones – some soul who had died in torment in the old prison. In amongst the overgrown allotments swarmed plentiful bees and clouds of butterflies. Giggling boys and girls pursued the brimstones and tortoiseshells with jamjars; a captured red admiral brought the curious around until allowed to flutter free.

Fry's timber yard was on the other side, bounded by the flats, Bowling Green Lane and Newcomen Street. As well as a sawmill they had a huge open-air timber store laid out over one of the ruins, twenty-feet high in places. The wood was mostly stacked horizontally, making it easy to climb. It became the headquarters for several gangs who managed to burrow into secret apertures

ELEPHANT BOYS

right inside the store, to be concealed from probing watchmen's eyes.

Because wood was stacked horizontally it was common to have a plank protruding from the rest. If it was of suitable length it became a springboard; we bounced into the air and crash-landed on the rubble beneath and a split lip or bloody nose was never a deterrent to such pleasurable pastimes. In later years, when the timber was surrounded by barbed wire, one young trespasser managed to bounce himself into a tangle of the stuff and was seriously injured. We took some comfort from the presence of Guy's Hospital, which was close enough to frown over our goings-on.

In front of the flats was a 'square', where ball games, 'he' and piggy-back fights would pass the time. From a balcony a man tossed pennies and ha'pennies in a game of 'scramble', delighting as ragamuffins pounced on his philanthropy. A woman scrubbing the step of No. 2 cast a scolding stare at this man encouraging hooligans on her doorstep. Adults shouted from the windows when a ball rattled a window pane. Girls did handstands against a wall showing their bloomers to shyly peeping boys. Other girls skipped, sometimes singly; sometimes a long washing line was turned by two girls as their friends darted in and out in some recognised ritual. Some older girls bounced balls off a wall, catching them with great agility while reciting a chant. In nearby Bowling Green Lane an oil-drum provided a wicket and somebody's dad showed the techniques of off-spin and leg breaks, while a boy with a piece of wood for a bat stroked the rubber ball the way he knew Dennis Compton would; each bowler took turns at six deliveries, hit the ball beyond the set boundary and you were given 'Lost ball, six and out'.

Comics were a pleasant pastime. I was heavily into Captain Marvel and his family, Captain Marvel Junior and Mary Marvel. I suppose the thought that anyone could call 'Shazam' and put the world to rights was some solace to boys who could do little to change their surroundings. DC comics also featured Superman and Batman and were highly prized for swaps. Picture comics included the *Beano*, *Dandy*, *Radio Fun*, *Film Fun* and *Knockout*. *Beano* and *Dandy* were stocked with their own original characters, as was *Knockout* – my favourite, alas now defunct. *Radio Fun* and *Film Fun* featured comic strips of famous comedians such as Laurel and

ELEPHANT BOYS

Hardy and Abbott and Costello and there was a heavy American influence: Joe E. Brown was featured and I confess I didn't know who he was until, late in his career, he appeared in the movies *Some Like It Hot* and *Showboat*. British comedians featured were Derek Roy and somebody called Izzy Bon.

Comics were swapped. Clumps of boys and girls would sit on the stairs of Balin or in their bedrooms, leafing through stacks of second-hand comics, some of which were very tatty from constant swapping. An early edition of the *Eagle* was freely distributed around the flats at the time of the Coronation, when we also received a day off from work. I think I am right in saying we became acquainted with Dan Dare as the Queen was trundling towards Westminster Abbey.

Another hobby was the collection of cigarette cards. They came in a great variety of subjects: series of fish from the oceans, butterflies, birds, sportsmen, cars, soldiers from present and past, and just about anything you could think of. Swaps helped make up complete sets. They could also be flicked against a wall in a game of pitch, where cards could be won or lost, or pocket-money staked; inevitably some wise kids glued two cards together to make a more formidable cast. These were the same smarties who hollowed out the centre of conkers and filled them with cement – or when that didn't work, would slightly bake them or soak them in vinegar – since winning was all-important in the quest for reputation.

We also collected cigarette packets. Either the whole or the cut-out front were stuffed into bags and dragged out for swaps. Before I began to smoke I was familiar with brands of the time: Gold Flake, Craven A, with its black cat emblem, Capstan, Kensitas No. 1 and No. 2, Piccadilly, Woodbines, Players Navy Cut and Weights. Rarer varieties – very collectable – were Park Drive, Sobrani, which had coloured papers and was a posh 'cocktail' smoke, and certain Turkish brands. Throat-burning Turf and Minors were a later addition aimed at young smokers: they were cheap and desperately horrible. Players Weights were most popular, being a good cheap smoke and sold in twenties, tens and fives (or a tobacconist would split a packet and sell in fives or singles).

Smoking started at a young age while sitting on the ledge of the electricity substation tucked away in a corner of the square. To avoid tell-tale signs of yellow stained fingers, we bought miniature pipes which had a bowl just the right size to poke a cigarette into. We would then inhale through the pipe. To avoid becoming sick, smoke was not 'taken down' – that is, until I was standing one day on the edge of the platform at London Bridge railway station, having a precocious puff when a fast train went through, wafted the smoke into my lungs and introduced me to the pain and the pleasures of real smoking. I stayed on cigarettes for ten years.

Evening indoors activity centred on the radio. People sat in clumps around scratchy wirelesses listening to *Dick Barton, Special Agent* and *It's That Man Again* featuring Tommy Handley. They erupted in hoots of laughter when Mrs Mopp barged in and asked 'Can I do you now, sir?'; later favourites were *Take It From Here* and, for the younger generation, *The Goon Show*.

From an early age I liked to read. Recognising the importance of getting me to read anything, my mother used to traipse to a newsagent in the Borough High Street every Saturday morning, to spend some of her scant income on amazing story comics for me to read in bed all through Saturday morning until I had devoured my favourites. Avidly I read the *Champion, Rover, Wizard, Hotspur* and *Adventure*. Favourite stories were Smith of the Lower Third, Ginger Nut and Rockfist Rogan who was so manly that he slept beneath a single sheet even in the coldest weather (when I tried something similar the result was to wake Mum for an extra blanket). Serials included an intriguing story of ten strong men marooned on a tropical island in a contest to the death: each week, two or more would engage in a grim struggle or lay traps for their adversaries until only one remained. I'm sure the Brit always won.

My Mum's earnings came from being a part-time tea lady at Odhams Press in Long Acre Lane, near Covent Garden. She also worked in the BBC's Bush House for a while. I'm thankful now for the thousands of words I read; it may not have been Dickens, but it gave me a vocabulary sadly missing from today's youngsters.

Mum was long suffering. She came from very respectable folk from Poplar, east London. She tolerated the kitten that Stan, my brother, brought home one day – Dad nearly sat on it because he didn't know it was sleeping on his armchair. We were not allowed to keep pets in the flats, so the creature was never let out to give away our secret. When the door knocker went, the wretched thing ran up the wall, or hid under the settee where it resisted all attempts to shift it – we then couldn't sit on the settee in case our

weight squashed it. It was allowed to attend to its toilet in a dirt box on the balcony. Eventually the kitten managed to get out and we found its remains in Long Lane where it had been run over.

Where Mum drew the line was the stray dog I brought home. It had followed me home from school and must have thought its luck was in when I led it to our door. Did it shift when Mum came out with the broom!

Dad was fairly quiet, but he was no slouch with his fists. Occasionally he would take a swing at Stan, especially if his Sunday afternoon nap was disturbed. He was not beyond chasing me and Stan from the flat when his blood was up. When I hit Kenny Anderson, he went for his dad, who tried to belt me; Dad observed this from the balcony outside No. 60 and he was down the stairs and on to the debris by Bowling Green Lane before Kenny's dad had departed. Imagine my pride and Kenny's humiliation when my dad put his dad on the deck. Kenny's dad got up and took off across the ruins like a doodlebug with his tail on fire.

As all small boys, then and now, I was interested in dinosaurs. I delved into H.G. Wells's *History of Mankind*, obtained from the reserved shelves of the school library with the aid of my form teacher. I even tried Darwin's *Origin Of Species*. My favourite book was *The Lost World* by Sir Arthur Conan Doyle: a party of adventurers led by the formidable Professor Challenger and growling Professor Summerlee enter the Amazon forest in search of a lost plateau where time has stood still. In my mind I travelled with Lord John Roxton, the irascible professors and the young fit reporter, Malone – the outsider struggling to impress his peers with reckless deeds. He was a perfect role model for a young would-be adventurer. The book was later made into a disappointing Hollywood film. It still awaits a good treatment from the film industry. Interestingly, the title was used by Michael Crichton in his sequel to *Jurassic Park*.

Through comics and Saturday morning cinema club I acquired an interest in wild west characters such as Billy The Kid, Wild Bill Hickok, Jesse James and (the then obscure) Wyatt Earp. As I grew older I came to terms with the fact that these bizarre stories could not be entirely true. I developed a lifelong interest in separating the fact from the fiction, to get to the real characters beneath the outrageous stories. As usual the fact is much more interesting than the fiction.

One reason for sitting on the yellow brick wall was as a lookout. Across the debris, which reached almost to the Borough High Street, was the approach route of a rival gang called the Red Cross Boys. They came from Red Cross Way, led by a boy named Curtis. We were the Balin House Boys and the two gangs frequently met on the battleground between us. Weapons were the abundant stones and bricks. These 'stone wars' lasted as long as the debris was there. The more flats that were built, the more gangs were born.

Roughly in the middle of the battle zone stood the remains of air-raid shelters. Slanted roofs of concrete were the entrance to a myriad of tunnels beneath; one, known as the Deep, was London's biggest dormitory air-raid shelter. During the war these tunnels were lined with bunks and makeshift beds and helped foster that indomitable, 'chirpy' spirit which really did exist among Londoners at the time.

I lay there many a night listening to the sounds of ack-ack, droning aircraft, muffled explosions and the thud of incendiary bombs on the roof overhead. There were several entrances, the main one being in the Borough High Street near the corner of Newcomen Street. After the war ended these shelters deteriorated into dark rubbish heaps. Even the hardiest of us was loath to go in alone, especially after a screaming nun wielding a bloody knife had been seen advancing on a party of explorers. After hearing this tale, some of us braved the darkness with the aid of a candle and proposed to navigate the tunnels to the Red Cross entrance on the other side of the Borough High Street – close to which was a United Dairies milkbar. *En route* we came face to face with an old man carrying a lantern coming out of the darkness. I don't remember leaving the place, all I know is that it was a quick exit. Probably he was searching for scrap, but tell that to nine-year-olds expecting to meet that nun! I don't recall going down there again.

Stone wars could be big affairs with perhaps a hundred boys of all ages taking part. Some of the little ones would stack stones behind the yellow wall as an arsenal for the bigger boys to draw on. The wall was our last line of defence before fleeing if we were getting the worst of it. When things were going well we used the above ground part of the air-raid shelters as a forward base and cut our enemy to pieces. I seem to remember that we won more than we lost, but maybe that is false pride. Wounds could be appalling. Heads split open as a barrage of sharp flint missiles came showering down. Broken bones were not unusual. Guy's Hospital, strategically placed in sight of our flats, must have got much of its custom from us. My brother Stan had his head stitched there, after being ambushed one day by assailants who sneaked away unseen.

It was because of Stan that I had my first brush with the man in blue. After a stone fight had been broken up by a police raid, Stan was grabbed by a 'copper' and was frantically struggling. I did my brotherly bit by 'steaming in' with fists and feet. Stan got away, I got caught. We were of the mature ages of twelve and nine respectively. Punishment was a good clump round the ear and delivery to long-suffering parents for more of the same. Those coppers knew how to deal with a situation. It was expected, nobody complained.

The wars culminated in one huge conflagration known as the Battle of the Borough. Many gangs allied to form armies for a final 'sort out'. Much of the fighting was done with stakes taken from fencing which surrounded the dwindling debris. Complete fences were demolished to provide six-foot wooden staves. The battle was fought in several stages and flared up at intervals throughout one weekend. In the mêlée nobody knew who was fighting who and no side was victorious. Hundreds took part on battlegrounds stretching from Great Dover Street to Southwark Street. The affair was talked about long after the last of the ruins had been resurrected into yet more council flats.

The call to arms came one Friday evening when kids from Balin House spotted a mob from Red Cross Way examining the timber store and probing for hiding-places. Word passed quickly around the flats and youths of all ages appeared in the square. Once it was established that the invaders were not a large force they were approached. They fled before contact could be made. Pursuit was rapid and stones followed the fleeing gang as they made their escape towards Newcomen Street. We were hot on their heels when we ran smack into a larger force. Their scouting group disappeared behind their front ranks and we were subjected to a hail of stones and bricks.

The exchange continued as we were pushed back to the shelter of the wood store. Reinforcements came as more boys poured out of Balin House and from Otford, Aylesford, Eastwell and Crayford Houses who were our traditional allies. The enemy were driven back and pursued into Newcomen Street. For a while gangs of

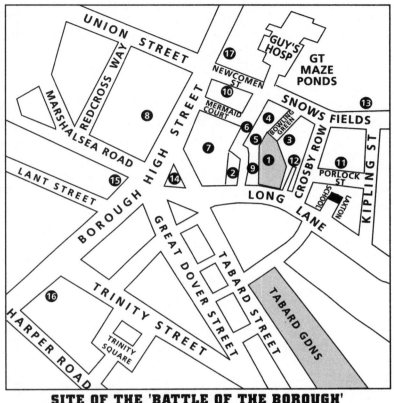

SITE OF THE 'BATTLE OF THE BOROUGH'

1. Balin House
2. Water tank
3. Fry's Timber Yard
4. Fry's timber store
5. Yellow brick wall
6/7. Debris
8. The 'Rec'
9. Allotments
10. The 'Carbolic' (King's Arms)
11. Site of bonfire
12. Cul-de-sac hidden camp
13. Dad's shed
14. St George's Church
15. Borough Underground Station
16. Stones End Police Station
17. Entrance to 'Deep' shelter

about fifty strong glared at each other. Ammunition was suddenly scarce. To our left was a six-foot-high wooden stake fence. The stakes were wound together by wire. Ronnie, one of our older members, pulled a stake from out of its wire fastening; the fence was demolished in a matter of seconds. A spontaneous charge followed. After a furious fight the Red Cross Boys were clubbed down. Those who didn't go down were driven into the Borough High Street where they ran for the safety of the Red Cross 'rec', the recreation ground used as their headquarters. Those left behind were badly beaten.

We considered we had won a great victory. Only the arrival of a police car caused the straggling withdrawal back to the yellow brick wall. The injured were being tended when, from the alley adjacent to the Blue Eyed Maid pub, there appeared a fresh challenge. A bigger mob, also armed with stakes, advanced across the debris toward us. There was considerably over a hundred and they came on swiftly, even though we bombarded them with stones as they approached. Suddenly they were upon us. We were forced back into our square where we ran through to the Long Lane exit, leaving behind some of our gang who had been knocked down and were receiving the same treatment we had recently dished out. The police had not been able to intervene but were now reinforced. Cars and foot police from a Black Maria raced to the buildings. They drove off the gangs and were left only with the wounded. It was all over for the night. Yet it couldn't end there. I remember the seething anger of Balin House residents. Their dwellings had been attacked. People were very parochial in those days.

Saturday morning came. People collected in the square. Not just kids and teenagers, but fully grown adults. Led by the Balin House Boys, all of the gangs of the Long Lane area made a raid on a building in Red Cross Way which was occupied as a sort of community building. There was a furious fight but the Red Cross crowd drove the attackers back along Marshalsea Road. That day, fighting spread as far as Great Dover Street and Tabard Gardens. A policeman who tried to intervene was badly beaten. Later that evening the Balin Boys – reinforced by the Otford House Gang – marched on Red Cross Way, cornered a bunch of the Red Cross Boys in a pub, dragged them out and clubbed them with bricks and iron bars. The community building was wrecked, furniture smashed, the floor torn up and its stock of booze greedily consumed.

News of the onslaught reached Red Cross Buildings and their boys tumbled out of their flats, supported by their allies from Union Street and as far away as Blackfriars Road. The gangs came upon each other on the 'rec' and immediately began the most ferocious free-for-all of the battle. Terrified residents contacted the police at Stones End police station. A vanload of policemen was sent to quell the disturbance, but when they marched along the Borough High Street the gangs united against them. They were forced to retreat to the Borough underground station where they were reinforced. The police went in again and grabbed a couple of ringleaders, who were promptly retrieved by the gangs.

The police rallied and pressed on up the Borough High Street, coming under a hail of bricks and stones. Upwards of two hundred people, armed with clubs, bricks and iron bars, were involved. No-goods from around the battle area came on to the streets relishing a good fight or a chance to loot shops and houses; women came out from the flats to urge their men on. A division of the gangs on both sides of the Borough High Street brought about a lull in the fighting, barricades were erected and, sensibly, the police sought a conference with the leaders. The barricades were then reluctantly dismantled and the gangs lumbered slowly home. The wounded were carried to Guy's to be stitched and mended. It was over.

A few more fights broke out between dedicated enemies, but it never again reached the intensity of the Battle of the Borough.

Apart from attacking the police, there are only two other occasions of alliances between Long Lane and Red Cross Way that I remember. One was when word spread that a baby had been assaulted in its pram in Marshalsea Road. Such an act was barely heard of in those days and it brought scores of people on to the streets to scour the area. Vigilantes questioned a few unfortunate and terrified passers-by, but I do not recall any positive result.

The other occasion was the horrific bombing of Mosers during the war. The building stood on the corner of Marshalsea Road and the Borough High Street, opposite the Borough underground station, and was hit by the first V2 rocket to land on London. I was playing in the square, kicking a ball against a wall, when the explosion a quarter of a mile away knocked me off my feet. My mother knew a Red Cross Way woman whose daughter was one of the twenty killed. For some time after the tragedy this woman

ELEPHANT BOYS

couldn't stop hearing the clicking of her daughter's typewriter as she practised at home. The general feeling was that the real target was Durrances in Great Dover Street, said to be a manufacturer of munitions. If that was so, the rocket fell short by about a quarter-mile and instead hit Mosers – an important engineering firm. I suppose it was a random lucky hit for the Germans.

My actual memories of the war are faint. I remember gathering shrapnel, the molten remains of bombs and ammunition; peculiarly shaped pieces of it adorned many fireplaces in the vicinity. We kids peeped over the mortuary wall as bodies carried in had their blankets removed to reveal torn torsos and dangling limbs. Then there was the old lady standing in Newcomen Street, as we hurried by heading for the Deep, shaking her fist at an aircraft with its tail on fire, rejoicing in its being shot down. Dad reckoned it was a doodlebug. People used to watch them go over. They had a measured amount of fuel, just enough to get them over London; everyone ran for cover when the flames went out bringing them plunging towards random targets.

I spent part of the war in the Evelina Hospital in Marshalsea Road with pneumonia and a suspected 'spot on the lung', the dreaded forerunner of tuberculosis. I remember getting out of bed after five weeks and being too weak to stand. A decision was made to send me to a convalescent home for three months, followed by three months in an open-air school. Tearfully I was packed off from Waterloo Station with a group of other kids; but the open-air school closed because of an epidemic, so I spent six months' convalescence in Lynton, Devon, during which time they found out I wasn't tubercular. Dad persuaded them to keep me for the full six months to keep me away from the war – at least that's what they told me. The home, Clooneavin, was perched on the steep hillside between Lynton and Lynmouth. It had a timbered walkway which we scaled rather than walked. We were taken on rambles by streams rippling over stones, and walks on purple hills; when the escort wasn't looking older boys pulled the tail feathers from pheasants and we would roll down the steep hillsides. Once, I tumbled so far that I crossed a roadway and rolled down another slope, cutting the inside of my mouth open. There was scant sympathy from the irate nurse who rinsed my mouth with salt water. Even so, I didn't want to come home!

Evacuation followed: first to Folkestone, which was immediately bombed; then to Bishop's Waltham, near Southampton and in equal danger, so in a short while we were back home. My only recollection of Bishop's Waltham is of being abandoned in the woods when Stan decided to hide. I went off thinking I was lost and Stan had to return to our lodgings without me; a search party found me halfway up a tree, don't ask me why.

On VE day dad took us to Trafalgar Square where we joined in all the rejoicing. I was only seven years old. My recollections are of sitting on dad's shoulders watching a parade. Somewhere nearby a coloured man was standing on a box addressing a crowd; a Yank in uniform took exception to what he said, grabbed him by his ankles, jerked him to the ground and kicked him in the head. It's a fact that violent acts provide the most lasting memories. The end of the war was marked by street parties for children. I don't remember where ours took place, but I can still picture the different coloured jellies and paper hats and children's entertainers. It must have been a generous sacrifice for hard-up adults.

The warfare was over, but the debris still remained – a source of industry for penniless kids. Firewood could be gathered, chopped or split and tied into sixpenny bundles for sale around the flats. Fires in grates had to be started with newspapers and kindling to set the coal alight. Coal was often of a cheap variety: my dad was always complaining about the slag mixed in with whatever variety he had purchased, and he changed often. Welsh nuts were his favourite.

Mixing slag with coal was not the only trick perpetrated by coal delivery companies. I, or my brother Stan, had to stand on the balcony and count in the sacks deposited in the coal cupboard. These hundredweight bags were carried on the backs of coal-blackened delivery men who tipped them into the coal cupboard. The unwary could end up with one less bag. The coal cupboard stood in the passage inside the flat and it had removable slats of wood, so coal could be reached as the quantity reduced. Even with the cupboard door closed there was always a faint whiff of coal dust.

Another way of setting coal alight was to use paraffin-soaked bars which were purchased from Fogarty's stores next to Balin House in Long Lane. Even better were 'tarry blocks', as we called them. They could occasionally be found among the rubble. Soon it was realised that they were road blocks. This brought back

memories of incendiary bombs setting the surface of Newcomen Street afire. Here and there smouldering gaps in the surface of the road evidenced where the small fire bombs had landed. After the war other gaps began to appear as young entrepreneurs prised the blocks free and sold them for use in the grate.

Dad had a small workshop in Snowsfields where he made crates to sell to the boxman in Long Lane. He also manufactured small pieces of furniture, kitchen tables, blanket boxes, stools and the like, and also made repairs to household furniture. I used to sweep up for him on infrequent occasions and was usually up to my knees in wood shavings which I bagged and sold for kindling. The advent of tarry blocks, which were apt to flare up in the grate and tumble coal from the fire onto the floor, brought about increased demand for fire fenders, which for a while became his best sellers. The economics of supply and demand could be altered by something as insignificant as a tarry block. The surface of Newcomen Street became pitted to a point where it was unsuitable for traffic and a hazard to the meandering patrons departing the Kings Arms (popularly known as the 'Carbolic' because it always smelled of the stuff). The Council stripped the street and resurfaced it with asphalt. In Snowsfields, close to dad's workshop, there was a scrap metal dealer who – between police raids – would buy the bounty garnered from the bombed sites and lead stripped from roofs.

Camp-fires were built on the debris and huge Guy Fawkes night bonfires were erected. One of these very close to Fry's woodyard caused great consternation, not only for the danger, but also for the appropriation of 'surplus' timber. The piles of wood, thrown-out furniture and rolls of unused lino, were gradually assembled in pyramids. My dad actually heaved a settee and two armchairs over the balcony from No. 60. They dropped like stones and crashed into the square, much to my mother's embarrassment. She didn't want her old furniture publicly exhibited. The old man had to wait for his tea that night.

Stocks of wood had to be guarded against marauders, particularly those from Red Cross Way, who would sneak off with wood that we'd worked hard to collect. We in turn would scour the neighbourhood for unguarded supplies. One bonfire occurred every 5 November in the centre of Porlock Street. It was adjacent to council flats and, when I think back, unbelievably dangerous. It left a great scar in the road.

Fireworks purchased from hard-earned pocket-money were mostly penny bangers and threepenny rockets. Other favourites were squibs, which shot across the ground and made everybody jump, and jumping crackers (usually tossed at girls or unsuspecting passers-by). Accidents were commonplace: a rocket fired from a milk bottle which toppled and misdirected its fiery missile towards a downstairs window; bangers about to be thrown exploding in the hand; fingers blown off, and so on. The worst I knew was Stanley Pell bending his arm to throw a banger, bringing it near to his face, where it exploded and caused a very nasty black powder smear which lasted for weeks. Naturally he was known as Blackfaced Stan for a while.

Unpopular residents would receive a firework through their letterbox. An old lady, known as 'Hoppy' due to one gammy leg, was given to wielding her stick at youngsters who disturbed her inebriated slumbers. She kept a bucket in the passage on firework night.

Another form of revenge on recalcitrant residents was 'knock down ginger'. In its simplest form a knocker would be banged and by the time the door was opened small boys were nowhere to be seen. A fit resident would give chase and it was a perilous occupation if you were not fleet of foot. Dave Parker could always expect to be last in our group and most in danger of getting caught. I was always out in front, Johnny Rose thought he was the craftiest: he would turn a corner, pull up sharp and casually saunter back in the direction of the pursuer. This worked several times, but then one alert chaser grabbed him and shook the living daylights out of him.

We tried a number of remote-control knocking devices. The square in Balin House had washing poles, between which was stretched a washing line for residents' use. On a dark night we would lower a line and tie it to a piece of string attached to somebody's door knocker, then hide and wait for someone to walk into the line and knock on the door. On one occasion an angry resident grabbed hold of an entirely innocent victim. Attaching a piece of string on a downstairs flat's knocker and operating it from a balcony above was another innovation. We were in danger of becoming trapped if the victim rushed upstairs, but we could gain access to the roof and descend in another block, or we'd run on to the first-floor balcony, climb over, suspend ourselves from the

ELEPHANT BOYS

railings and drop to the ground. It gave us a considerable jolt, but we did it anyway. A family who occupied a downstairs flat, which they furnished with orange boxes and tea chests, suffered from just about every kid in the buildings to the point of being persecuted.

In a cul-de-sac in Long Lane, between Balin House and Crosby Row – just next to the bootmender's shop where you could also buy two pennyworth of cat's-meat among the smell of horse oils, boot leather and horse meat – stood a row of derelict houses. Most were open to the sky, holes gaping where bombs had passed through. In the middle of the row stood a three-storey house with the rafters, where the floor had been, providing a catwalk. The stairs were rickety but still intact and upstairs at the back was a room barely touched by the war. We managed to rig the door with a sliding panel so we could open and close it from outside without using a padlock which would have attracted rival gangs of youngsters. Only the inner core of our gang knew about the room: we decked it out with old posters, a calendar, clock, candles and even a small Primus stove, together with some scrounged furniture smuggled in. For months it served as a comfortable headquarters until it was discovered and wrecked by intruders in our absence.

Climbing buildings was a daring pastime. Probably it began by retrieving balls lost during games of football and cricket. A coat thrown over walls topped with broken glass did not always provide sufficient protection to the hands, but cuts were no deterrent to adventure. Some boys became so skilled that they could scale the most difficult precipices, walk along narrow walls, shin up and down drainpipes and leap across chasms. Balin House is sixty feet high and many times drainpipes were climbed to the top floor in order to climb through a window after a doorkey had been lost. A nimble lad could earn sixpence from a locked-out resident. I wonder if this was practice for a life of cat burglary for some. Scaffolding around new building work, sometimes as high as a hundred feet, was scaled for a dare; and factories were entered, not so much for their wares, but for a challenge. Freddie Wake was once retrieving a ball that had been kicked over a wall from Balin House: after clambering over the pram sheds, he edged on to the wall only to find the ball had dropped into a deep 'area' by a factory wall. He was climbing down a drainpipe when it came away from the wall and he fell onto a jagged pipe that was pointing upwards. It penetrated his backside. In agony he tried to climb back up, then had to wait for help. He was rescued by a party of boys and firemen and rushed to Guy's for major repairs – fortunately he survived.

Hanging on to the tailboards of lorries was another daring pastime. It was a convenient way to travel. Sometimes the objective was simply transport along main roads, in the assumption that the lorry was going where you wanted to be. Sometimes it was just for the thrill of it. Imagine leaving the Trocette cinema in Tower Bridge Road, walking back towards Long Lane, then seeing a lorry heading in your direction. It saved a long walk for short legs. One, two or three small boys with their backsides sticking out of their trousers, clinging to the back of a lorry, knees bent to keep feet off the ground, was not unusual! If they noticed this the lorry drivers either grinned and put up with it, maintaining a steady speed, or they stopped and shook a fist at disappearing ruffians; or occasionally they would speed up and weave for their own delight. It could be terrifying when a lorry accidentally or deliberately picked up speed. If your hold was not secure you could end up in the road severely grazed, or worse, fall into the path of a vehicle. Stories of kids falling under wheels was, of course, no deterrent to the incorrigible. Some tailboarding had a more industrial purpose: jump up on to a tailboard, climb up on the lorry or open the back door to a van, roll off whatever you could see and hope to find something profitable in the wreckage. 'Off the back of a lorry' became a term for pilfered goods. In later years some kids formed gangs of 'jump up' artists.

Another expression which came about at that time was 'latch door kids'. It was common practice to hang a key on a piece of string inside the flat which could be reached by feeling with fingers through the letterbox. The key could be pulled through and parents could go to the pub without trusting a key to a child who was almost certain to lose it. The risk of burglary was surprisingly slim. I suppose there was little worth stealing. Those who did not have access to a key would sit on the steps of The George in Long Lane or its downmarket rival, the 'Carbolic', awaiting the departure of a family member. A packet of crisps with the salt in a little piece of blue waxed paper twisted to keep it closed, or an arrowroot biscuit, would turn up every now and then with a glass of lemonade or a weak shandy. My mother didn't like the stigma of her children being seen sitting on the pub steps, so she made only

ELEPHANT BOYS

infrequent visits to The George. This afforded my dad plenty of opportunity to carouse with his friends.

Balin House had its own 'square', an area of asphalted ground within the flats which served as a useful playing ground. It was two squares, really, and the smaller of the two overlooked by our flat was at the rear of the building. The front square had a row of pram sheds, used mostly for storage. Every now and then nosy neighbours watched as some suspected person turned out his shed in the presence of the police. A soldier, standing in the square, once caught a baby as it fell from a first-floor window; it was rumoured that the mother was unmarried, so not too much fuss was made.

The most popular game was buzz, which had a number of variations. Basically one person on one side threw a ball and anyone on the other side who got hit either dropped out or increased the number on the other side. They could pass the ball to each other, with no running with the ball allowed, and attempt to trap the remaining opponents whose aim was to avoid being hit. The game could go on for hours, or more usually until a misdirected shot broke a window. As the cost of repair was a half-crown, the square emptied very quickly.

Cannon was a game where sticks were placed against a wall and broken by throwing a ball; then one side had to swoop in to rebuild the sticks into a kind of wicket without being hit by the ball thrown by the opposite side. Tin-can Tommy started with a can being thrown and, as the nominated person ran to retrieve it, everyone hid; he then had to spot you and shout 'Tin-can Tommy, one-two-three', banging the can on the ground and calling your name until everyone was caught.

British Bulldog and Hi-cock-a-rooster were similar to each other, but Bulldog was a rougher game. Opposing sides of equal numbers had to pass each other without being barged or bundled out of the arena. For bulldog you just ran and jinked at top speed, attempting to reach the other side without being scragged and brought down by an opponent. For Hi-cock-a-rooster you hopped on one foot and barged into opposing team members to eliminate them if they put a foot down. Imagine the arguments: 'Yes it was'... 'No it wasn't'...

Piggy-back fights were great fun and very popular, usually played with great gusto and resulting in scratches and torn clothing. Hi-Jimmy-knacker was played by one side leaping on to the backs of the other side who were lined up, bent double, in a queue facing a wall. They then had to withstand the combined weight of the team on top, whose members would shout 'Hi-Jimmy-knacker, one-two-three' and run one at a time, launching themselves as forcibly as possible on to the line of wincing opponents. Eventually everybody collapsed in a writhing pile.

Hopscotch was played on a chalked-out series of squares on the pavement. There were several versions including a large circle divided into squares around its perimeter. There were games where arrows were chalked on walls and in roadways, or the dank arches beneath London Bridge railway station. One team would seek out another, sometimes taking all evening and late into the night to do it. We could roam for miles and when we returned home an angry parent would glare from a balcony, hoarse from calling a name.

Alleygobs featured five coloured blocks which were cast on the ground. They then had to be picked up – within the time you threw a stone in the air or bounced a ball on the floor – and caught; once in your hand they were thrown in the air and caught on the back of the hand. I can't remember how the game was scored. It was one of those mysteries of science, like the gyroscope set spinning by the pull of a cord which kept it impossibly upright, or the yo-yo, which I never could retrieve after the first throw, or the bubblegum balloons deftly exploded on the lips of experts.

We played draughts, snap, rummy, chase the ace, Newmarket and, as we grew older, indulged in card schools of nap, pontoon, poker and solo. Cricket was played with an oil-drum or similar for a wicket and, where possible, a sorbo rubber ball. Football most often was played on rough ground with a tennis ball and goalposts marked by folded coats or chalked lines. Footwork was classier than most professional teams have nowadays: I remember boys who failed a test for Millwall who today would be candidates for top-flight teams. At school we wore boots which had to be softened with Dubbin, or else they were agony to wear – not like today's 'carpet slippers'!

Probably not befitting the description of games was 'bunking in'. Favourite for this was the Trocette cinema in Tower Bridge Road, Bermondsey, a fifteen-minute walk from Balin House. Saturday morning picture club cost 6d and at an early age I didn't mind paying that. Cartoons, short films and a serial were good value. I remember with fondness Johnny Mack Brown (whom my uncle Wag had known in Hollywood), Hopalong Cassidy and Dick Foran, who featured in a rip-roaring cowboy-and-indian saga which ended each week with a cliff-hanger – next week he would miraculously escape in the most outrageous fashion, or he was rescued by the Sons of the Pioneers, who always rode towards the action with a song. Unpopular with me were the 'cissy' cowboys Roy Rogers and Gene Autry. They also sang. Yuk!

For the general cinema, main features were rarely paid for: entrance was obtained by stealthily opening an exit door with a piece of wire and creeping in, or a dozen of us charging past startled usherettes and quickly sitting down while the film was on. Some were spotted and chased out, but as long as one was inside he could open doors for the others. If that failed there was always the doorman who would accept half the admission charge to let you sneak by him. On one occasion the Trocette was short staffed and could not cover all the exits through which we were sneaking, one at a time, at short intervals. I remember getting to a seat and then watching my mate Dave Parker stumble through the door when it was his turn. He was promptly caught in the crossbeams of several torches as he braved it out by calmly making his way down the centre aisle just like a German bomber caught in searchlights. Boldly he stopped at a row of seats with a vacant one in the middle then, while the paying patrons stood up for him, pushed his way through and sat down. A suspicious usherette kept her torch on him and beckoned. Steadfastly, he sat staring at the screen in total disregard. Eventually she was driven off by irritated patrons and he stayed for the whole show.

Other cinemas nearby were the Globe, Old Kent and Regal in the Old Kent Road; the Astoria, a short bus ride further on at Canal Bridge; and the Elephant's own Trocadero and Elephant and Castle. Meanwhile, a No. 35 bus went direct to the Regal and the Golden Domes at Camberwell Green. Cinemas had split programmes in those days. On Monday they showed an A and B film, with a complete change on Thursday and again on Sunday for one day only. This was usually a gangster film with someone like Humphrey Bogart, James Cagney or George Raft.

Fights in cinemas were commonplace. Dice games were played in the toilets. A chorus of catcalling in the auditorium was not uncommon, especially if the programme was not up to expectations. Uncommon was vandalism: on isolated occasions seats were cut up or had chewing gum squeezed into the fabric, but the daubing of paint or damage to property was not considered to be of any use. Buskers paraded outside most cinemas to entertain the queues. The most famous was known as Muttoneye, due to his singular socket, who played a small organ and was popularly thought to be a millionaire. One old fellow would sing 'I'm going to lock my heart and throw away the keys', then fling a bunch of keys into the road – he often had to struggle to get them back as some rascal tried to kick them down a drainhole.

Gangster films were popular viewing. Troublesome youngsters who upset their parents would get a 'clip' and be asked if they wanted to grow up like Dillinger, or be described as 'young Dillingers' – reflecting the notoriety of the cinema's best-known gangster. Teenagers generally visited the cinema at least twice a week, often more. It was easy to see a different programme any night of the week. Tickets were 9d or 1s and later increased to 1s 3d or 1s 6d, good value for young men resolved to drool over Susan Hayward or Linda Darnell. Erroll Flynn romped through the greatest version of Robin Hood with Olivia deHavilland as his Maid Marion. Johnny Weissmuller impressed us by wrestling crocodiles – though we would much rather have wrestled 'Jane', played by Maureen O'Sullivan. *Zorro* featured Tyrone Power and the best sword-fight with that master villain Basil Rathbone; unlike Erroll Flynn, they could actually fence. The brilliant *Hue and Cry*, starring Harry Fowler, depicts the romance of life on the bombsites of London. It featured hordes of young boys like ourselves in the sort of adventure we craved. It is the best reminder of how London looked after the war.

We mimicked our celluloid heroes. Cigarettes dangled from Humphrey Bogart lips (they'd take off a layer of skin if allowed to stick). American drawls were effected and perfected. We rode with old 'short-in-the-saddle' Alan Ladd, right up to his appearance in the greatest western of all, *Shane* (look for the shot after the opening titles when his approach is framed between the antlers of a deer, then a cut to what every young man believed was the archetypal hero of the West). We drifted into town with Henry Fonda, fought redskins with John Wayne and rode in posses with Randolph Scott. We too outdrew the baddie, and I dare say rode into the sunset with the girl.

'There are heroisms all around us' – so goes the title of a chapter in *The Lost World*. I longed to be a hero just like Lord John or

Malone. My moment came when we visited a place called the Rising Sun, near Whipps Cross, on the edge of Epping Forest in east London. The area was a series of ponds which were fished sometimes by rod but more interestingly by dragnet. This could be an old piece of clothing trawled through the shallow pools to see what turned up. Newts, beetles and all sorts were eagerly inspected. Kids also fished with nets on the end of a pole. Suddenly, that day, a young girl stepped into a bomb crater and an alert was screamed by her friends as she struggled in the water. They ran from adult to adult sitting on benches around the ponds only to be ignored. By now her face was turning blue. Impetuously, I jumped in and grabbed her hand, only to step into the same hole. I couldn't swim. Now two of us thrashed about until cool Johnny Hooper reached out with a fishing net. I grabbed it and held on to the girl as he dragged us out. The girl was promptly attended to by adults. I was left sopping wet to get on a No. 35 bus back to the Borough. It was a long journey. When we arrived at our flats I was hoisted on the shoulders of my mates and enquirers were told of my valiant deed (Johnny Hooper didn't get a mention). I couldn't get into our flat. On this occasion my mother had joined dad in The George. Word reached her and she was much embarrassed at having been sought out, as though this was a regular activity of hers. Would you believe it? – I was told off for not going to my aunt Doris's home in Walthamstow, instead of getting on a bus and risking pneumonia. Such was the reward for heroes.

My aunt told the story to the local paper and a report duly appeared which was posted to my dad. He wasn't at all satisfied with the small squib, which did not contain my name and address, and he wrote to the paper and told them so. The next week a fuller account appeared and as a result we received a visit from the young girl and her dad who gave me ten bob. My Mum was embarrassed because I was wearing a set of soiled cricket whites. She kept the clippings for many years but eventually they disappeared. I have forgotten the girl's name, but I remember that she lived near Old Street, Islington.

My half-brother Jim was appointed to give me swimming lessons in Kennington Park open-air pool. I did moderately well and felt able to join the improvers' class during school swimming lessons. The PE teacher had his own method of teaching us to swim a width of Grange Road Baths pool. He lined us up facing six

ELEPHANT BOYS

feet of water, told us to swim to the other side and blew his whistle. Either you made it across, or you hastily turned around to grab the wall. For quite some time afterwards I swam 'arms only', a method based on the memory of the desperate struggle to haul myself across the pool to safety.

Youth clubs were popular, except that many of them expected to include attendance at church service once a week. The trick was to put in only enough chapel visits to avoid expulsion. Snooker was as popular then as now. Outdoor sports were encouraged and so was boxing. Charterhouse club, sponsored by the famous Surrey public school, was just around the corner in Crosby Row and had our gang as members on and off over several years. We would get chucked out, then somehow manage to rejoin, placing a burden on ever-suffering clergymen who ran the club and tolerated us remarkably well. Dancing classes were held in the girls' club further along Crosby Row. We attended because it gave us an opportunity to have a clumsy grapple with the opposite sex. The practice was to stand the boys at one end of the upstairs hall and the girls at the other; on the command we would advance upon each other and our partner would be the one we walked into. No matter how I tried, jinking, weaving and jostling, I never got to dance with pretty dark-haired Maureen, but Brenda always managed to get me. We trudged around the floor, arms rigidly keeping a space between us – one two three, one two three – lacking any notion of rhythm and style. I still dance the same way.

I joined the boxing team and had my first representative bout when we were visited by a club from Herne Hill, Dulwich. The priest had matched me with an opponent who was said to be a district age-group champion. I had no experience at all at boxing and wasn't expected to get through three rounds. But he hadn't come up against a slugger. He stuck out a few left jabs and I swung some roundhouse punches. Suddenly he went down, coughing and wheezing. His coach retired him halfway through round one claiming he'd been hit in the throat and couldn't breathe. The contest was declared a draw. My mates reckoned they couldn't bear losing to a scruff like me. I was then considered too rough for the boxing team.

Fights without the protection of the Queensberry rules usually did not take place in the club. On one occasion two older boys fell out; we followed as one chased the other from the clubhouse.

ELEPHANT BOYS

When we came on them the pursuer had spread-eagled his prey on the ground, sitting astride him with his knees pressing on his upper arms, pinning him to the ground while he gripped his hair with both hands and banged his head on the pavement. These were educational occasions.

All youngsters like mysterious places. We had many. Whites Grounds in Bermondsey had a cork factory which had been abandoned. Sprinkled all around the factory grounds were pieces of cork of varying sizes and shapes – it was Lego without the pins and could be used to build model forts for use with lead toy soldiers, or to construct entire model cities on the dining table at home. The 'sulphur mines' was a piece of land at Great Maze Ponds, on which the new wing of Guy's Hospital now stands. The sulphur was from furnaces in Guy's and was dumped amongst other rubbish on the wasteland. We dug it out of the ground and when burnt it gave off an eerie bluish light. Wrapped in paper soaked in saltpetre, which could be bought in a butcher's shop, it made a splendid smoke bomb. We once raided Charterhouse girls' club, which was segregated in a building around the corner in Crosby Row, and tossed in a smoke bomb, entirely disrupting their dance night.

Great Maze Ponds was a wasteland of dumped rubbish, with hidden spoils lodged inside secret hideaways and behind bricks loosened in broken walls. In my innocence I hid, in a hole in the ground marked by a stake, my Mum's Christmas present: a small mirror and a pretty notebook, wrapped in a cloth together with a perfume bottle which my Mum had discarded and I had filled with blackcurrant juice (well, who could afford perfume?). When I retrieved my treasure the mirror was broken and damp had penetrated the notebook. Only the 'perfume' remained, which on presentation received a knowing look and consequently did not spoil my mother's clothes. Tarry substances made midnight torches as we played secret games. When Johnny Rose waved his torch as a signal he shook off the dripping tar onto my hands; I never complained, but I still bear the circle of pale skin on the back of my hand.

We burrowed into back gardens and abandoned houses. On one occasion we tunnelled under a wall and found ourselves in some old dear's parlour – it's even money on who was the more startled. We fitted ourselves up with 'junior detective' cards and badges and set about solving crimes and following suspects. One time, when we peeked around a corner at a boy acting suspiciously with his girl accomplice, we discovered his trousers around his ankles; giggling our presence, we made off when he hobbled towards us shaking his 'fist'. Sexton Blake and Tinker never had such interesting investigations. Johnny Rose told a story of a man who not only gave live sex exhibitions, but also molested young boys. Every new place we explored was accompanied by the expression 'Watch out, Bill Gooch will get you'. I never believed he existed, till an unshaven rough man spoke to Dave Parker and me in the Borough High Street and invited us to a party. He looked pretty much like Johnny's description of Old Bill Gooch. We stammered words to the effect of 'Do me a favour' and 'Leave it out' and walked into the Post Office.

We invented a hidden language where we coughed and uttered words at the same time. It was quite effective for a word or two, as it didn't get picked up by those not in the know, but occasional fits of coughing when we got over-excited gave us sore throats and brought about enquiries to our health.

Once I climbed a fire escape ladder which stood erect against the wall of a factory adjacent to our sulphur mines. At the top was a platform, beyond which a difficult climb was required to negotiate a protruding ledge to reach the top of the building. The climb had been made by our best climber, Stanley Pell, on a previous occasion. With two friends I climbed to the platform and then alone made a terrifying climb to the roof. I had discovered a fear for heights and only the thought of humiliation in front of my friends enabled me to get to the roof where I sat covered in cold sweat. I then found I couldn't make the return climb – probably it was going backwards and downwards, which terrified me even more than the climb up. I made several attempts, only to return to the roof. My friends below the ledge couldn't see me, so I kept up a dialogue about the view and the fact that I could not see any lead (which was supposed to be part of the roof covering) and found all sorts of excuses not to climb down. Unfortunately it began to get dark. I had to nerve it again. The worse horror of humiliation overcame my reluctance and I made the return climb without giving away my fear to my friends. They must surely have suspected the truth, but in the true tradition of loyalty to mates they never let on. After that climb I never made another anywhere near as difficult. The respect of my friends was reason enough to make that difficult climb. It was not necessary ever to repeat it.

ELEPHANT BOYS

Near Tower Bridge, on the north side of the Thames, we could change into our swimming 'cossies' in a cave situated below the river bank. We actually swam in the Thames, which in those days was no less dark and oily than it is now. It was not unknown for a boy to swim across to the south side. For some reason logs, twenty or thirty feet in length, floated in the river. I suppose they were waiting to be hauled to a mill somewhere up river. We would sit astride the logs and some older boys would run along them, arms outstretched for balance, as they bumped and rotated under their weight. This all ended when a boy named Dagon fell off and was sucked under a barge.

The Borough Market is situated near London Bridge railway station. It is a fruit and vegetable market. Although it was patrolled by watchmen, we used to scale the tall wire fence and pinch fruit. Stanley Pell played football with a brown paper packet he found lying in the gutter outside the market. When it burst open he found it contained fifty pounds. He took it to the police station and that was the last he saw of that. The opinion of his friends is not easily expressed here. Our greatest expedition was a raid to capture bananas. We had never seen them and the first shipments after the war were a major talking point. Some of us decided that we couldn't wait for prices to come down to ones our parents could afford, so we raided the place they were being stored in. Balin House was pleasurably surprised to have these strange forgotten fruits sold for a penny a time in the 'square'. Similar raids were made on the many wharves which lined the river Thames. For some reason we only ever seemed to find copra, the hard part of a coconut – it was terrible to eat. The bonded warehouses were too well guarded for us to take on, although they did not deter older villains who were prepared to be violent and to risk serious consequences. We were not yet at that stage of our development.

School was a crude affair. The worst was, without doubt, Riley Road in Bermondsey. It accommodated the roughest of the toughs from that part of London, including Frankie Chapman and a boy named Kemp whose reputation was widespread. My brother Stan was sent there for a short spell. Fortunately for him our mother obtained a transfer to Camberwell School of Arts and Crafts, where his natural talent as an artist could be developed. It shaped the rest of his life, as he made his career around the art side of magazines and comics.

I went first to Snowsfield School. It still stands by the ancient Guinness Buildings off Weston Street, Bermondsey. I did moderately well. I actually passed my eleven-plus (then called the scholarship) but because there were not enough Grammar school places to go round I was sent to Bermondsey Secondary Central in Pages Walk, off the Old Kent Road. The building still stands but is now some sort of depot for the local authority. It was the equivalent of today's technical schools. Youngsters from our part of the country were not expected to do well and certainly were not encouraged. My mother tried valiantly to get me into Wilson's Grammar School, where one of my best friends had gained a place, but they would not budge. Jobs were not particularly scarce and immigrants were flowing in from abroad to fill shortages in the labour market. I suspect the governments of the day saw no great advantage in educating many of us to be anything other than factory fodder. When a girl from our flats, Jean something or other, gained a place at Loughborough College it was so unusual that all of the flats turned out to give her a good send-off.

I played for the football and cricket teams. To be fair the school was far less severe than Riley Road. Discipline was stern, though. Caning was commonplace for lateness as well as more serious offences. At one time a new headmaster, Mr Smith, took it upon himself to dish out the punishments. He was a rotund little man who would take the cane back well behind his head; from there it would curve in an arc to land like a piece of wet lettuce on the hand (previously lubricated with orange peel if we had prior warning of a caning). Although he used his full might, all he could raise in place of a blister was a stifled snigger on the lips of his victims. We positively looked forward to a caning from Smithy.

It was to our considerable discomfort that on a later occasion, when we were summoned to his office for the usual farce, we were confronted by another teacher who was a different type altogether. Cold and sadistic, today he would probably have the nickname of 'Jaws'. He split the end of his cane so that when it landed it pinched the skin and drew it upwards as he prepared to swing again. He gave short measured strokes from the shoulder. Nobody sniggered when Jaws was operating. Six strokes from him left a very red, sore and often split hand. Then there was the PE teacher, whose name I have forgotten, who did what PE teachers always did – used a slipper across the backside or back of the leg. We also had

ELEPHANT BOYS

a Mr Lewis, whose form of punishment was to arrive behind you, when you were least expecting him, and bring you out of your daydream with a bang on the head from whichever textbook he was carrying. As he taught physics it was usually a weighty tome that left your ears ringing and stars circling around your brain. I actually remember first understanding what 'seeing stars' meant after being landed a ferocious blow from what might well have been Newton's *Principia Mathematica*.

Our other Mr Louis was my form master in my last two years of school. I thought a lot of him. I believe he tried very hard to change our expectancy of what we could achieve in life. He was not known for his ferocity, unlike Mr Slapton who sounded and acted like something out of Dickens. Slapton had the boys of our age who could not get into Mr Louis's class. He was fond of caning the backs of their legs: I remember boys with smarting legs wincing in the playground after a bout of Slapton. Our deceptively soft Mr Louis could sometimes be driven to violence. The occasion came when the school decided to clamp down on lateness. Prefects were placed on every stairway at several levels. A bunch of us arrived a few minutes late and negotiated our way past the first prefect who took one look at our crowd and wisely decided to observe the wall as we slipped past. On the next level a boy took down my name as I led our bunch past him. I moved on but heard the crunch as one of the lads back in the queue administered his own form of corporal punishment with a right-hander. Louis was furious. He lined six of us up in front of the class and gave us three strokes each from a wooden ruler – not the flat side, but the edge. Three of those across the seam where the fingers of my right hand met my palm left me with red eyes. It did hurt, but I was determined not to cry. Emotion was not to be shown at any cost: only babies cry. When I shut my finger in a door of the school toilet I told nobody and walked the mile home with my fingernail hanging off and blood spotting the pavement. I remember reciting to myself 'It doesn't hurt, it doesn't hurt'. It was then I learned how to switch off pain. Years later, on my wedding day, when the door slammed on my hand as I was getting out of the car to go into the church, I went through the ceremony in much the same way.

The best fighter in the school was Roy 'Nosher' Norris. I was part of his gang until we fell out during one playful fight on the coal heap. In a general mêlée I jumped on his back and sent him

ELEPHANT BOYS

sprawling in the coal, ruining his brand-new blazer. I had to hide for the rest of the day in the toilets. In one school fight a boy named Watling picked a fight with a quiet classmate who used to sit next to me. Watling began to get the worst of it as his opponent, John, peppered him with straight jabs and a few tasty hooks. Watling's friends began barging John, pulling his clothes and spitting at him; even so he persevered until Watling had to be rescued by a teacher. The next day Watling sported a fat lip and a black eye and a new-found respect. John went on to become a good amateur boxer.

School dinners had their own ritual. First in the queue, either by early arrival or displacement, was the best school fighter or one of his cronies. Dinners were substantial enough, for in those days there was a determination to build children up. It was the eating habits that made me stay away, especially on a Wednesday which was salad day. Bowls of green stuff were spaced along the tables for kids to dip into. In the scramble to get to the bowls first they were often tipped over and bits were thrown back in, some half chewed. I was too fussy for that and walked a mile home for one of Mum's home-made meat pies. Mums had other ways of building us up, with bread and dripping sandwiches – unhealthy, perhaps, but certainly delicious – and we were given spoonfuls of malt and bribed into swallowing cod liver oil or halibut oil pills.

On the brighter side there was a photography club run, surprisingly, by the headmaster's cane-wielding substitute, and sports could be continued after school. There was a range of extra-curricular activity. The one we would have most liked would have been with Miss Fletcher, a young English teacher, with the form and looks to leave a warm impression on impressionable fifteen-year-olds. Her classes were very popular indeed, partly because of her fashionable New Look skirts that ended marginally above the knees. School debates gave me an opportunity to develop the vocabulary I had gained through reading. I was an enthusiastic contributor and had an opinion on everything; 'Know it all' was my reward for being too talkative.

In keeping with my aspirations as a junior detective I became crime reporter for the school newspaper. And classroom revues, in the form of a radio programme filled with acts, allowed me to write short scripts and recite monologues. School plays were best avoided, as they placed demands on time for rehearsal. I had the misfortune to be cast as an understudy in some domestic saga

ELEPHANT BOYS

which only required me to walk on with a bucket and place it in some designated spot for an imaginary cow to be milked by someone else. Of course I didn't bother to learn my part; equally of course, on the day of this Christmas play the actor didn't show and I was thrust into the part. I put that bucket everywhere but the right place. Howls of laughter met Miss Fletcher's gesticulations and my wanderings all over the stage. My mother, bless her, was in the audience. I was so flushed I must have looked like a beetroot. Bang went my chances of ever getting off with Miss Fletcher.

There were occasional visits from Chuckaway Charlie. He would arrive outside the school gates with a suitcase full of chocolate bars and sweet packets, which he would hurl into the midst of grateful youngsters with outstretched arms. I suppose nowadays he would be considered a threat, but I don't recall any trouble from that slightly batty, kind man.

Aged fifteen, I had an awakening. It was like stepping out from a tunnel into broad daylight. First, I saw a vision in the sky. I was standing on the balcony outside No. 60 when I looked up and saw a cloud crossing the sky. Stretched out on a divan was the body of a Roman soldier; sitting by his head was a figure that I cannot determine as male or female. I watched this apparition as it passed above me and disappeared into the distance. Then I looked down on to the paths and grassy verges of the new estates which had been built since the war. As kids we were familiar only with sparrows and pigeons. Now I saw starlings and blackbirds, and from this point on I saw things I had never noticed before. Television had been watched mostly for children's programmes; I had tried to follow political discussion and had been completely lost, but suddenly I could understand and, even more, I could discuss and form opinions. Dad and I watched a programme of political discussion featuring Bob Boothby, Michael Foot, Bill Brown and often Dingle Foot. It was lively, often heated argument – and no less so in our household, as dad took the Labour point of view and I, contrarily, the Conservative one.

My second vision took place in our flat when I sat in my brother's bedroom and watched a pageant of colour passing before me on the wall. Strange robed figures in bright colours paraded in silent splendour. When it faded I felt awakened and from that point became much more articulate and logical. It's the sort of thing you tell no other. Perhaps it is experienced by all growing youngsters. All I can say is that it was startling reality in place of colourless existence. It was as if, up to then, I had seen life through a veil which was now suddenly lifted.

After school I gained an apprenticeship as a compositor with William Jones Clifton & Co. Ltd in Hanson Street, round the back of Warren Street and near Tottenham Court Road, in the West End. My English was good and I obtained the job as one of two successful applicants from over a hundred. The job trained me well for what was to be a successful career in printing and publishing until the industry was destroyed by that worst of all West End villainy, Thatcherism. When the firm moved to King's Lynn, Norfolk, I decided to remain in London. After I left, the company premises were pulled down to become a bus depot.

Those are my fondest memories of work. Apprenticeships, as they were in those days, were a thorough training and preparation for a career. If I had not been indentured immediately on leaving school I may well have got into serious trouble.

Johnny Rose became a machine minder with the Haycock Press in the Old Kent Road. The skills were less demanding, but his pay was higher than mine, courtesy of the domineering Natsopa Union. Dave Parker joined the local 'mafia', called dockers. I once saw a dockers' local union meeting where the stewards entertained voters with a display of chair legs and iron bars – guess if they won the vote. For a spell Dave was involved in salvage work until one day they brought up a sunken tug and, on searching it, he discovered the skipper wedged behind a stove pipe looking down on him with a bloated grin.

ELEPHANT BOYS

3. LONDON'S ROARING TWENTIES

As a family the McDonalds of Balin House were held in good esteem. We were three generations, in a sense, all known as Mac. My mother often had to ask callers, 'Big, Middle or Small?'

My father, Arthur James (Jim), was foreman at the British Trolley Track in Copperfield Street, Southwark. Periodically he had to turf out unsatisfactory employees. He was a real hire-and-fire foreman who heaved out burly Irish navvies and any others who were workshy. He told me he used to find them asleep under benches. I remember him being hit with hammers, threatened with knives and all sorts of weapons; he would come home bloody, but if he said 'Out', out they went – peaceably or otherwise.

I was at home when, after filling his cigarette lighter from one of those little rubber-like petrol cylinders, he tried the lighter and the spark set the vapours on his hands alight. I threw the lighter into the fireplace and even though his fingers were covered in huge blisters he still managed to tell me off for fruitlessly stamping on his lighter. After applying some preparation that my mother bought from the chemist in Long Lane, he went to work that same morning.

Jim was as honest as any man I have known. He disapproved of my association with the Elephant Boys, although he never tried seriously to dissuade me from joining other boys from our estate who gravitated to the collecting point at the Elephant and Castle. Parents realised there was little to hold inquisitive youngsters at home; television was in its infancy, while ludo and snakes and

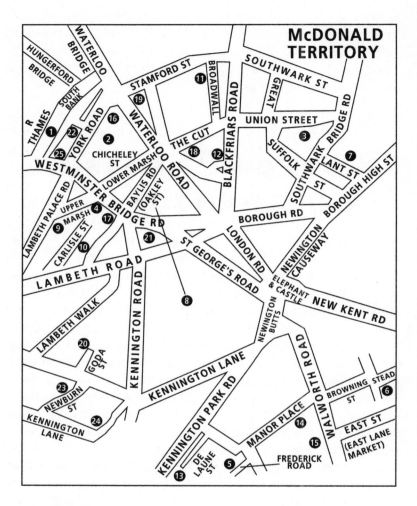

1. County Hall
2. Princes Buildings
3. British Trolley Track
4. Canterbury Arms (notorious Music Hall)
5. Birthplace of Stanley and Brian McDonald
6. Ada (Grandma Mac, Wag)
7. Jim Grace, Stanley and Brian McDonald (bombed)
8. Morley Glassworks
9. William McDonald, Snr
10. First recored McDonald home
11. Broadwall
12. Valentine Place
13. Ada and Dan Johnson
14. Manor Place Baths
15. Temple Bar
16. Waterloo Railway Station
17. Necropolis Railway Station (to Brookfield Cemetery, Surrey)
18. Old Vic
19. Duke of Wellington (Wellington Arms)
20. Site of the later attack on Johnny Carter
21. Morley College
22. McDonald family cottage (and Stinie Morrision)
23. Birthplace of Pheobe (Grandma Mac) Morley
24. Vauxhall Gardens (notorious pleasure gardens)
25. Billy Kimber

ladders no longer satisfied the needs of the daring. He did make sure I got a job when I left school at fifteen. It was through a friend of his I became an apprentice compositor and I've got him to thank that I have a trade which has always provided me with a good living.

Jim was born in 1887 at 20 Princes Buildings, Lambeth. The family were still living there when the youngest of thirteen children, Thomas, was born in 1891. Some time after that the family moved to a cottage at 116 York Road, Lambeth. The eldest of the boys, Sam, was by trade a baker working in Clapham. Working with him was a tall, slightly odd young man named Morris Stein. Stinie, as he liked to be known, had learnt bakery during a spell in prison for burglary. On his release he took a temporary job in the Clapham bakery to avoid the attentions of the law. Sam said he was always arriving late, mostly because he had been active at night prowling the neighbourhood for possible burglaries. He lived at a number of different addresses in the East End and south London, with a number of different women. Stinie was always trying to sell bits and pieces, so Sam introduced him to the landlord of the cottage in York Road – a jeweller named Max Frank, who also had jewellery shops in the Walworth Road and Southwark Bridge Road where he offered services for those wishing to dispose of dodgy merchandise. Stinie did a lot of business with Max, sometimes selling, sometimes buying stolen jewellery which he sold around the East End.

The McDonalds moved out of the cottage to live at 138 East Street – better known as East Lane Market, Walworth – and Max let the York Road premises out to an assortment of disreputable characters. On the top floor was Abel Grizzard. Brother of a notorious jewellery thief and receiver, Abel had a number of women working the dives around Lambeth. A middle floor was occupied by the Franks and there were other rooms let out to tradespeople. Part of the ground floor was occupied by Jack and Flo Dellow, although it appears Jack was only using her name. Her real husband had left Flo with a young son some years earlier in Lincolnshire; how she came to be in Lambeth is not clear. Jack was a bookmaker who ran with a crowd of racing toughs who headquartered at the Horns Public House in Kennington. One night Jack fell out with Larry Rappers, one of Billy Kimber's boys, and stabbed him with a butcher's steel (one of those things you use

to sharpen knives). He took off when Kimber's crowd came looking for him. To earn a living Flo became one of Abel Grizzard's girls, but told Max Frank she wanted someone to move in with her as a 'husband'. Max saw something of mutual benefit and invited Stinie around for tea. Immediately it was decided that Stinie would move in with Flo.

He had hardly moved in when he was arrested in 1911 for the sensational murder of Leon Beron, a police informer, fence and pitiless loan shark, whose bludgeoned body was found on Clapham Common. Some people thought his was a ritual killing, but more likely it was the equivalent of what we would call today a serious mugging. Beron was known to carry gold sovereigns and some expensive jewellery. Stinie was the last person to have been seen with him in the East End on New Year's Eve; and the fact that the body was found in Clapham the following morning was more than a bit suspicious. A bowler hat found in the York Road cottage revealed a cloakroom ticket hidden in the lining. This led to a parcel that was stored at St Mary's railway station, Whitechapel, where Aldgate East now stands. When opened, the bundle revealed a revolver and ammunition. This bundle had been deposited a few hours after the murder, adding to police suspicions. Stinie, who was a streetwise criminal, was said to own the hat. Although reprieved from a death sentence, and comforted by many letters and visits from Flo Dellow, he starved himself to death in protest in Parkhurst prison. Despite overwhelming evidence saying 'he done it', Stinie Morrison has become something of a *cause célèbre* for rough-justice seekers.

The McDonalds were London Scottish and had settled in the area around Lambeth before Jim's birth. They had been located in Upper Marsh, moving on to Broadwall, off the then notorious Stamford Street – abode of libertines, roughnecks and honest labourers who were obliged to live among them. Broadwall is still there but it is now completely changed. The family then moved to Valentine Place – still there today, tucked away behind Blackfriars Road, a graphics studio standing on the site of No. 12. The oldest building in the street dates from 1886, built at about the time the family was moving on.

There were thirteen children, nine brothers and four sisters (but one, Rosina, died at an early age), all ruled by a surviving matriarch known as Grandma Mac. Life was a permanent struggle. William, who had fathered the thirteen kids, died in 1896. He had been in the forces; a petition from his wife, Phoebe, to Queen Victoria after his death resulted in the princely sum of two pounds as a one-off discretionary grant. William junior became head of the family at twenty-five. He had a strict code which included early-evening curfews to keep his younger brothers out of trouble. Jim's fondest memory of him concerned one night when, having climbed out of a window to go across the river for a night in the West End, and sneaked in on his return, he was met by a grotesque ghostly figure in the passage entry. Afraid to come in lest the ghost got him, he stayed out all night. In the morning he discovered William had draped his coat and bowler beside the lit gas mantle to cast a huge shivering shadow!

Jim was the third youngest. Some of the elder boys had fought in the Boer War and also the First World War. Sam, the eldest, died in 1912. Second eldest brother, William, was a marine. Third eldest, Lance-Sergeant George Robert McDonald, B Company, 15th Battalion, Royal Scots, was one of 20,000 mown down by machine-gunners at Thiepval Wood on the first day of the Somme, 1 July 1916 – the 'big picnic'. His name appears on the memorial at Thiepval; he was forty-two. Tom, the youngest of the brothers, was lost at sea in 1919. For some reason, at the time he was using the name Thomas J. King.

Jim married his first wife, Janie Hobart, in 1910 and they had a son, Arthur James junior (Jimboy). The marriage didn't work out. Jim had followed his brothers into the mounted artillery and while he was away Janie stayed with Jim's sister Alice and her husband Bill Hayman, a train driver who drove the Royal Scot. She met another train-driver friend of Bill's named Jack, who had a club foot, and took up with him – leaving Jimboy on the doorstep for Alice to find. To be fair to her, she probably got fed up with Jim's brothers dragging him off to the pub when he was home on leave. He hired a private detective, who found Janie, but she was afraid to return home. Eventually she married the fellow who had limped off with her.

One brother, Charles, known as Wag, served in the Boer War as a cavalryman and was at Vereeniging at the time of the Boer surrender in 1902. In 1914 he re-enlisted as a mounted infantryman. He was at Woolwich Barracks when his brother Bert

ELEPHANT BOYS

enlisted in the Royal Field Artillery, closely followed by Jim. As the First World War got under way they were transferred to the Queen's Infantry.

Jim, my dad, was captured by Germans and rescued by Scots Guards in 1917. He used to tell me he was lying on the ground while the Germans seemed to be deciding what to do with him and three others, when the Scots came on them. In the rush to get away one German soldier thrust a bayonet through his wrist. (The scar would then be shown.) After that Jim and Bert were posted to India, stationed in Calcutta where they won the Calcutta Cup in the tennis doubles championship. After that, they were posted to Secunderabad as part of 4th Brigade RFA. German and Turkish agents had succeeded in stirring up a number of tribes – particularly the Mahsuds – which meant the British had to station forces from Britain in India to put down the uprisings. This they did in 1917; conversely Indian troops, who were not trusted to fight their own, were deployed outside India.

One sister, Anne, and her husband, Bill Burnup, were living in India where they had a business interest in a company named Hinton which dealt in silk and was associated in some way to a company the Burnups ran in Britain. They commuted between continents, living the high life with a large residence in India, servants and all, and a house in Brixton (at that time a desirable London suburb). Another sister, my aunt Ada, also bought a house in India.

Ada was the great fount of information on the family. Many early photographs were discovered in her house when she died in 1963. She was a great storyteller, particularly with tales that featured Wag. Born Ada Louise McDonald in 1879, she led a very businesslike life. From an early age she ran various commercial enterprises from home. She eventually became a freelance buyer and seller of fashion garments from her houses in Bedford Street and later Stead Street, Walworth, south London. She wasn't always easy to get on with, falling somewhere between harridan and grand vizier, with the wisdom of Solomon tinged with the cunning of Lucretia Borgia and the impatience of Margaret Thatcher.

Ada married Dan Johnston in 1910 and they lived in India for a spell in the 1910s. Bella, Dan's sister, was a rampant suffragette and found a ready umbrella-wielder in Ada. Dan and Wag became friendly and Wag was to draw him into the way of south

Londoners hovering on the edges of the underworld. Dan had been born in Crown Court, off Dean Street, Soho, scene of many an adventure in my mis-spent youth. He was 'well to do', working as a currier in his dad's leather business, but liked dicing with the illicit. When I knew him he had become a withdrawn, miserable man – not at all like Ada's description of his earlier life. Probably he'd had a surfeit of Ada's forcible personality and retreated into acquiescence.

Wag was the mischievous villain of the family. When Jim first joined him in the mounted artillery, his initial greeting at Woolwich barracks consisted of some veteran picking up his kit from the bunk he thought was his and strewing it all over the floor – not knowing Jim was Wag's brother. Wag arrived and promptly threw the other fellow's stuff out of the first-floor window. Most of it blew across the parade ground, only the boots remaining! Wag always looked out for my dad.

Wag had become friends with the actor Victor McLaglen. Vic was born in 1886 in Tunbridge Wells, Kent, and had served in the army after lying about his age, as so many adventurous young men of the time did. His true age was discovered before he could join the fighting in the Boer War. Vic liked a good fight, having taken part in numerous amateur boxing bouts and a handful of professional contests. His most interesting was in 1909 when he went six rounds with the giant World Heavyweight Champion Jack Johnson. Not too many people wanted to exchange blows with the toughest man of his time, who had chased Tommy Burns around the world before getting him to put up the world title. Burns virtually surrendered and new contenders did not last long, forcing Johnson to fight short exhibition bouts to get some money in. But during the first round with Jack, Vic was caught with a jarring straight jab. Vic remarked that they were being paid for six rounds; at that they danced and wisecracked in an exhibition of outrageous posing.

Wag and Fred, the youngest, were the only uncles I knew. The rest died or disappeared before I was born, although I did know all three aunts.

Ada told stories about Wag all the time. On a day when he was entitled to have a lie-in, he would deliberately set his alarm clock so that he could throw his boot at it when it went off. He was an experienced horseman. When Jim was being given a hard time during training by a sergeant, it was Wag who advised Jim to pull his horse's head in as the sergeant galloped at him, the result being the launching of a very unhappy sergeant into the air. I have Bert's Great War diary in which he constantly refers to Jim and Wag, mostly for being late back from leave, and their various pub visits. There are also interesting passages describing walks through gas chambers in preparation for the fields of France and Belgium.

Tom, the youngest, appears in Bert's diary as Thomas J. King. Bert often referred to him by his army number. It may be that Tom had enlisted previously and departed without benefit of discharge, then re-enlisted under another name. After the war Tom worked on a number of British warships and visited Australia, where he joined HMS *Polladern*. Disembarking at Port Said, Egypt in 1919, he joined HMS *Canberra* as a trimmer to return to England. No more is known. Wag put a notice in the *South London Press* asking for news of him. Family history records that he was lost at sea but the detail has been lost.

Phoebe Morley, who became Grandma Mac, was the daughter of Samuel Morley and his second wife, Anne Cater. Samuel fathered Phoebe at the age of sixty-five. Phoebe's father and grandfather had some connection with Morley College in the Westminster Bridge Road. The family were glassmakers with premises in Oakley Street, Lambeth, where they created stylish cutglass decanters and tumblers. One method of sustaining her brood was the dangling of a giant stewpot by the open fire, where her children could help themselves to a cup of stew. The children contributed what they could earn to keep the pot supplied. One by one the boys joined the army as a source of income and survival. Jimboy, my half-brother, said Grandma Mac was 'intoxicated' by the movies which were then in their infancy: she would walk him miles to see the latest film. She was constantly on the move, living all around Lambeth and Southwark, and her home was in Walworth by the time she died in 1934, aged eighty-five. She is buried in Streatham Park Cemetery.

The brothers mixed with the hard men of south London. It was virtually impossible to avoid that. A few doors away lived Billy Kimber whom Jim, Bert, Wag, Tom and Wal went around with. Visits to horserace courses were a popular family-and-friends outing. When I went with my dad after the Second World War, I recall the colourful tipsters. One, dressed as a jockey, sold folded bits of paper with an air of secrecy and mystification. Prince Monolulu, crowned with a feathered headdress and draped in colourful robes, yelled 'I gotta horse, I gotta horse', and sold the same tip to everyone, but it was part of the fun to buy from him. My dad said he was an East End con man named Pete Mackey; whoever he was, in the tradition of all true spielers he certainly could whip up a crowd.

It was at Kempton Park that Kimber recognised the opportunities available. He set up a book and Jim worked for him at Kempton, and on a street pitch off the Waterloo Road, until he joined the army in 1914. Wag worked for Kimber at Hurst Park and controlled a number of illegal street pitches around the Elephant and Castle and Blackfriars. His activities attracted the attention of Tom Divall, at that time a Metropolitan Police Inspector. The day Wag referred to the policeman as the 'divil in disguise', Divall – who was not known for his sense of humour – offered him out in the street and both removed their jackets for a stand-up fight outside the Duke of Wellington in the Waterloo Road. During the fight Wag's hand was broken and even though he was prepared to go on, Divall put his coat on and walked off.

Divall was a powerfully built, old-fashioned copper who came from the same tough area as our family. He was particularly pally with Billy Kimber and allowed him to operate his illegal bookie pitches on the basis that it is better to know where the enemy can be located than go looking for them. Although he did let illegal gambling go on, he was considered 'dead straight' locally and he kept good order. Gambling was considered a social problem, not high on the list of police concerns.

The lads used to meet at Billy Bristow's Walworth beer shop for cards and a regular late-Saturday-night game of pitch and toss. Divall would wander in, look around to see if anyone he wanted to talk to was there, look at the game to ensure everyone knew he was permitting it, create an atmosphere of discomfort, then stroll out again leaving no doubt about who was in control. One Saturday he did his usual tour and sauntered off. He was back in an hour to shut the game down, rousting everybody who was there; apparently on his earlier visit someone had lifted his pocket watch. Bristow, a street-corner seller of racing tips, paid a heavy price, as he was driven out of Walworth by Divall. He then tried his luck over the

water in the East End's Canning Town, but he was arrested there when Divall marked his card. Tom Divall knew his business and was not a man to be mistreated. Ada said he considered himself the match of any hardnut, which was a fair opinion until he came up against fairground fighter Bert 'Bombardier' Banks, who knocked him out.

Billy Kimber was one of the Elephant Boys whose behaviour caused him to be warned off the racecourses in the 1910s. In the little-regulated regime of the courses close to London he had set up a 'co-operative' which excluded anyone who did not pay into his mutual fund. The disenfranchised were liable to have their stands overturned and their satchels emptied. When the courses were overhauled he was driven out. He then robbed a wholesalers off the Old Kent Road. On the run, he enlisted in 1916, but was back around his old haunts within a short time. Most likely a deserter, he disappeared from the Elephant and resurfaced in Birmingham where he had family connections. At the recommencement of horseracing after the First World War, he set up a new book.

Jim described Kimber as a big, jovial, well-liked fellow, respected as a settler of disagreements and disputes. He could fight and was a natural leader. From his base in Hospital Street, between his aunt's home in Bordesley and the centre of Birmingham, he organised the working of the courses and again got up to his old tricks. He recruited from the Elephant and Castle and dominated the allocation of bookies' pitches at racecourses from the north to the south of England. Most bookies contributed to his fund for protection. They didn't seem to mind, for he had displaced the toughs who fought each other and beat up bookies who were reluctant to pay everyone who demanded their money. Although only in his twenties, he brought order to racing's criminal fraternity.

In 1918 Jim McDonald's older brothers, Wag and Wal, were in a fracas in the Walworth Road. In Kimber's absence, and because of the First World War, there had been no clear leader of the Elephant Boys. Wag was a natural and may have been making a bid for leadership. Warrants were issued for Wag and Wal, who promptly shipped for India, where Jim and Bert were serving in the army at Calcutta. By 1920 they were back and Wag and Wal beat up Billy Endelson and Freddie Mason to wrest control of the street pitches from Endelson's boss, George Hatfield (the leading south London bookie of his time). Hatfield also specialised in welshing schemes, setting up bogus books on the free side of courses and 'doing a runner' before paying out on the last race – or earlier, if he was having a bad day.

To cement his position as gang leader, Wag led a raid on some racing rivals, the Titanic Gang of Hoxton, who were located on the borders of central and east London. At that time the Titanics had established themselves as the leading London team by hammering the East End Jewish gangs and the Clerkenwell Italians. It was important for the Elephant Boys to reassert themselves as the premier London gang if they were to reap the rewards from renting out pitches to bookmakers. The Titanics were reeling from police pressure after a pitched battle with the Cortesi and Sabini gangs, in which they had been superior but had lost their top men to the police. A succession of fights around the Angel and Hoxton settled the matter. Alf White, Charlie Wooder, Freddie Gilbert and Sandy Rice agreed to Wag's leadership.

Wag had chosen his time well and was now master of south, east and north London. Success prompted Kimber to appoint Wag and Georgie Sage as his representatives in the south of England to control a network of street and racecourse pitches.

Kimber now set up his headquarters in Warren Street, a turning off Tottenham Court Road. Wag took control south of the river Thames, which included the popular courses Hurst Park, Sandown, Kempton Park, Ascot, Lingfield and many others. George, better known as Brummy Sage, took over north of the river. He was a villainous bookie, well into his forties, but a real roughhouser employed by Kimber to strongarm the opposition.

One branch of the Elephant Gang had never lost its supremacy. It was an all-female gang of shop boosters led by Fliss Diamond. One of its members was Maggie, sister of Billy Hill, a nine-year-old tearaway working for Wal as a runner. Maggie would one day take over the distaff side and become 'Queen' of the 'Forty Elephants' (a nickname taken from the tales of Ali Baba and his forty thieves). Billy and Maggie were from central London. Billy was learning his trade and would become one of London's craftiest thieves; and, thirty years later, a crime boss. Another of the Forty Elephants, Florrie Holmes, parked a huge Sunbeam car under the Lambeth railway arches and sat there taking bets for Bert.

Wal McDonald had a fiery relationship with another of the

female gang, ace booster Ada Wellman. According to aunt Ada she was a dissolute, wanton, through-and-through piece of south London low-life living on Minerva Street, Blackfriars, too close to home for Wal's comfort. She wouldn't leave him alone. It was a wearing affair. When he didn't want to know (which was often) she would come round to try to find him, and frequently made a public spectacle. It was usually left to Grandma Mac to shift her with a 'give-as-good-as-you-get' street row.

Then Wal had a great slice of luck. Ada Wellman was pinched leaving the Army & Navy Stores at Victoria wearing her extra-wide coat with its extra-deep pockets, inside and out, and a cummerbund, all stuffed with enough plunder to open a fashion warehouse. She appeared at Westminster Police Court where she was described as one of the 'Forty Thieves gang' and drew six months' hard labour. When she came out Wal had moved.

In the early 1920s Kimber paid the price for too rapid growth: his empire was a sprawling diseconomy of scale and into it stepped Charles Sabini. Known as Darby, Sabini was more ruthless than Kimber. Not only did he charge protection and collect fees for the best pitches, he also made 'offers' the bookies 'couldn't refuse' with ancillary services such as printed race cards, board wiping and supply of chalk. He really began to muscle in. His gang – by no means all Italians, and many of whom had been pally with Kimber's boys – came from around the area known as Little Italy, which stretched from Saffron Hill and Clerkenwell Green to King's Cross. They systematically bribed police and manipulated bookies into changing to their services without fear of being prosecuted. The result was a series of gang fights and razor slashings across the south-of-England racecourses.

Darby had started out at small point-to-point meetings and trotting tracks and still had an interest in many small profitable sites where he could rig the results and run a book at the same time. He formed alliances with other gangs, including the Titanics from Hoxton – now led by Alf White – who were still smarting from their humiliation by Wag. The Titanics were a thoroughbred team of organised pickpockets and con men who plagued the racecourses as well as the trains running to and from them. The White family themselves were also great con men. One scam was to get a girlfriend to go into a jeweller's and examine an expensive ring, taking it to the

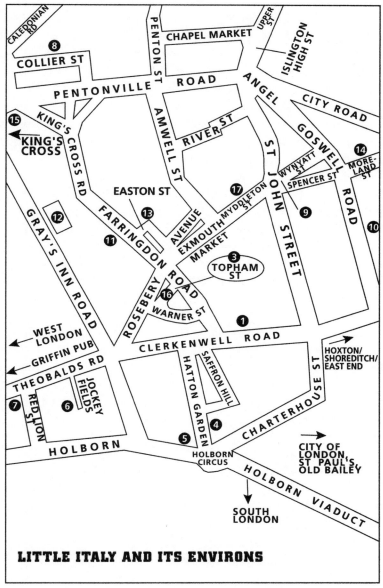

LITTLE ITALY AND ITS ENVIRONS

1. Clerkenwell Green
2. Albert Dimes
3. Fratalanza Club
   (once Gt Bath St)
4. Hatton Garden
   (jewellery quarter)
5. Gamages
6. Bullion raid
7. Old *Daily Mirror*
   building
8. Darby Sabini
9. The Bull
10. Post Office raid
11. Alf White
12. Royal Free Hospital
13. Harryboy Sabini
    and Queen's Head
14. Freddie Gilbert
15. The Bell
16. Cortesis
17. Billy Blyth

light of the doorway for a better look; then one brother would come up and snatch it, making off while others got in the way of pursuers. They had an arrangement with jewellers Joe Grizzard (brother of Abel, the pimp who once lived in the cottage in York Road) and Mike Spellman to shift the loot. That was until they went down for twelve months apiece. Prison was so hard that Joe Grizzard, who was in poor health, died soon after early release. Another White scam was to wait outside hotels for taxis to pull up and 'take charge' of luggage while arrivals went in to register . . . They would then find that their baggage had taken a different holiday.

Among the Hoxton crowd was country-house burglar Georgie Ingrams, who in a moment of madness with ace partner George Smithson stole two Gainsborough paintings from Benham Park House in Berkshire. Desperate to leave the country to escape the unwelcome heat, but without his usual fencing services of Grizzard and Spellman, he asked Alf White if he could put him in touch with some racing men who might be willing to buy the paintings. Alf dressed a bunch of racing toughs – including Wag and Wal – in soft trilbies and herring-bone suits and brought them to George's flat, where they posed as landed gentry. After poring over the paintings and other dry goods, they decided they didn't want to buy. When they had left, Ingrams found they had snaffled some of his hot jewellery items and while he had been kept occupied, someone had been through his bedroom drawer and lifted his cash. He never much associated with racing gangs after that.

After one pinch Ingrams's partner Smithson had shared a cell with Stinie Morrison, who was on his hunger strike and pretending to be mad (he probably was). Stinie had been removed to hospital and force-fed until he died. When Ingrams was pinched for the Gainsborough job he remembered Smithson's tale about Stinie and went on his own hunger strike. He too was force-fed. Then he was shown a photograph of the emaciated Stinie just before he passed away – at which Ingrams suddenly regained a full appetite.

At the August Brighton race meeting in 1920, Kimber's boys fought openly with the Sabinis. Fourteen men were arrested and severely dealt with by police magistrates. It was the first time the Sabinis looked like an organisation big enough to challenge Kimber's control. Brighton was a free course where spectators could watch the races from the Downs free of charge. Previously punters had been plagued with all sorts of crooks and con men until Kimber had chased them off. Many of these cut-throats saw in the Sabinis the chance to get back to the old ways. Among them were the East End bookies, mostly Jews, whose presence on the courses in the south was barely tolerated by Kimber. They resented his charging for their pitches and so they brought their strength and organisation to Darby Sabini. In March 1921, when two Jewish bookies refused to pay their royalties, Kimber's men upturned their satchels and watched a free-for-all as money and tips blew around in the spring breeze. The bookies complained to Darby, who ordered a retaliatory beating. Kimber could not let it go. He sent in Wag.

Wag hunted for his one-time friend at Greenford Park Trotting Track in Middlesex, where he came upon Darby's brother Joe and set about him in the betting ring. Darby arrived, pulled a gun and fired a shot into the ground. Wag, Dan Johnston, Billy Endelson and Chalky Brown did the only thing possible. Run. Police arrested two Hoxton bookies, Freddie Gilbert and Sandy Rice, who had quit working for Darby's new friend Alf White, as they were not happy with his deference to the Sabinis. They had stuck with Wag and fingered Joe for a beating.

Darby, who was questioned by police for having a shooter, organised himself very well and with police abetment the charges were dismissed. They were also dismissed against Gilbert and Rice, which may have resulted from Darby's connivance. Soon after, Gilbert, a former professional boxer, was repaid for his betrayal by being hacked about with a machete one Good Friday by some of the East End Mob. He received over seventy stitches in his wounds. Rice was stabbed in the buttocks by Joe Sabini, but slashed Joe's arm in return. Hardly recovered, Gilbert was spotted near one of the Jewish bookies' dives in the East End by Eddie Emmanuel who went and fetched ex-boxer George Langham. Gilbert fired a shot at Langham. The bullet struck a wall, sending splinters of stone into the eye of Langham, who ran off to get it seen to – leaving Emmanuel to a good hiding from Gilbert. Guns were becoming a trend as weapons from the First World War filtered through to the underworld. It is said, nowadays, that guns were not used by old-style villains. Certainly they were not as available as now, but they were willingly used when accessible. In their stead razors, knives, coshes and knuckledusters obtained tolerable results.

Kimber, Wag and Sage received an invitation to visit Darby's

ELEPHANT BOYS

King's Cross home to attempt to patch things up. Wag and Sage, suspecting a trap, tried to persuade Kimber to reconnoitre the scene and have men standing by outside. Kimber was not convinced. He believed the Sabinis had seen the futility of drawing the sort of adverse Press comment which had followed recent gang fights: the Sabinis had had the worst of the fighting and he judged they were willing to come to a sensible sharing arrangement. He was right as far as Darby Sabini was concerned.

On Sunday, 27 March 1921 Kimber, Wag and Sage walked from Kimber's house in Warren Street, Marylebone, to Gray's Inn Road, King's Cross, stopping for a few bevvies on the way. At 10 p.m. they were picked up in a taxi by Darby Sabini and two others and taken to Darby's house in Collier Street, which was located between the Pentonville and Caledonian Roads close to King's Cross railway station. A party was in progress – later described by police as an open-all-hours drinking orgy run by Mrs Sabini – and the three added to their already well-oiled dispositions.

At about midnight, four members of an East End Jewish gang who had teamed up with the Sabinis arrived. Kimber, who had lorded it over the Jewish bookmakers, could not stomach Alf Solomon, their leader. Kimber, the worse for drink, persistently denigrated Solomon and then exchanged blows with one of Solomon's minders who tried to get at him. Darby, Wag and Sage patiently attempted to calm the situation. Then Kimber suffered a gash over his eye from a life-preserver wielded by Jim Ford. At this, Sage floored Ford and Solomon pulled from his trouser pocket a revolver which went off as Kimber grabbed his arm – shooting Kimber in the side. The bullet passed through him, inflicting a painful wound that bled badly, then rebounded around the room, finally lodging in the brim of a hat on the mantelpiece.

Wag snatched the gun from Solomon and threw it through a window. He and Sage then tried to get Kimber out of the house while Solomon was being subdued: he now had Darby Sabini sitting on him. Kimber was too heavy to carry far, so they sat him down in Collier Street and called a taxi. The driver, thinking he was contending with drunks, drove off and returned with a policeman who put Kimber into the taxi and took him to the Royal Free Hospital in Gray's Inn Road. Wag and Sage scarpered to King's Cross railway station, where they took a taxi to Sage's house in Mornington Crescent, Camden.

Solomon gave himself up for the shooting, claiming Kimber had the gun and it went off accidentally in a drunken struggle. Kimber, who was not badly hurt, refuted Solomon's version but proved to have the usual amnesia associated with gang fights. On 27 April, a month after the shooting, Solomon – who described himself as a humble fruiterer from Long Acre, Covent Garden, but was described in court as having a string of convictions against him – was acquitted through lack of evidence. Ironically Kimber, described as the leader of a gang of desperate men, was fined five pounds for not having appeared at a previous hearing to answer a charge of beating up Matt McCausland (one of Sabini's toughs), a charge that had since been dropped. At one of many court hearings, frustrated police stated there was an agreement between the gangs that they would not assist in the prosecution of each other's members.

The Saturday after Kimber was shot, Brummy Sage, whom Billy had put in charge of the Camden Town Mob, led another attack on the Sabinis at Alexandra Park. Careful Darby had deposited his gun with a friendly thug named Tommy Mack who, inconveniently, had gone off to buy a round of drinks. When trouble started Darby reached for his revolver, only to find it was in the bar with Tommy. In a pitched battle in the silver ring before racing started, plainclothes police mixed in the fighting; but still they could not prevent the shooting of Darby's chauffeur and bodyguard Joe Best. Sage knocked Best down and Tony Martin, a Birmingham bookie who had lost part of his ear in the retaliatory beating the previous week, pulled a gun and shot Best in the head as he lay on the ground. Steward Tom Boyce had his teeth kicked in by Brummies who mistook him for a Sabini man. In the usual tradition Best, who nearly died, could not identify his assailant. Boyce accepted a payment of one hundred pounds, presumably to buy a new set of teeth.

Wag was without Kimber who was still recovering from his wound. In the face of mounting police and Press interest, he decided to make peace. He had been told that Solomon was not all bad and had only intended to shoot Billy in the leg. Wag spoke to Solomon at Sandown Park, only to be hit on the head with a mallet by one of Solomon's crowd. Apparently he was not aware his boss was only misunderstood. Wag waited for Epsom's Derby week to get even.

On Derby Day there was an uneasy peace. Among the heaving mass of spectators could be seen the hard faces of men bent on mischief; but hammers and knives remained out of sight. On the next day, Thursday, 2 June 1921, it was different. All-day feelings of displeasure manifested themselves into jostling and shoving and the occasional slap. Wag wanted revenge. He and his crew, mostly Brummies augmented by a handful of Elephant Boys, eyeballed the combined Sabinis, Whites, Cortesis and Jews, but left quietly at the end of the day's racing so their enemies would think they had been driven off. Instead, they lay in wait on the Epsom Road near Ewell for the lorry which always carried the Sabinis back to London. When the lorry showed, they drove a taxi into it and swerved their open-topped motorcoach to block the road.

As the lorry disgorged its contents, appearing to be ready for a fight, Wag's gang swarmed over the side of the coach and attacked. In the pitched battle they cut and battered Larry Green's gang from Leeds which Darby had been making overtures to (he had lent them the lorry to go to the Brick Kiln pub). None of the Sabinis was present. The Leeds bookies were smashed and battered by thirty to forty men in a fight reported to the Kingston Police as a riot. The law turned out in strength, arriving when the fight was over. Wag, his head gashed, was put into the Sabini lorry by his runner Fred Smith and driven to East Lane, where Grandma Mac put a stitch in his scalp using a sewing needle and thread. Many of the Birmingham crowd lingered a few miles away at the George and Dragon (now the Kingston Lodge Hotel) on Kingston Hill. There they were surrounded by an unexpectedly large armed police force, by now convinced they were dealing with Sinn Feiners who were very active at the time.

Rounded up for questioning, twenty-eight of them were charged with conspiracy to commit grievous bodily harm. It was a major news event, generating a lot of heat. Before the twenty-eight came to trial the East Enders staged a reprisal at Salisbury races. The police, who were expecting trouble, had put out a large force. When the bother erupted in the evening near the railway station, where the two gangs came together, they arrested East End ringleader Jimmy Ford, then had to bring up reinforcements when an attempt was made to rescue him. A police constable was clubbed to the ground and a police open tender was boarded in a general free-for-all resulting in nine arrests (this time all East

Enders). Somehow, bookie's clerk Frank Sundock fell under the wheels of a taxicab containing some of Kimber's men.

At the magistrates' court a gang of south Londoners, among them Wal and Bert, created a disturbance. The magistrate threatened to refer the case to the assizes, saying it was obvious a fair trial could not be held in Salisbury; presumably he thought south Londoners came from Wiltshire. Later the nine received sentences ranging from being bound over to keep the peace to six months. Among them was Jack Levene, whom Wal thought had hit Wag with that mallet. He went down for four months.

The battlefield shifted to Bath Racecourse, where Alf Solomon and his gang attacked George Riley, only to find he was a lure. Wal and a large force bent on avenging Billy Kimber set about Solomon and his crowd. The police arrived in time to catch Alf – leaking blood from a head wound received from a hammer wielded by Freddie Mason, waving a revolver. He stood trial as Henry Solomon to avoid previous form; it didn't prevent him getting a month's hard labour.

The Epsom twenty-eight, mostly Brummies, came up at Guildford Assizes where they were reduced to twenty-two and endured an unusual case: the judge, Mr Justice Rowlatt, decided after summing up the general case that he would make a 'for-and-against' statement for each of the accused. He asked the jury to make up their minds after each individual statement and write down their verdicts, to be delivered at the end of the trial. Probably he was trying to be fair: there was a distinct feeling of guilt by association, since nineteen of the defendants had been on the same charabanc and some had been armed with knives, coshes and pistols – although it was not clear who, as the weapons had been found under the charabanc seats.

After the judge made his statement for each defendant, the jury left the court, trudged along a corridor and up two flights of stairs to deliberate, then did it all over again for each of the accused. Five were found not guilty. The seventeen going down included the Brummagem Hammers brothers Tom, Henry and Eddie Tuckley. One of the Banks brothers from Waterloo received fifteen months. Sentences ranged from nine months to the customary 'carpet' of three years. It was a considerable blow to Billy Kimber. It didn't bother Wag too much. Before the police came for him he had shipped for Canada, in time travelling on to Alaska and then working his way down to Los Angeles – a trip recorded in a diary of his American travels which would last ten years.

It has been said that the Elephant Boys were 'all rough house' and did not have the brains of the Sabinis, but you only have to look at who got away and who got caught to see the error in that. The Elephant Boys almost always escaped; the Brummies were nowhere near as careful and, like the Sabinis and East Enders, were always going down.

The troubles continued. Sabini men George Langham, an alias of Alfie Solomon's brother, and Jim Ford slashed Sage-protected man John Phillips when he refused to hand over a tenner (he collected fourteen stitches for his thriftiness). A riot on Brighton beach occurred when Wal broke up a Sabini dice game: police arrived too late to catch the attackers, but arrested the gamers. Vince Petti, already suffering from a beating by Wal's team, suffered again at the hands of the police and was charged with assault for his pains. Petti, a relative of the Sabinis, had just been released from Borstal after three years for theft: this time he got a month in the penitentiary, his bail having been stood by British Cruiser Weight Champion Jack Bloomfield, another Sabini soldier. Going down with Petti was Tom Basciano, another candidate for the accolade for hitting Wag with that mallet. It has been speculated that Wag had offered a reward for the name of the mallet-wielder.

Kimber, Bert and others raided the Bell pub, right in the centre of King's Cross, which Darby Sabini used as his local. Bert was glad not to have found anyone worth beating up. He found out afterwards that Kimber intended to shoot Darby and put an end to his pretensions.

George Baker and Joe Jackson led a team from the Elephant against the Hoxton side of the Sabini operation, which developed into a gun fight in the Gray's Inn Road. Jackson was charged with shooting at Detective Constable John Rutherford, who thoughtlessly got in the way, with intent to murder him. It brought him a seven-year term in HM accommodation, while George Baker got five years. Sabini man George Fagioli received nine months for possession of a firearm. Next, Sage, Alby Medes and professional boxer Freddie Rye were pulled in by the police after being seen in Rosebery Avenue, Clerkenwell, close to the Queen's Head where Harryboy Sabini (who lived next door) was a frequent visitor. Rye, who was armed with a revolver, later lost his licence to box. Many, many boxers and ex-boxers made their services available to the gangs.

A short time later, Brummy Sage was taking the air with his wife Helen, Freddie Gilbert and a party of friends outside the Southampton Arms in Mornington Crescent – headquarters of his Camden Town manor – when Joe and Harryboy Sabini, Alf White, George West and a dozen others jumped out of three taxicabs and fired shots at them. Gilbert was stuck with a sword stick and hit with hammers. Sage grappled with Joe Sabini to prevent him getting in another shot and a general fracas began. A young constable, who was passing, chased Joe Sabini and took his gun from him, then held on to him despite threats from the Sabini team. Sage took a cosh away from Tommy Mack and proceeded to beat him over the head with it. To get away Mack jumped on to a passing tram, with Sage in pursuit. By now a large crowd had gathered and the tram was brought to a stop. Young passenger Amy Kent grabbed hold of Mack to shield him from Sage's blows, then continued to hold on to him for the police. Sage, who later claimed he was trying to rescue Mack from the hostile crowd, was arrested when he went back to help Gilbert.

Joe Sabini's gun was a long-barrelled repeater with a stiletto attachment. After firing at Sage he had used it to stab Freddie Gilbert; Alf White was said to have fired the other shot, but no other gun was found. At his trial Joe Sabini craftily swapped coats with brother Harryboy, then invited counsel to ask him how he could have concealed such a gun in his pocket. But a sharp-eyed policeman recognised the coats had been changed and that Joe's own coat was perfectly adequate to conceal the gun. At this time the woeful Mack was found guilty of wounding Amy Kent by stabbing her in the arm – he got eighteen months for riot, with a further six months for wounding. West was acquitted. Helen Sage had identified him as one of the shooters, then withdrawn her statement, causing an angry judge to allow her to be questioned as a hostile witness; even so, in accordance with the code, she refused to recall much of the incident.

A police constable brought a laugh when he described how Alf White had jumped into a taxi to get away: the policeman himself, standing on the running-board, redirected the taxi to Albany Street Police Station. White called the celebrated boxer Kid Lewis as an

ELEPHANT BOYS

alibi witness; and he called none other than Tom Divall, who liked racing men and was now a private security adviser to racecourses, to speak of his good character. It did him no good. White, said the judge, was part of a powerful organisation which frightened people, and would go down for five years.

George West was soon rounded up again, this time for his speciality. He would telegram a bet to an accommodation address, retrieve it and alter the horse to a winner. He would then don a post office uniform and deliver the resealed telegram, which was obviously timed before the race had been run, to a bookie for a certain win.

A week later the two teams from north of the Thames came face to face inside Paddington railway station. Freddie Gilbert, who now saw himself as a leading light in the Camden Town Gang, had a go at Alf Solomon and his brother George Langham – at which Harryboy Sabini jabbed a revolver into his midriff, threatening to blow his oddly located brains out and preventing him getting on a train. Police officers tried to arrest Harryboy who, having dropped the gun on the platform, coolly picked it up and boarded the departing train while his boys frustrated the police.

Gilbert, Sage and Elephant Boy Freddie Brett were arrested later that week and charged with demanding money with menaces from Sabini gangster Harry Margulas. According to Ada, it was a blatant set-up to counter the Mornington Crescent shooting charges – all the witnesses to the threats were Sabini men. Margulas then caused the arrest of Freddie Gilbert's brother John, George Moore and Joe Smith for allegedly offering him money to leave the country or 'twist' the evidence. They were acquitted when the case against Sage, Freddie Gilbert and Brett collapsed. Harryboy Sabini, already on bail for the Mornington Crescent fracas, was recognised in a police court by a policeman and charged with threatening Gilbert with a gun on Paddington Station. Harry, although only in his early twenties, was the worst of the Sabini brothers.

Everybody was fighting everybody: Kimber and the Sabinis, the Sabinis and the Cortesis (who, after splitting with Darby, were trying to take over). Newspapers reported the strife and questions were asked in the House about armed gangsters and racecourse gangs. In 1922 Joe Sabini got three years for shooting at Brummy Sage outside the Southampton Arms. Somehow Harryboy never

ELEPHANT BOYS

x

came to trial, but he and Eddie Emmanuel were bound over to keep the peace for the threat to Freddie Gilbert on Paddington Station. When Alf White received the five-year sentence for his part in the shooting at Mornington Crescent, there was uproar in the court. Alf collapsed while his family beseeched the judge to reverse his decision. In no time at all he was back on the streets. He had won his appeal on the grounds that the judge had misdirected the jury on the matter of Helen Sage's evidence (that she did not recognise him as one of the men who had fired at Sage and Gilbert).

Sage and Gilbert couldn't act. Therefore Bert, Wal and Jim McDonald, Billy Endelson and others called on Alf very smartly as he celebrated in the Bull public house on the corner of Wynyatt Street and St John Street, not far from the Angel, Islington. Alf, Jim Ford and Wally Cleal were dragged from their wives into the street where they were given a good going-over with coshes, Alf was flung into the back of a builder's lorry parked outside and had tubs of paint and turps poured over him. Someone suggested striking a match, but the brothers wouldn't have it.

With Joe Sabini inside, strong family ties meant that Darby had to keep him in some comfort. To facilitate this he had approaches made to two Maidstone Prison officers to carry messages and presents to Joe for two pounds a week each. The guards reported the incident. Alf White and George Drake – a terror from Paddington who once slashed a Soho prostitute who owed him thirty shillings, becoming known as the thirty-bob bastard – were arrested. Alf, lucky to be out after his sentence of five years for the wounding the previous year had been quashed on appeal, appeared in the dock heavily bandaged and with a walking stick. Allowed to sit, he constantly winced, but it didn't stop him getting eighteen months for the attempt to bribe the warders. Drake collected two years.

In the beer tent at Hurst Park races my dad, Jim, was badmouthed by Eddie Emmanuel – a Jewish bookie reputed by some to have invented many of the racecourse scams, and to be even more powerful than Darby Sabini. Jim did not consider himself a major player in the wars and told Emmanuel so. Eddie kept up the banter. Ada, who knew him through the rag trade, described him as a smallish, oily, bad-tempered piece of work, generally regarded as a grass and police collaborator. To Wal's amusement, Jim upended his pint of wallop over the detestable

ELEPHANT BOYS

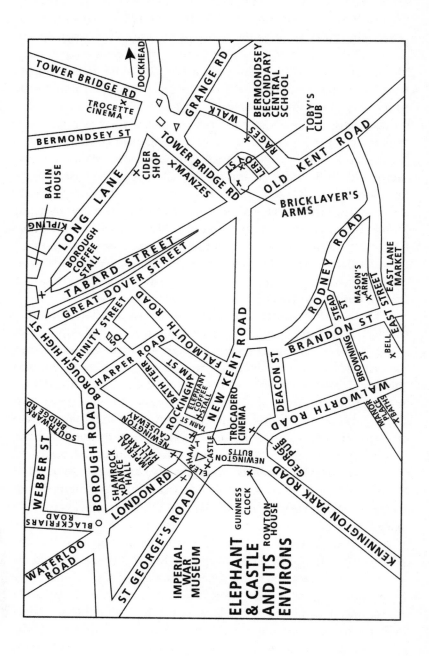

ELEPHANT & CASTLE AND ITS ENVIRONS

little rascal. Freddie Smith added to Emmanuel's indignity by lending him a helping hand but undoing the buttons on his braces, causing him to grab his receding trousers, to roars of applause.

Freddie was a young tearaway who once tricked himself into the driving seat of a van and drove off from Camberwell Green with a load of silverware. Stopping in a side street to paint out the tell-tale words on the van, he proceeded to East Lane where he flogged the silver to street traders. Arrested at the Borough, he managed to put the frighteners on witnesses, so by the time he came up at the Central Criminal Court even the driver who had been duped (into examining his rear doors so Freddie could hop into the driving seat) could no longer recognise him. In a surprise move the jury stopped the trial and he got off. He escaped again when he led a raid on the post office in Goswell Road, Islington with his brother Jack and two Peckham tearaways, Bill and Harry Thompson. Three got caught, Jack was acquitted. The Thompson brothers were found guilty, but then released after another gang who had been arrested for a series of raids up north took the rap for the Goswell Road job. Freddie, who never came to trial, had promised to watch out for their families if they coughed to an extra robbery.

Freddie, who lived at the Bermondsey end of Long Lane, was an associate of master thief Ruby Sparks. Ruby launched a celebrated career of cat burglary, shared occasionally by Lil Goldstein – whom the Press nicknamed the Bobbed Haired Bandit – and eventually married Billy Hill's sister Maggie. Freddie followed a different path as con man, extortionist and armed raider: he was typical of the satellite members of the Elephant Boys and his own small gang was the forerunner of what became known as the Bermondsey Boys.

The Sabinis came under a fresh threat when Alex Tomaso – the real name of Sandy Rice, who had been acquitted with Freddie Gilbert for setting up the attack on Darby and Joe Sabini for Wag's punishment squad at Greenford, and was high on the Sabini hit list – formed an alliance with Darby's former colleagues, the Cortesis. Saffron Hill racketeers, the Cortesis were aggrieved that Darby did not share enough of his crooked proceeds. Older brother Augustus (Gus) Cortesi considered himself a godfather. This title was being thrust more and more on an unwilling Darby Sabini, who in fact preferred to keep out of the limelight. So Gus was becoming jealous.

A major scrap occurred when Alex Tomaso, Gus, Enrico, Paul and George Cortesi burst into the Fratalanza drinking club in Great Bath

ELEPHANT BOYS

Street, Clerkenwell. Gus Cortesi's hand was knocked away by club secretary's daughter Louisa Doralli as he took a shot at Darby; the bullet went through a window. Tomaso laid Darby out with a wine bottle. Louisa, having saved Darby, then jumped in front of Harryboy Sabini who gallantly pushed her out of the way just as Enrico (Frenchie) Cortesi shot him in the abdomen. A general wrecking of the place followed. When the police later tried to arrest Frenchie, they were obstructed by a crowd who got him away.

The five assailants surrendered themselves to police. At the magistrates' court Mr Bingley commended Louisa Doralli for her bravery. She later admitted to being sweet on Harryboy, a favour he never returned when he recovered. Gus and Frenchie got three years, the others got off.

The general war continued. Jim and Wal were in the Temple Bar in the Walworth Road when Alf Solomon and a team from Aldgate turned the place over, threatening to do Jim. Wal, who was just leaving with his girlfriend, Mary Stanford, hid behind some dustbins and escaped being done. Mary said she took the lids off the bins and pretended to be rummaging for scraps to help shield him. Jim reckoned he himself only escaped being cut because some of Solomon's crew didn't want to have his brother Wag after them. Wag, by this time, was in America, but they might not have known this. In any case, Wag did one day repay Solomon for threatening Jim, shooting his mate Billy Kimber, and having his own head tapped with that mallet.

A retaliatory attack followed. Wal, Bert, Jim and others raided the Bottle Club in Whitechapel. Hunting Alf Solomon, they cornered his older brother Mark and gave him a good hiding. A week later, Camden Town bookie Georgie Williams had shots fired at him by Mark Solomon. Wal, Bert and Jim thought they had overdone the beating and wondered which direction the bullets would come from. Then Mark Solomon was arrested by suspicious police on a loitering-with-intent charge in an attempt to get a deportation order, but it was thrown out at Old Street police court. It turned out that Williams had been gaoled for a month for welshing on payments at Sandown – some of them to the Solomon brothers – and they had their own little feud going on. It could all get very confusing.

Harryboy got away with an attack on three London bookmakers, Harry Fellowes, Joe Turner and Joe Taylor, at Wye races. It was a clear case of demanding money with menaces. Tommy Mack, who had just come out after his calamitous meeting with Amy Kent, got another month. With him went a nasty little piece of work known as 'Babe' Mancini and a senior Sabini soldier, boxer Pasqualino Papa. These events were commonplace: Jim said they were almost always the Sabini crowd terrorising bookies who were not allied to any of the gangs. Joe Turner, who steadfastly refused to pay 'contributions' to anybody, was doubly unlucky when a crowd from the Elephant raided his Hampstead house, beat up his missus and emptied a bedroom safe of cash and jewellery. Charlie Say got nicked, but Freddie Smith escaped again. It was no wonder Freddie was called Lucky from then on.

Alf Solomon was a real badman who considered himself the enforcer for the Jewish gangs. In 1923 he and Alf White were found not guilty of causing grievous bodily harm to bookie Bill Homer, who had defied them. Matt McCausland was found guilty of assaulting Homer under provocation. He was bound over for twelve months after a police officer told the court the event was not related to the now notorious racecourse troubles. Generally it was felt that a few bob had changed hands.

One day in 1924 Solomon was sitting with Eddie Emmanuel in the Eden Social Club in Eden Street, a turning off the Hampstead Road, just across the Euston Road from Warren Street where the Euston Tower now stands. In walked one of Emmanuel's many grass victims, bookie Buck Emden. Seeing the informer sitting on a stool, he gave him a tongue lashing and when the impudent Emmanuel answered back, Emden smashed a glass on the counter and shoved it in his face. Solomon, who may have been minding the little Jew, came off his stool with a carving knife in his hand and stabbed Emden in the back of the head, killing him. Solomon claimed self-defence, saying his friend Emmanuel was 'bleeding like a pig' and he thought he was about to be stabbed again. Even though Solomon had been restrained from also killing the doorman, Mike Abelson, that amazing barrister Sir Edward Marshall Hall (retained by Solomon's friends) provided one of his celebrated theatrical defences. Flashing the jagged points of a broken glass in the faces of twelve quivering jurors, he got murder reduced to manslaughter and a sentence of just three years.

Pitched battles on racecourses, at wayside pubs and in London streets reached a climax in 1925 at the 'Battle of Waterloo', where

a huge fight took place outside the Duke of Wellington in the Waterloo Road. It flared again in 1927 at the fight in Ham Yard, near Shaftesbury Avenue. The battle at Ham Yard brought together two of the main protagonists, Wal McDonald and Harryboy Sabini, with a half dozen others on each side. The Yard, just off Great Windmill Street in the heart of Soho, was mostly derelict and strewn with rubble where building work was in progress. The fight with bricks, razors and knives left four men seriously injured and Harryboy with a stripe across his cheek given him by Wal. It may have had later repercussions. Darby Sabini wanted to call a truce, but Harryboy wouldn't have it.

At least eight deaths had resulted from the fighting and profuse cuttings and clubbings. Questions asked in the House of Commons caused the Home Secretary to do what home secretaries do when facing a crisis: promise masses of law and order. Seeing the writing on the wall, Billy Kimber and Bert McDonald fired shots into the bar of the Griffin pub in Clerkenwell, home base of the Sabinis, as a farewell message of goodwill. They then took off to join Wag in America. The exact date of Bert and Kimber's departure is uncertain. Ada believed that night-club queen Kate Meyrick went with them – if so, it must have been in late 1927 or early 1928, for certainly she was back in England in May 1928 when her clubs were raided and she was gaoled for six months.

Jim reckoned Kimber used his racecourse proceeds to provide him with interests in a number of West End clubs. He also had some association with disgraced American lawyer Abe Hummel, who achieved notoriety for his controversial defences of New York's gangsters until things got too hot and he skipped to London. Most likely Hummel intended to provide the same services to London's gangs, but he died in 1926.

Kimber frequented Kate Meyrick's society night-spots where he supplied bouncers and paid off police. Aunt Ada said he never paid for anything and senior members of his gang, including some of the brothers, often got treated to free drinks and meals. The gang's favourite West End watering-holes were Kate's Forty-three Club in Gerrard Street, where my dad worked as a stockman and did duty as a doorman in 1924, and the Silver Slipper in Regent Street. Both establishments practised after-hours drinking and gambling. Kimber would often remain in the Forty-three when the others had stumbled into the early-morning hours. There was a secret back door, really a hole knocked through the wall and covered inside and out by sliding panels. The inside panel was covered by a sofa which Jim had to pull away to open the exit, pushing toffs through when the club was being raided by police.

On one occasion, having pulled the panels aside, Jim observed a pair of legs belonging to a police constable who happily took a quid for not noticing what was going on. Jim could only get a few out and managed to push the sofa back before the police came back to question him. Satisfied he was only a doorman, they let him go, but Billy Kimber and several dozen others had the indignity of having to pay forty shillings – or twenty-one days – for drinking on unlicensed premises! The club had lost its licence after previous raids and was masquerading as a dance-club.

Kate, although fifty, was a good-looking woman and was enormously popular with patrons from the monied classes who would visit her many night-clubs, considering them a cut above Soho's usual joints. She had prosecutions against her and served time for abusing strict drinking regulations. But she managed to sweeten the police for much of the time.

When Kimber pulled out, Kate lost her protection and her clubs were constantly raided by police. Jim said that because they no longer received payments for staying away, they kept finding excuses to raid what were, for the most part, respectable clubs in an attempt to reinstate payments. The climax came in 1928 when Met. Sergeant George Goddard was caught in a trap accepting bribes to tip off various clubs about police plans. Banknote numbers paid out to Kate were found in Goddard's safety deposit box and both were arrested. Goddard received eighteen months' hard labour and a £2,000 fine – a small amount from his total take of at least £10,000. Dad said he was a shrewd copper, bent as a nine-bob note, who made enough for a luxurious retirement. Kate was sentenced to fifteen months' hard labour. This proved to be too much for her, as she died soon afterwards in 1933.

The police's part in West End club life is often not fully appreciated. Nor is the complexity of gang membership in London at that time. It could all get a bit confusing; see page 82 for a simplified chart.

ELEPHANT BOYS

CHART OF LONDON GANG MEMBERS

BIRMINGHAM/ELEPHANT/ CAMDEN TOWN

George Hatfield

Billy Kimber
George Sage
Harry Brown
Tony Martin
Tom Tuckley
Henry Tuckley
Eddie Tuckley
Bert Banks*
John Phillips*
Arthur Phillips*
George Williams

Wag McDonald
Wal McDonald
Bert McDonald
Jim McDonald
Billy Endelson
Bert Banks*
Billy Banks
Joe Jackson
Fred Smith
Jack Smith
Dan Johnston
Albert Medes
Fred Rye
George Baker*
Fred Brett
Bill Thompson
Henry Thompson
Charles Say
Fred Gilbert*

Spot/Hill
Spot/Carter
Frank Fraser
Richardson

HOXTON

Fred Gilbert*
Sandy Rice*
Jimmy Spinks
Matt McCausland*
Frank Sundock*
George Riley
John Phillips*
Arthur Phillips*
George Moore
John Gilbert
Joe Smith
George Baker*
Alf White*
Charlie Wooder*
George White
Charles White
Bill Martin

Gus Cortesi
Enrico Cortesi
George Cortesi
Sandy Rice*
Al Scasini

Bobby Ramsey

Nash

Kray

CLERKENWELL

Darby Sabini
Joe Sabini
Harry Sabini
George Sabini
Vince Petti
Matt McCausland*
Alf White*
Charlie Wooder*
Pasqualino Papa
Jack Bloomfield
Tom Basciano
George Fagioli
Tommy Mack
George West
Kid Lewis
Wally Cleal
George Drake
Antonio Mancini*
Luigi Fiori
Jim Dutton
Jim Baldwin
Paul Boffa

Harry White

Albert Dimes

Hill/Fraser/Dimes

Dimes/Fraser/Richardson

EAST END

Arthur Harding

Alf Solomon
Simeon Solomon
Mark Solomon
George Langham
Eddie Emmanuel
Jim Ford
Antonio Mancini*
Frank Sundock*
Jack Levene
Harry Margulas
Mark Frater
George Sewell
Sid Baxter
Sam Nyberg

Dodger Mullins

Jack Spot

Kray

*Dual membership

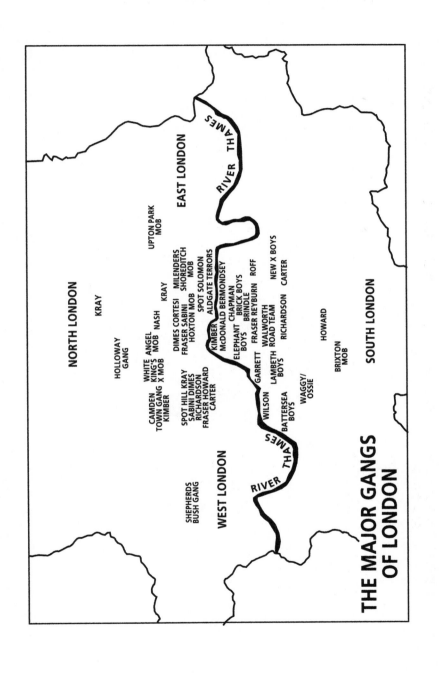

THE MAJOR GANGS OF LONDON

NORTH LONDON

EAST LONDON

WEST LONDON

SOUTH LONDON

RIVER THAMES

RIVER THAMES

KRAY

HOLLOWAY GANG

UPTON PARK MOB

WHITE ANGEL KING'S MOB NASH KRAY
X MOB

DIMES CORTESI MILENDERS
FRASER SABINI SHOREDITCH
HOXTON MOB MOB

SPOT SOLOMON

CAMDEN
TOWN GANG
KIMBER

SPOT HILL KRAY
SABINI DIMES
RICHARDSON
FRASER HOWARD
CARTER

KIMBER ALDGATE TERRORS

McDONALD BERMONDSEY

ELEPHANT CHAPMAN BRICK BOYS ROFF
BOYS BRINDLE
WALWORTH FRASER REYBURN NEW X BOYS
GARRETT ROAD TEAM
LAMBETH RICHARDSON CARTER
BOYS

WAGGY/
OSSIE

WILSON

BATTERSEA
BOYS

HOWARD

BRIXTON
MOB

SHEPHERDS
BUSH GANG

4. AMERICA AND . . .

Wag had taken the boat train from Waterloo to Southampton and the SS *Empress of France* across the Atlantic and up the St Lawrence River to Quebec. Hearing there was work further on, he took a train to Winnipeg and was taken on as a harvester. When the season finished in November he and two friends bought an old Ford and set off for British Columbia, stopping on the way to help clear snowed-up passes and repair railway tracks. They also worked at a lumber camp and as track-layers, arriving in Vancouver in December. After some months Wag crossed into the USA and saw the sights of Seattle. He then took the SS *Rodman* to Craig, Alaska, where he was engaged as a cannery hand. His diary, which rivals many a travelogue, tells the story:

> After working around the cannery for a few weeks, word came in that pirates were busy around the salmon traps on different parts of the coast. These pirates rob the traps of all the fish if they see they are not properly guarded.
>
> A salmon trap is a large square raft connected with the shore by cable. The raft is composed of large logs. The outside logs have wire netting tacked on and drop about fifty feet in the water to prevent the fish from getting out. They enter at one end of the raft through a funnel shaped net and once inside escape is impossible. One of these traps was in considerable trouble one night. Pirates came on the trap and enquired whether they could buy any fish. These pirates are men going about in high-powered motor boat, either robbing the traps by means of holding up the watchman or

buying the fish then selling it to the canneries. If they want to buy fish they will offer about ten dollars for 1,000 salmon. Not a bad investment. Some of these men are very well off and own their own motor boats.

This trio who came on this trap were informed that there was no fish for sale. They then tried to hold up the watchman. He being an old Texas Ranger was more handy with a gun than they thought. A few shots were exchanged, the trap watchman getting shot through the leg.

News came in to the cannery of this shooting and the excitement and hustle around the cannery was beyond description. I don't know if the cannery officials thought I was accustomed to shooting, but I was asked if I would go out and relieve the man who was shot so he could come in and have his wound dressed. One has no help whatever on these traps. You are all alone, miles from the cannery, and well away from the shore. After packing a few things, a motor boat was waiting for me at the wharf in which I was simply whirled away through foam and spray to the scene of hostilities.

After a somewhat breathless journey of about eighty miles we arrived at our destination at dusk and found the man none the worse for his adventure, only for a slight limping and bleeding. He was hurried back to the cannery for medical treatment in the motor launch and I was left alone on the trap, not a living soul within sight, just the boundless ocean south of me and the vast forests east of me 1,800 yards from the shore. I surveyed the position and started to put the trap in a state of defence in case of attack. I had a 30-30 Winchester rifle and a 45 Colt's automatic with me and felt secure knowing I could protect myself in case of attack. I rolled logs into position and cut out a groove to rest my rifle in, also to take cover behind it. I was never worried by the pirates, although at times I had some restless nights when boats came steaming by without any lights which is contrary to all navigating rules of the coast. Next day when the news had spread afar, I had many visitors to see the trap. One was the United States gunboat *Cygon*, a boat to protect the fishing industry of Alaska. The Commodore came on the trap and took particulars of the

ELEPHANT BOYS

86

shooting affair. I explained to him as far as I knew of the affair and showed him the bullet holes through the shack. He took several photographs of the shack and myself. He said they must have kept up a warm fire to have all those bullet holes through the shack. 'Well,' he said, 'we are all neighbours I guess, and all friends on this coast, and why these guys should put up all that shooting fairly licks me.' He gave me a friendly handshake and asked me if I had sufficient supplies to last me till our relief boat came out. I told him I had plenty and he departed, wishing me the best of luck. While steaming away he blew three blasts on his siren which is the custom of bidding farewell to men on these traps as the life is so lonesome and dangerous at times.

Numerous other craft called next day and the trap looked like a busy day at one of our famous seaside resorts with the different kinds of boats that were tied up there, but I was glad of their company and told the boys to stay as long as they wished. Eventually, by evening, all had gone and I was left alone again. My worst experience was to come yet. The next morning I awoke to find a strong wind blowing from the north and a choppy sea, till later on in the day it came to a regular gale. I saw the great waves washing over the trap and I knew this was a warning to be prepared for stormy weather. About 8.30 p.m. the storm seemed to be at its worst stage. The sky seemed to open with sheets of lightning and the roar of thunder seemed to shake the whole earth. Owing to the metallic nature of the country around here storms are more violent than anywhere I know of.

High waves were now washing over the shack and thundering against it like a herd of wild elephants. I expected every moment to get washed away. I tried to open the door of my shack, but the pressure of wind against it made it impossible. I managed later to open the door and poured gallons of oil on the waters, but that had little effect on such an angry sea. I got prepared for the worst in case I got washed overboard. I put some matches in waxed paper then put them into a small bottle which I corked and sealed, thinking if I did get washed ashore, I would have the satisfaction of knowing I could make a big fire and have a good dry up, but I was glad to see the storm dying out and the sea getting calmer.

I felt ever so grateful and pleased that I passed through that terrible ordeal without occasion to use my matches. I must confess here that I gave myself up as lost. There was no earthly chance of using my row boat in such a sea. The strangest part of this ordeal is what strange things comes to one's mind when in such difficulties. I remember quite clearly things that happened when I was at school. I was also wondering whether anyone would know of my fate if I were missing, thinking of all the family at home. All these things seemed to rush through my head quicker than I can relate them. I should like to thank the carpenter, if I could have seen him, for the way he built that shack to withstand such battering by those heavy seas.

The storm gave over about 11 p.m., but it was too dangerous to go out in the dark and see what amount of damage had been done. I knew there were loose logs about so I waited until morning; then what a sight met my eyes. The first thing I saw was a dead seal which must have been dashed against the logs by the great waves and killed. All the deck around my shack was washed away and my provisions had been washed away too. All I had left was a tin of carrots and a bottle of castor oil, not a very appetising meal in face of my difficulties. My rifle was dry and in good condition so I decided to get ashore in the row boat while the going was good and look around for a bear or whatever was good with my few carrots.

I was uncertain when the relief boat would call. Not seeing any bear, I shot some wild ducks with my Winchester, but sorry to relate that there wasn't much duck left after a 30-30 bullet hit it. I returned to the trap with the intention of smelling roast duck and have the few carrots I had left. I then saw in the distance the gunboat coming in my direction and the Commander informed me that my mast light was out on the night of the storm and he had called to see if I was safe. A friend in need is a friend indeed . . . I told him of my food shortage, when I was given plenty of supplies from the ship. They stocked me up with all kinds of provisions. I told the crew to help themselves to all the salmon they wanted.

As the fishing season was drawing to a close I was taken

off the trap and went back to the cannery again and felt pleased to be among some people again after being out on that trap for thirty-three days. All alone. I worked in the cannery cleaning up the fishing gear and put the boats and everything in order away for the winter. I was then informed by my boss that there was nothing else doing around the cannery as the season had finished. The last cargo of salmon had left about a week before by the last steamer out before the freeze-up. The big boss called me in his office this day and asked me whether I was interested in a new adventure. He wanted a crew to take one of his boats down to Seattle as her engines were disabled. We would be towed down. We were wanted just to steer her and look after the cargo. As I was saving my fare to Seattle and getting paid for this job, I accepted the offer. I left the cannery amidst cheering farewells and was told to come back again next season.

On our first day out we ran into some dirty weather and arrived at Ketchikan next day. Our third day out we encountered more bad weather and as our supply of cooking utensils was insufficient for our needs we were compelled to make our Mulligan [stew] in a bucket which I am sorry to say always managed to slip off the stove with the rolling of the boat when we were not there to attend to it. We gave that best and had bully beef and biscuits for the remainder of the trip.

We anchored in Safety Cove this night and saw to our cargo, as on the morrow we would be crossing a nasty stretch of water through Queen Charlotte Sound. It happened that the weather was fine at our time of crossing. Next day at 11.30 a.m. we entered Seymour Narrows. Owing to the strong current running we were unable to get through and had to turn back where the waters were calmer. We made another attempt at 2.30 p.m. and managed by a miracle to reach the other side of the narrows. The strong currents and the whirlpools in these narrows beggar description. We dropped an oil barrel overboard and down it went in those whirlpools, out of sight.

Today with steady steaming we entered the Gulf of Georgia at 6 p.m. and steaming on through the night we entered Active Pass, another Niagara. After we got through safely and bid farewell to this place. This place goes by the name of

ELEPHANT BOYS

Misery Island owing to the number of wrecks that have happened here. We passed Vancouver Island on our starboard in splendid weather. Going full steam ahead we enter Puget Sound and arrive at Seattle and civilisation.

After touring Washington State's countryside, including a visit to Mount Ranier, Wag travelled by steamship to San Francisco for a look round and then on to San Pedro, seaport town of Los Angeles. He was quite taken with the place:

Los Angeles, I think, is without question the most talked-of city in America. Its glorious sunshine, its wonderful climate, wonderful fruits and flowers, magnificent boulevards, pretty parks and nearby ocean resorts make it a most beautiful city.

Far out from the city one may see miles upon miles of orange and lemon groves. The vast vineyards extending for thousands of acres. One can see the flowers and palms nod a beckoning welcome. What a change from the snow and ice of Alaska. When I was there Los Angeles had a population of a little over one million people and from all accounts is still growing gradually.

I think my object in visiting Los Angeles was mostly to visit the moving-picture colony of Hollywood I had heard so much about in London. The suburbs of Los Angeles have grown rapidly in the last five years, the chief place being the flourishing suburb of Hollywood about eight miles from Los Angeles, home of the pictures and the glorified bungalows of the famous picture stars. I was told that in 1900 there was next to nothing in Hollywood except scenery and climate.

I took a trip into Hollywood to see whether I could run across any of the famous picture stars. I took the Pacific Electric Railway from Los Angeles, a ten cent fare, five pence in English money, and after riding about twenty minutes one enters Hollywood without being aware of the fact. The bungalows, palm trees, drug stores, beauty parlours and beautiful stores make it quite a busy town.

Hollywood is no sleepy hollow. It is full of pep. I found many prominent picture actors lived in the neighbourhood. Although the great picture-loving people of London may think of Hollywood as a place where the streets are thick with movie stars from morning till night, one of the most disappointing features of the casual traveller is the absence of any stars at all on the streets and the idea of seeing any are soon shattered. You run into movie stars on the streets with about the same frequency as you would see the King and Queen on the streets of London.

You would not recognise most of your favourite movie actors if you met them. They are far different seen in the flesh than on the screen. I was beginning to feel a little disappointed at not seeing any of the stars, but I found out after that the only places where strangers in Hollywood can be sure of seeing the actors during the daytime are at the studios. One may see a company sometimes making a film in the streets in the early morning. These little incidents happen daily with the big film companies and they pass unnoticed by those living there. One day last summer, when the thermometer had stood about all it intended to stand, I was sheltering in the shade from the blazing sun when I was the target of a score of cinema cameras. A shot was being taken on Hollywood Boulevard of an alleged bank bandit who escaped with his ill-gotten gains only to be congratulated by the producer on a realistic piece of acting.

The movie studios at the present time are about as easy for sightseers to enter as Buckingham Palace. There was a time when strangers were allowed in the studios, but I hear the visitors often interrupted the actors in their work and so spoilt the scenes that the privilege is now stopped.

Wag's diary goes on to record the climate of California, which he called 'wonderful':

Thousands from the east and middle west spend the winter in this garden State. This is the land of pictures I had heard so much about in England. Made by nature and by man. The air is so clear and the sky is so blue that the mountains, twenty minutes away, seem only a short distance. Sunshine and health are lying loose and if you've got life enough in you to draw one long breath you won't have to draw another before you realise how it tastes and how it makes you feel like a youngster again.

ELEPHANT BOYS

91

The Californian sunshine seems to throw a glow on everything. It gives all the fruit and flowers life. It gives all those beautiful blue gum trees life. It is wonderful. All the flowers here seem to have brighter colours than one ever saw before. The hills are carpeted with green velvet as far as the eye can see. The abundance of fruit and the quantity one sees here is amazing. Oranges growing in January, the different varieties of grapes, walnuts in April and May. Lemons all the year round. Pears in December. Pomegranates from August to January. Cantaloupes about April, apples all the year round. Figs, nectarines, olives, plums, raspberries, all so plentiful. It was well named God's country. God never fashioned such another wondrous spot on the entire surface of this earth. I cannot describe it enough to you, you should go and see for yourself.

Wag was determined to see a lot of the country before settling into some sort of employment. He teamed up with a party of hunters, one of whom was Red McDaniels, an Englishman and 'racing man' of previous acquaintance. It is difficult, nowadays, to imagine the little spoilt environment close to Los Angeles, Wag describes it in his diary:

What I saw of California on this trip was surprising to me. It all seemed to beckon to come on, offering a state-wide panorama of inspiring grandeur. Thrills galore. The delight of leaving a crowded city. Beauty. Scenic charms everywhere. A gorgeous land full of life and colour. Rivers and dashing cataracts that boom and roar in their wild leaps over the mountains where peaks are lost in an ocean of white clouds. Forests of giant redwoods and fir. The invigorating smell of the eucalyptus and pine. What a contrast to London's stuffy streets. We travelled over a very large area of the State. From the Sierra mountains to the coast. From the coast to the hot sands of the Mojave desert. We had what they term out here a swell time. We made up our minds to go out on the Mojave desert (pronounced Mo-harvey) about 125 miles from Los Angeles in search of game and adventure.

After leaving Los Angeles by way of Cahuenga Pass and

out through Ventura, we go to Calahass, on over the Georgia Pass and drop down into the beautiful Santa Clara river valley, noted for its fine fruit that grows around here. The scenery here was magnificent where one can feast eyes on mountainous scenery never to be forgotten. We leave the valley behind us and cross the Cajon mountains where giant redwood trees reach up lofty arms hundreds of feet towards the sky, where forests come down to the vast and peaceful valley of the Santa Clara River.

All this is too beautiful to leave behind hurriedly, so we stop here to view this scenic landscape. From the top of the mountains we can see thousands of streams glittering in the sun and piercing the wooded mountains on the other side of the valley. South Africa and Cape Colony are noted for beautiful scenery, but nothing can compare with this beautiful view.

Leaving here we soon enter the town of San Bernardino, the last important town reached before we enter the Mojave Desert Plateau. San Bernardino is situated in the centre of the fertile San Bernardino Valley which in point of beauty is not excelled in the whole State of California. The lofty mountain peaks which attain a height of from 11,000 to 12,500 feet are a familiar sight to all who motor out this way. I ventured to a height of 5,500 feet up on the mountains and the panoramic vista that unfolds itself is truly beautiful. When I view such wonderful scenery my thoughts turn to smoky London Town. Everything comes in one's mind whilst viewing such splendid scenery.

Leaving San Bernardino through the foothills of the mountains we enter some rough country. The road leads straight at this point for more than fifteen miles without a single bend. The closest watch is now made for boulders strewn across our path that have rolled down from the surrounding hills. The road leaves the hills and skirts high hills of white sand on each side of the road which indicates we are nearing the desert country, but what is approaching us in the distance in this sort of country. Our eyes are tired from the glare of the sun and dust. We stop and look to make sure our eyes are not deceiving us. These parts are what one would term bad man's country where a hold-up is of

ELEPHANT BOYS

frequent occurrence, but we are prepared for such emergencies.

Our mysterious travellers get quite close now, and what a surprise we had. It was two covered wagons and a few saddle horses. One of the wagons carries the white canvas top of the old prairie schooner which I thought to be extinct. It is the covered wagon in real life of story and pictures. They are bleached grey, canvas and wood alike. The wheels red with desert dust. A hatless boy holds the reins with his mother beside him. She wears an old-fashioned sun-bonnet with the long sides to shade her face from the sun. They were piled high with household goods, no doubt moving into a nearby settlement. We exchanged greetings with one another, but never stopped to ask any questions as the horses were fatigued and no doubt it may have been a job to start them again. It was truly a sight to see such a thing looking exactly like we see in the pictures when the Indian war whoop was no doubt the signal for disaster along these trails.

We start off on our journey again and the car is skimming across very flat country. No longer do we see the green vegetation, but dry scrub and sage brush and small mounds of white sand. Barren country meets us in all directions. We must be on the edge of the desert. Reaching the northeast section of the San Bernardino mountains we enter Cajon Pass, pronounced Cahone, at dusk. There is a roadhouse where we stop for refreshments. It is now about 7 p.m. when we hear a terrific rumbling and snorting in the distance. We are near the Santa Fe and Union Pacific railway tracks. Along comes the Continental Limited of the Union Pacific with a double header (two engines) dashing through for her trip over the summit of the mountains.

If you, dear reader, want a thrill, just watch this baby come flying through here at breakneck speed with two ponderous locomotives with their headlights penetrating the darkness for hundreds of yards ahead of them, their bells clanging and whistles blowing, echoing through the mountains for miles around. One of the engines went by the name of Big Irish Mike. These engines are used only for mountain traffic and what I saw of the surrounding country they would need them. One trembles to think what would happen if an overhanging rock I saw in the railway cutting was to fall on the tracks and the Limited coming on at that speed. Maybe there's a reason why they reach this point in darkness. Compared to the dash through that cutting an aviator's life is a pastime.

We now started our trip to the summit of the mountains. Climbing the grade for close on five miles we were beginning to feel the cold now. We saw moving objects on the mountainside which we took to be mountain sheep grazing, we never stopped the car to look as it is rather dangerous to other cars coming along here. The sharp curves and bends on the mountain are all shapes. Figure eights and zigzagging all over the place. We can see overhead a road running alongside the mountain which we must travel over. We cannot see down into the valley, but we are looking clear out into space up in the clouds. We can see yawning chasms down the mountainside, but cannot tell the depths.

We must be very high up on the mountain as my ears have a drumming and throbbing feeling. Whether it was air pressure or the rarefied air I cannot say, but at this time it was very cold at this altitude. We rounded a figure eight curve with a large white fence on each side of the road which told us it must have been a dangerous spot. A run of a few hundred yards and we reached the summit. What a sight met our eyes. Far out in the distance down in the valley we could see thousands of lights twinkling in the darkness. Just imagine putting a very fine sieve in front of a large lantern and you have some idea how these lights looked to us. It was the town of Pasadena far away to the south of us.

It was so cold now we closed the car windows and put on some warm clothing. After viewing this wonderful sight we were off again on the down grade into the valley, but the numerous turns we took, it was impossible to get a true bearing as to which direction we were travelling. As it was the only road off the mountain we could soon find our bearings again this side of the mountain.

After finding our direction of travel we found we were travelling northeast and by our maps thirty-five miles ahead of us was eighty miles of desolate desert. We had a plentiful supply of water and were determined to reach the desert

before dawn, find a suitable ground for camping and get a few hours' rest before morning.

It was quite warm down here in the valley so we were high in spirits for a good rest. We were now in some wild country. Nothing whatever to see on the plains. We try and find some suitable camping ground, but there isn't a bush or tree for miles. Still travelling on we come to some small sage brush which we knew must lead to something bigger. A few more miles and we were on the desert. We saw some large trees and bushes and we made our camp for the night.

After hot coffee from our flasks we unloaded the car of our guns, frying pans, blankets, food, stove and water, and rolled ourselves up in blankets and waited for the thrills of the morrow. Several times before falling to sleep I woke my chums up with my laughter, all I could get from them was some very sharp words and 'What was all the laughter about?' I informed them that whatever game we met on the morrow they won't know which direction to turn as they'd get such a fusillade from our arsenal that there won't be anything left of them.

We had a 22 gauge rifle, a 30-30 Winchester, two 12 gauge shotguns and a 32 Colt's automatic. By the early hour of 4 a.m. I awoke to look up in the desert sky with its millions of stars twinkling bright in the sky. A crescent moon was in the east shining its silver rays over the desert. The transparent blue sky with the silvery half moon and stars was a truly beautiful picture.

Far out on the desert we heard the howl of the coyote. Have you heard a dog howling when he's near music? Well that's how Mr Coyote howls, but he seems to go yap-yap after every howl. As we had our breakfast bacon under the car, and being impatient at the others not getting up which they had promised to do at daybreak, I thought it advisable not to take any chances with Mr Coyote. They have a sense of direction and will sneak around and walk off with a whole piece of bacon or meat and you'd never know where it had gone to.

I got out of my blankets with my Colt handy in case he was too near, but I never saw anything. All I got for getting up was 'What time do you call this for getting up on a Sunday morning?' 'Come on,' I shouted, 'there's something

ELEPHANT BOYS

crawling around here, over by those bushes a few yards away.' Guns in hand, they all jumped up only to find they had been fooled out of their slumbers. That was the only way to get them out, otherwise I'm afraid they would be there now.

We soon had bacon sizzling in the pan, with hot coffee and biscuits and were prepared for our great hunting adventure. I should like to mention the desert when we saw it at daybreak, miles of white sand, sage brush, giant cactus and Joshua trees in every direction we looked. Not a sign of human habitation as far as the eye could see. We were in the real desert here, miles from civilisation. Away to the west we could see the mountains we travelled across overnight all in their rugged splendour.

The sun came creeping up over the horizon with a dull red glow which warned us we were in for a hot day. With final preparations we started off on our hunt. We formed in line in skirmishing order to cover as much ground as possible, also to drive everything in front of us we saw. The first living object we saw was a horned toad, a small harmless animal with a small body something like an alligator, spiked tail and horns poking out the side of its head. These things are quite harmless, they feign death when anyone approaches them. They are the same colour as the ground and are not seen very quick. We never molested it as long as it was harmless, but we were on the lookout for rattlesnakes. One doesn't seem to have any pity for these reptiles. They lay so quiet till one is nearly on top of them. By a quick move they rear up and strike you. It may cost you your life if you don't act at once and attend to the bite. Glad to relate we never encountered any of them.

Bang, bang, goes two guns on my right. A large jackrabbit is dashing through the brush. Bang goes one of my barrels. Two more on my left and down he came. When we saw Mr Rabbit he put me in mind of that Klondike ballad – Dan McGrew pumped full of lead. Our first kill. I think there was more lead in him than the whole weight of his body. We left him where he lay, a feed for the coyotes. Advancing a few yards we saw some chipmunks, belonging to the squirrel family, quite harmless and playful.

ELEPHANT BOYS

Bang goes another gun and Mr Rabbit fell right into a bush and stayed there. He only had one charge in him so we took him along with us. In a few hours we had all the rabbits we wanted so we strolled back to camp. I then expressed a wish to explore some of the yet remote parts of the desert. This was a desert in real life, what I had read so much about in my school days. I now had the opportunity to see it for myself. We loaded up the car and we were off again in search of bigger game. Travelling away to the east we crossed what seemed to be the end of the world. The heat was terrific. The glare of the sun. A mirage ahead of us all the time. These mirages which have enticed men on to their deaths when being mistaken for water. Here we came to a small creek which did contain water, but we could never see where it came from, but what a drab and lifeless stream it looked. No doubt the water was poisonous as our examination of the ground told us there was arsenic and alkali all over where we trod. The desert in some parts is thick with this poison. Yet this water in contrast to the dry and parched desert was a welcome sight to us.

A few more miles brought us to a spot where we thought there would be some likely chance of some good shooting, but after walking a mile or two we only saw jackrabbits and lizards so we decided to travel back to the mountains. All day long we never saw a living soul although we had travelled many miles. After a few hours' run we came to the foot of the mountains again and into a clearing in a thicket before us, where we stopped in sudden surprise, for there in front of us in one of the most unlikely places imaginable was a house. Have you ever had surprises when you think somebody is dead and you suddenly run across them on the street? Well that's how we felt. Nobody would ever dream of seeing a house in these parts. I cannot fail to give you an account of this uncanny incident in our travels. A house, or rather an old shack, alone in a rusty, dried coloured clearing. The nearest human habitation about fifty miles away. We thought it may be an old desert rat's shack (a nickname for a kind of hermit) who lives and believes he will find gold out on the desert some day.

Just to unravel this air of mystery we decided to have a look around here. We approached very cautiously with our guns all ready in case we were met with a fusillade of buckshot. Over the gateway was a large name, EL PARADISO. We somehow knew the place was deserted. We called and called, but received no answer where men have been living, maybe have suffered or died of thirst. There was no knowing what we might find inside. Slowly we approached as though fearful that the place concealed something of evil. As we stood for a moment in front of the porch we could hear no sound from within. We knocked, then looked through its stained windows covered with cobwebs. Then finding the doors unsecured we entered. I may mention that I never gripped a gun as I did my automatic when I entered that house. On these kind of stunts at home we used to say 'Oh, that made me feel goosey'. Out there they say 'I am full of goose pimples', but I will admit I had plenty of both.

It looked to us the place had been deserted for years. In one corner stood an old rusty stove, quite an unusual thing to see out on the desert. Things were scattered about as though the occupants had fled in haste, but no doubt there may have been visitors there before us who may have taken away the movables. The most surprising thing of all was to see some magazines scattered about the floors. There was the *Edinburgh Review*, the *Atlantic Monthly* and the *Nineteenth Century*. The dates they bore were 1900 to 1904.

After exploring the interior and seeing all we wanted to see and failing to find out who the occupants were, we decided to make for the car as some uncanny feeling came upon us to see whether our car was safe outside. To lose our car in this wilderness would mean the end of our exploring expedition. We gradually walked out of this creepy place, but not without giving an occasional backwards glance to know we were in no traps. So that was the house of mystery in this wilderness.

We got into some hilly country and camped for the night. We were up at daybreak and explored the hills for animals and game. We came upon a lynx eating a rabbit. It saw us, hunched its back and stood there spitting at us, its hair all standing erect with fury. We were about to fire when it scurried off into the bush leaving the half-eaten rabbit on the ground. We were in hopes of finding some mountain

ELEPHANT BOYS

lions about here. There is a State bounty of $25 (£5) for any mountain lions captured dead or alive, but sorry to say we never saw the sign of one.

We now decided to get near the creeks in the mountains in hopes of finding duck and quail, but after travelling all day we never saw any game at all. We had a camp fire musical party at night over our hot coffee. Our instruments consisted of a mouth organ, a banjo, a comb wrapped in paper and an old tin can for a drum. We enjoyed the performance very much. I think we were all beginning to feel a little disheartened at our hunting trip as we only got jackrabbits, so we decided to make our way homewards, but I must say hunting mountain lions is rather dangerous and a trifle risky at times. It generally happens the hunter gets caught sometimes. One has to watch every tree, also the bush too, they generally lay out on the protruding branch of a tree and watch their opportunity to spring and when they do they tear one to pieces. It is also dangerous to shoot when man and lion are in combat. These mountain lions are dangerous and ferocious. They are the size of a leopard and the colour of a lion. They are very destructive to cattle, generally horses. They kill just for the love of it. They will partly devour sheep then go and kill more, hence the £5 bounty on their hide. Bill Hart, the once-famous movie actor, who is a great lover of horses, offers a £5 reward for any one brought to him. You may guess the reason why we were anxious to bag a few.

We now made our way out to what is termed the citrus belt, through the beautiful orange and lemon groves, the magnificent vineyards around Riverside and Redlands. Thereabouts are some of the quaint old Spanish missions dated 1814. Near here is a monument commemorating the departure of General Sherman of the Civil War when ordered east during that period. We felt very interested to know why the monument was erected to his name. We halted at a nearby ranch for refreshments and enquired of the old lady who served us whether she could give us any information concerning the memorial. She seemed pretty well acquainted with its history and related the following story to us.

As far as she knew General Sherman lived around these parts when he was a young lieutenant and became so infatuated with a Spanish girl by the name of Señorita Bonificia, who was considered the most beautiful young miss around here, when he made his farewell call on this Spanish miss he wore a rose in the buttonhole of his uniform. She took the rose from his coat, saying: 'Together we will plant this, and if it lives and flourishes, I will know that your love is true.' He is supposed to have replied: 'When it blooms I will come back and claim you.' Thus they vowed to remain true to each other until he returned for her. Year after year went by. She cared for the rose tenderly until it covered the walls of her little cottage. It bloomed with great masses of sweet roses, but the young lieutenant never returned. The Señorita grew old, but remained as sweetly beautiful as she was in her youth. She finally died under the same rose vine true to the vow she made by it. The way the old lady knew its history, I thought it interesting to know this romantic love story.

We now decided to make our way homewards and on our way visit Harry Carey's ranch out at Saugas and see all the cowpunchers in action in real life. Harry Carey, of movie fame, owns a large ranch and an Indian trading post about thirty-five miles from Los Angeles. Convalescing at the ranch was the infamous Wyatt Earp who was in the habit of making the rounds of Hollywood studios trying to sell his memoirs. He was a famous lawman but is now regarded as something of a braggart and is willing to adapt his many famous exploits for as much as he can get. He has many versions of his gunfight at the OK Corral. We hoped to get a first-hand version, but the old gentleman had been very ill and Carey had graciously offered him the comfort of his ranch to recover. [Earp died in Los Angeles in January 1929.]

I cannot fail to give you a vivid description of what we saw there. The thrills we saw that comes from straddling amidships of a Californian cow pony, the marvellous feats of horsemanship, the cowboy's chaps (leather trousers), the size of handkerchief he wears around his neck. There are horses everywhere, cattlemen from the plains of Texas done up in every shade and colour. Suddenly we hear a shot and

ELEPHANT BOYS

out of the corral charges a big red bull ridden by a cowboy who seems to have plenty of ups and downs. We see plenty of thrills here, the rider now seems to take a tighter grip on the saddle and raises both feet up along the bull's neck. Roaring and plunging like an avalanche the bull charges a dummy and then becomes weakened and exhausted. Weakened at last from the unnatural exertions he hunts along the fence for an exit while the cowboy watches for a chance to grab the fence and escape. What with bronco-riding, chasing one-eyed cows, broncos going backwards with their riders and the clouds of dust, we decided to get into town and have a wash up and leave the cows and bucking horses to those who were more familiar with them than us.

We toured through Hollywood and arrived back in Los Angeles. Back to civilisation and the whirling traffic, but better in health and spirits. We saw something out of the ordinary, something that took our minds off the city for a while, a land of sunshine and flowers, a land of magic. Nowhere else in my travels have I found such mighty silences as out on that desert, nor in those canyons such brooding mystery. I think it was fortunate of me that I made my way down into this wonderful State of California, through its forests of giant redwoods, fragrant meadows and cloud wrapped mountains. It has given me that spell that seems to hold all men here in the far west. The people here are more friendly, one is given to feel that these people have abundant leisure and their enjoyments were made for sharing with the stranger. I could go on writing for ever of the wonders of this beautiful country, but all good things must come to an end, even holidays.

Wag was in Los Angeles in 1923 where, in the turmoil that followed the passing of the Eighteenth Amendment bringing about prohibition, he was arrested and bailed after a bar brawl. Subsequently charges against him were discontinued.

Through McDaniels he became a strongarm man for the emerging gangster Jack Dragna who, in the absence of any other top gangster, decided to emulate the Chicago racketeers. Although aged only thirty, Dragna effectively ran the Los Angeles rackets.

ELEPHANT BOYS

Money and style surrounded racketeers: Wag wanted his share, enjoying his percentage for collecting gambling debts and being Dragna's accountant. His duties included keeping a check on expected receipts and persuading recalcitrants to pay up. Dragna also controlled a number of speakeasies or 'blind pigs' as they were called. Wag related, 'You can get drink at all kinds of prices. If you drink the cheap stuff you want a copper-lined stomach, because many people have been stricken by paralysis and poisoned through drinking it.'

Dragna was not in the class of Al Capone or New York gangsters such as Owney Madden, who held ruthless control over their soldiers. Jack was constantly struggling with insubordinate troops probing for signs of weakness. Wag, who described himself to Ada as a sort of 'tally man', struggled constantly with fractious debtors and he built up a strongarm team which included a boxer named Tommy Carroll. When Wag had a routine collection to make in Chinatown, he took Tommy along to show him where to go on future occasions.

Chinatown was a collection of notorious gambling dens run by Triad gangs who were tapped for some of their proceeds by Dragna. Never happy to part with any of their moolah and always testing Dragna for signs of weakness, the Triads confronted Wag in Ferguson's Alley. As he backed away, a long-bladed knife narrowly missed his arm as a Triad tried to chop it off. It sliced through the Gladstone bag he was carrying; even so he raised the bag to ward off another blow. Before it landed, Tommy dropped the Chinaman with a left hook and felled another just as swiftly. Wag made it to his car while Tommy waved the knife at the assembled Chinese. With Tommy on the running-board, Wag careened away with a crowd running behind them. Ada remembered his words as he related the story: 'As I clutched the wheel I counted my fingers.' Wag and Tommy were firm friends from that day.

Both Wag and Tommy were prolific practical jokers and constantly wound Dragna up by placing ticking gadgets near him. They would hide them under cushions and pretend to search while 'frantic Jack' became a bag of nerves, but he couldn't afford to be without his minders.

Tommy Carroll, who it was rumoured had a number of petty convictions for brawling and auto appropriation, was a good-looking genial Scots/Irish American trying to get walk-on parts in

ELEPHANT BOYS

the movies. He was a sharp-witted trickster with the ability to spot an opportunity in just about everything. When Nancy Carroll, one of the few good silent screen idols who would make it to the talkies, became a sensation on her arrival in Hollywood, Tommy immediately passed himself off as her brother. She was a beautiful hellcat who could easily be mistaken for a relative of Tommy's, and it paid dividends in parties for Tommy and Wag. He also took Wag along to crowd casting sessions – so my uncle Wag and Tommy Carroll are in many crowd scenes from those early movies. Wag also managed walk-on parts in *All The Brothers were Valiant*, starring Lon Chaney, and had a presence in *The Big Parade*, an epic starring John Gilbert.

Chatty and popular, Tommy inveigled his way into parties and it was at one given by Basil Rathbone that he met Ann Harding. An aspiring stage actress, she visited Hollywood in 1923 aiming to get into the movies. She was ice-cold beautiful, not the typical starlet. Taken by the charms of Carroll, she plunged with him into an affair that was largely consummated at the apartment he shared with Wag – much to the annoyance of Rathbone, who had his own designs in that direction. It amused Wag that Rathbone, a stern, charming and physically fit South African, kept turning up at the apartment on the flimsiest of excuses when all the time he was checking to see if Ann was there. Although married, he was obsessed with her.

Carroll was a swift operator who moved around a succession of beautiful women. He had wangled his way on to the security staff at Paramount Studios, a situation Wag called his 'paramount concession', when he saw him escorting Bebe Daniels and other beautiful women who enjoyed his charming personality. One of these, Jacqueline Logan, was a dark-haired beauty looking for opportunities to impress movie directors with her voluptuous proclivities. It was the age of the siren when many actresses slunk around in flimsy dresses that emphasised their attributes. Having Tommy on one arm deterred molesters. Jacqueline's boyfriend, Maurice Flynn, objected that Tommy was being too protective – at which she dumped Maurice for Tommy. Maurice, a fitness fanatic, went to take the matter up with Tommy, who grabbed his arms in an iron grip, which was enough to impress Maurice that it was a matter best forgotten.

Tommy's most dangerous dalliance was with Madge Bellamy, who punched him in the face when he messed her about. She was volatile and so unpredictable that eventually she was sacked by Fox Studios. After an absence from movies she returned in a series of B films that did not provide well for her lavish spending. She ended up broke. Tommy was lucky, in that she only punched him: a later lover was shot for much the same thing.

When Ann Harding disentangled herself from Carroll, Basil Rathbone attempted to step in, only to find Wag had nipped in before him! They had to be separated when Wag came upon Basil hiding behind a car parked outside the apartment. Basil, who was a gentleman, offered Wag the chance to make his point in the boxing ring. Wag described it as a very hard three rounds. Rathbone was a cultured sportsman, a superb swordsman and rower, and he boxed in the traditional English style – straight jab and hook – which peppered Wag as he threw his punches in the fashion of a streetfighter. Both were marked up and agreed after three rounds that the row was over. Wag complimented Basil on his skills; Basil pointed out that it had crossed his mind to offer swords. It was a curious business.

Wag would have been about forty-seven to Basil's thirty-two and Ann's twenty-two. Wag, who was always taken to be younger than he was, called Ann his little Texas Rose. Before she became a movie star she moved to New York where she became a successful stage actress. Wag gave way to Harry Bannister, whom she married in 1926, although they remained friends. She returned to Hollywood in 1929 when she made it to the silver screen, portraying herself as a sober, emotionless actress taken to be from the 'East' – off screen she was a Texas spitfire. Ada always believed Ann led Wag on for the protection he offered, and that he willingly played along.

Tommy Carroll was well in as a bodyguard and managed to get to guard numerous Hollywood movie stars. Through Tommy, Wag found himself 'minding' his screen hero Charlie Chaplin. Charlie grew up in Lambeth and was Britain's most famous export to the United States. He was born in Kennington in 1889, a stone's throw from where I was born in 1937. His family were poor to the point that his mother was once resident in Lambeth Workhouse. Like many in Lambeth he knew hard times. He was persevering enough to gain parts in London music-hall shows and pantomimes which, in 1910, gave him a chance to tour in the United States. The rest is legend. His movie image as the little, but not too helpless, tramp

ELEPHANT BOYS

endures to this day. Wag soon found out that in private life Chaplin still bore the tough attitude to winning that he'd learnt on the streets of Lambeth. He was mobbed everywhere he went and paid for a small army of bodyguards. Part of Wag's duties was to pick Chaplin up late at night from his home at Cove Way and drive him to a beach house, or sometimes a hotel, where he entertained young ladies (too young to be legal). On one occasion Wag stayed on duty all night in the hall at the home of Charlie's brother Syd, while Charlie amused himself upstairs.

Wag had idolised Chaplin, but became disillusioned by his predilection for young girls, some as young as twelve or thirteen. There had been suspicious gossip, but somehow Chaplin managed to keep his well-known peccadilloes out of the Press. Wag hung around in the hope that his experiences in Alaska might prove useful to Chaplin, who was working on one of his most ambitious, and ultimately successful, movies, *The Gold Rush*. When it was clear Chaplin didn't want advice, and that the movie was not so much about Alaska as a novel way of showing off Chaplin's talents, Wag gave up. In later years he told Ada that the scene could have been set at sea, or in the desert or any lonely place, and obtained the same effect of melancholy. Anyway Chaplin was showing an interest in his young choice of leading lady, Lita Grey, whom he eventually got into trouble and had to marry.

Besides, Wag – who was proud of his veteran status – did not have much regard for 'war dodgers', as he called those like Chaplin who had not served their country.

Tommy Carroll was not so fussy. He earned a good stipend for paying off hotel staff and snooping reporters, to whom he also fed bits of information to keep columns filled with Chaplin's preferred items. In 1924 Tommy beat up a reporter and framed him by placing a revolver on his battered body and calling the police. The reporter was held at Georgia Street police station and only released without charge after he agreed not to relate a story that he had tracked Chaplin and a teenage girl to Westlake Park where they stayed for several hours at a private house.

Tommy got himself and Wag aboard the *Oneida*, newspaper tycoon William Randolph Hearst's yacht, as bodyguards to the rich and famous. In November 1924 Hearst threw a lavish party on board the boat which ended in tragedy. Sixty-year-old Hearst doted on his young girlfriend, Marion Davies. She had been a bit-part actress with modest talent going nowhere, until she turned her more considerable personal talents on Hearst. He lauded her mediocre appearances in dull movies and fêted her wherever she went. She, in return, shared her favours with whoever she fancied. Hearst was driven to distraction and devised ways of isolating and entertaining her at the same time, throwing parties at his spectacular San Simeon castle and on the high seas. Even then he did not trust her and set bodyguards to watch out for her dalliances. One such dalliance was Charlie Chaplin – although at twenty-seven she was a bit old for him, Wag thought.

The *Oneida* sailed for Catalina Island, but Hearst refused to sail into its capital, Avalon, because he was having a bitter row with Marion. Tommy and Wag heard the commotion as Marion launched into Hearst in their stateroom. She was accused of having arranged for a lover to meet her ashore in Avalon. Hearst thought it was probably Chaplin. Furiously she denied it. The argument became so heated that Marion, who stammered badly when she was excited, went into a convulsion and had to be sedated.

The *Oneida* steamed on to San Diego as things calmed down. However, on the night of 17 November, more guests came aboard. One of them was Hollywood producer Tom Ince, a forty-year-old unhappily married man who had developed a fondness for Marion Davies. She, in turn, knew that Ince was a very important Hollywood contact who could turn her career into something spectacular – which Hearst had failed to do with all his money and the power of his printing presses.

Wag was ashore with guests and on his return to the yacht came upon a shaken Tommy Carroll. Tommy was not one to panic, but he was in a state of near collapse and not able, or willing, to talk of what had occurred. Other guests had appeared shocked. Some were leaving the boat. It was a while after that Wag got the story from Tommy, and then only after rumours had appeared in the Press and Hollywood bars that something awful had happened.

In the evening Tommy had been carrying out his duties, which included watching over Marion. Because he was required to be 'not conspicuous', she had slipped away and he began to fear she had gone ashore. His search found Marion on the lower deck: she was alone and told him to 'beat it'. Tommy went to the upper deck and immediately bumped into Hearst who was also searching for Marion. Being cute, and wanting to preserve his job, Tommy said

ELEPHANT BOYS

not to worry, he knew where Marion was and he was watching from a safe distance. Hearst went down the stairs and moments later a shot was fired.

Tommy descended the stairs in dreadful anticipation, expecting to find either Marion or Hearst in a pool of blood. Instead both were standing there, amid a haze and a smell of gunpowder. On the deck, half hidden by a partition, was a man's body. The fellow was on the edge of death, with a hole in the back of his head from which blood was pumping on to the deck. Other guests arrived and Hearst escorted the stunned Marion through the curious spectators to their cabin. Tommy and some crew members covered the body with a windbreaker. Late in the evening, just before Wag arrived back with his party, they had taken the body ashore where it had been collected by a doctor.

Tommy had not known who the dead man was or who had shot him. He had seen two crew members mopping up the blood, which slewed across the deck and took some time to remove. The mops could not be cleaned and were broken and flung into the sea. The body, now described as ill, was in the hands of a doctor friend of Hearst's and would later be identified as Tom Ince. Within days Ince was cremated, his wife signed the papers and up he went in smoke.

Rumours took hold and an investigation failed to clear up the mystery. One early suspicion by the guests is said to have been that the dead man was Charlie Chaplin who'd been found in a state of 'amour' with Marion Davies. Hearst fostered this story although Chaplin was alive and well, bringing the whole thing down to a level of farce. Chaplin was forced to deny that he was aboard the *Oneida*, but many believed he was and that Ince – who bore some resemblance to him – got a bullet meant for the 'cheeky chappie'. Wag may not have seen the shooting, but much as he disliked Chaplin, he was quite sure the film star was not aboard the *Oneida*.

Tommy Carroll married his on-and-off girlfriend Vi and left Hollywood soon afterwards. He was a much-changed man, not least for his attachment to alcohol. According to Wag he had $5,000 of Hearst's money residing in his pocket. Wag received a $250 bonus. Whoever the guests and crew were who came upon the scene of that murder, they remained quiet. Some are said to have launched successful careers with the backing of Randolph Hearst.

Those in the know whispered that Ince had gone ahead of the *Oneida* to Catalina island where he was waiting at Tom Mix's house for a meeting with Marion. When she didn't show he followed the yacht to San Diego, where he came aboard as a legitimate guest – and either Hearst, or Tommy, killed him. In view of Tommy's later career it was certainly a possibility.

ELEPHANT BOYS

5. ◆ ◆ ◆ TRAGEDY

Wag renewed his friendship with Vic McLaglen who, after making a number of successful British films, had arrived in Hollywood in 1925. Both had a wicked sense of humour and were practical jokers. Wag wanted to surpass the fight with Jack Johnson, which he regarded as Vic's greatest practical joke, and he arranged for a boxer called Butcher to fight Vic in an exhibition at the Olympic Gymnasium in Hollywood. Vic was suspicious and wore his suit under his dressing gown in case he had to depart in a hurry. Even he didn't expect Jack Dempsey to step into the ring. Dempsey had just lost the world title to Gene Tunney and 'badly needed a victory'. Vic pulled a leg of lamb from under his gown to present to the 'butcher'. Dempsey said he would eat it after he had finished with Vic and then treated them all to a bar lunch.

According to Ada, Wag and Vic were inseparable. Wag knew a number of other movie actors, among them a successful British silent star, Reg Denny. Reg had a yacht aboard which Wag did duty as a bodyguard and occasional host. He would have reason to be thankful to Reg and his yacht at a later date.

Dragna had a speakeasy near Santa Monica Boulevard called the Vineyard, managed by Tod Browning. The cellar was blocked off by a cupboard at the head of the stairs through which only the well-heeled could enter. Wag took turns to operate a long lever that unlocked the door, allowing celebs to push through when no one was looking; it also flashed a red light downstairs to ensure that a host or hostess was in place to receive visitors as they entered. It was all a big game to grown-up kids like Fredric March, Buster

Keaton and Wallace Beery who would melodramatically act out their entrances. A narrow stairway led down to a large windowless basement; the only natural light filtered in from 'portholes' of hard glass in the pavement outside, where kids would stand by the cracked glass and listen to the ragtime music. Low lights lit up blue baize tabletops and walls painted with the silhouettes of spooks which gave the Vineyard its nickname, 'The Ghosthouse'.

From midnight the place was packed with the profligate, dedicated to the highrolling jangling of the nervous system and the measured dissipation of body and soul. Tod Browning was making his mark as actor, writer and director in early Hollywood movies, working with Vic McLaglen, Marion Davies, Douglas Fairbanks and Johnny Mack Brown. He was often accompanied by Australian vamp Mae Busch whom he insisted should be called Suzy. She was a good comedy actress and later featured in some Laurel and Hardy films. Wag said Browning had a dark side and was obsessed with the supernatural and other weird stuff: he was fastidious in his management; the club closed promptly at 4 a.m.; every man wore a black tuxedo; and Wag and others had orders to reject newly fashionable red, and occasional white, jackets. It was not a popular occupation – they once turned away Ramon Novarro, who'd already had a skinful, another taboo for entry.

Manning the downstairs was a mixture of Hollywood extras and tough guys. A number of future stars did duty in the Vineyard. Chester Morris, Ward Bond, Paul Kelly, Charles Farrell and William Boyd – who became one of my boyhood favourites, Hopalong Cassidy – lent their presence. Sophie Tucker, Edna Murphy, Dolores Del Rio, Janet Gaynor, Barbara Kent and Paul Kelly's mistress and friend of Wag, Scots lass Dottie MacKaye, hosted celebrities around the tables (strictly business). Jack supplied other females for cosier pastimes. Dottie was a party girl who was to lead Kelly into serious trouble.

Wag had his own troubles in the shape of a silent movie actress who had taken his fancy. Thirty-four-year-old Neva Gerber had made a number of unremarkable movies and was still working in the business. In 1926 she appeared in Westerns with Yakima Canutt (later the stuntman for John Wayne, performing the famous stunt in *Stagecoach*). Neva had been a paramour of William Desmond Taylor, a rapacious womaniser who was shot to death by an unknown party in 1922. Scandalmongers tried to implicate her in Taylor's death. Certainly she had fallen for the adventurer's charms and came close to marrying him, but Wag said she was no more involved in his death than any of the other female movie stars who had been desecrated by Taylor.

Although she was not a conventional beauty, Neva had something about her that brought men around her in droves. She was not making a successful transition to talkies, but was already wealthy. Before his death Taylor had lavished money, jewels and autos on her in exchange for which she broke their engagement. Taylor had become one of the early Hollywood successes – partly actor, mostly director and producer – he couldn't keep his hands off his leading ladies. First Neva, who made it pay; then a succession of beauties including Mabel Normand, star of many Mack Sennett slapstick movies and Sennett's live-in lover, who also starred with Charlie Chaplin. Mabel had a fiery nature and was to become the prime suspect in Taylor's murder when it became known that a woman was seen leaving his apartment after a shot was heard. At the time of his demise Taylor was using his charms on actress Mary Miles Minter and had added her underwear to a large collection of initialled lingerie found in his apartment after his death. Also there were gifts and letters from his conquests, many of which disappeared during police investigations.

Neva, Mabel, Mary and others had to tell their stories on the witness stand at the inquest and their careers never recovered from the publicity. Mary sank without trace. Mabel lived out her short life lurching from scandal to scandal, fuelled by booze and drugs. Neva became an object of interest and hired Wag as a bodyguard – the first of a number of female stars to use his services to fend off drunks and mashers. Neva told Wag that Taylor's seduction of the virginal Mary had led to Taylor's death at the hands of Mary's mother Charlotte Shelby.

Like Mary, Neva was also presented as a demure damsel, something entirely different to her nature. Wag was smitten and he enjoyed her company, although he knew his interest was shared by many others. He didn't mind her mixing with other movie folk: he used situations like that to get invited to parties, but what he objected to was the gangster hangers-on. In one of his protective or jealous bouts he told Vince Moore to stay away from Neva, and when he didn't Wag 'sorted him out'. The next day Moore and another took a shot at Wag outside Helm's Billiard Parlor on

Hollywood Boulevard. The bullet cut a crease across the back of his neck, sending him writhing in agony. No doubt thinking they had killed him, they took off. Moore, who was also in Dragna's bad books, left town before Wag recovered. Some years later he was found dead by the side of a highway where he had been dumped after being tortured and shot.

Just when Wag gave up his quest for Neva is not known. Contained within his effects at his death was a photo of Neva taken in 1917, long before he knew her. Perhaps he had deliberately sought her out in Hollywood after idolising her in the silent movie serial *Voice on the Wire*.

It was at the Vineyard that Wag met Douglas Fairbanks. At this time Fairbanks was a big name and was given to doing the rounds of parties and clubs. Wag said he was a magnet to women and he played them like poker, another of his favourite pastimes. He often had several tables placed in a circle to entertain friends and hangers-on, although in Wag's experience he never had Mary Pickford along and it seemed their reputation as the ideal married couple was not what it was pretended to be. Wag would enjoy a good tip for making sure the star was poured into a taxi with what remained in his wallet intact. Fairbanks was not above getting into a brawl and, although a fair fighter, had a higher opinion of his prowess than that held by his friends. He shaped up to Lionel Barrymore. Both were drunk and engaged in a 'slapping match'. When some of Barrymore's pals started into Fairbanks he had to be rescued by Reg Denny and Wag, who floored two of Barrymore's friends. It was all settled with a handshake the following morning. Wag felt that his chances of more bit parts were dimmed by the attack on Barrymore.

Drinking in the Vineyard was kept in check and debts were settled immediately. Dragna was not one to give credit. It all went very well until stingy Jack cut back on his 'business' payments. Wag was 'minding' tables when the cops swept aside the guards upstairs and crashed through the door without waiting for the lever to be pulled. Instead of panic, their presence was greeted with intoxicated disregard as merry bigshots accustomed to police ignoring their pleasures shrugged off the intrusion and carried on gaming.

This nonchalance did not last long. A frustrated cop smashed his stick down on a roulette wheel and dashed the chips from the table. Something hit Ward Bond's girlfriend in her eye, causing Bond to grab the cop and carry him to the nearest wall where he began to slam his head against the plaster, punctuating each thump with 'Where's your manners?' As other cops grabbed Bond he really got mad and started knocking them about. Wag and others were ushering toffs from the club amid whizzing bottles and chairs as some of the celebs took up Bond's cause. Wag recalled that he didn't need much help. Wag, locked in a struggle with a cop, crashed through a row of blackjack tables and tore a long gash in his hand. Wrapping a tablecloth around it, he struggled up the stairs and was taken by Paul Kelly to the Central Receiving Hospital to have it stitched.

Paul Kelly, who had a blossoming movie career, later was gaoled for the manslaughter of Dottie MacKaye's husband, dancer and libertine, Ray Raymond. After a spell of hard drinking Kelly had beaten him to death. After a short spell in prison he returned to the movies and became in steady demand for gangster parts. Dottie married Paul, but maintained her fondness for a tipple and a good row. In 1941 after a bout of both she was killed in an auto accident.

Wag, who had learnt vehicle maintenance in the Royal Field Artillery, opened a garage on 8th and Grand for his daytime occupation. He also owned an Auto Laundry on 9th and Hoover, had some share of the business at Dinty's fashionable sandwich bar on South Spring Street and dealt in mysterious polishes and potions concocted by a drummer known as Indian Tom (but whose real name was Walter Lippman). He also owned a piece of land and was part of a team selling land to speculators who searched it for gold – California gold rush fever still existed in some people, even though the likelihood of finding any substantial amounts of gold missed in the heyday of the mining camps was near impossible. He was doing nicely. The club, his commission on collections, his auto businesses and other enterprises were bringing in the dollars. The only thing he was short of was sleep.

Another burgeoning sideline was in protecting celebrities himself or commissioning, as bodyguards and attendants, others with an ability to perform all sorts of tasks like supplying booze, covering up scandals, providing escorts, warning people off and sometimes beating them up. There was much in Hollywood that required covering up.

The Vineyard did not reopen. Wag teamed up with Jimmy

ELEPHANT BOYS

Spenser, another English immigrant, who had worked for Owney Madden and Legs Diamond in New York. Starting out as a slugger, Madden did a spell in prison for murder, then began to challenge Dutch Schulz and others for control of New York's Hell's Kitchen. If Spenser had stuck with him his fortune would have been made. Instead he stole Madden's car and departed New York when he assessed that Schulz would wipe out the Madden outfit. However, Madden was no longer the small-time crook: eventually he oversaw the killing of Legs Diamond, Vinny Coll and Dutch Schulz to become the number-one New York gang boss. He retired to a life of opulence in Hot Springs, Arkansas, where he played host to America's criminal élite, and died in 1965.

Spenser had a job minding a Nick Licata casino near Hollywood Boulevard. He also took part in a number of hold-ups, drawing on his experience as a New York mobster. He recommended Wag as a bouncer and bodyguard: the two escorted the volatile Licata around Los Angeles night-spots where Licata made life difficult for Dragna by enticing his customers away to his livelier casinos. Licata was a Chicago gangster with connections to the big syndicate chiefs in Chicago, Detroit and New York. No doubt he thought Dragna's operations were easy pickings. Wag was treading a dangerous line. Technically he still worked for Dragna, but he managed to persuade him he could keep an eye on Licata's operations and feed back information. Dragna accepted the arrangement and Wag had a nervous time drawing pay from both and double-crossing the two of them. It was a time when bodies were turning up in the street at the slightest suspicion of the dreaded double-cross.

Bert and Kimber had sailed for New York and travelled overland to California. They stopped off at Flagstaff, Arizona, where Kimber had expected to meet a friend who had set up in business, only to find someone had shot him and the business no longer existed. While Kimber tried to establish other connections Bert took a job with a company called TOT and helped construct a highway to cross the Mojave Desert. Kimber and Bert finally crossed the Mojave Desert in 1928 to meet up with Wag in Los Angeles. Kimber rented a house and sometime later became the object of police interest: he was travelling on someone else's passport. The woman living with him called herself Mrs Kimber and apparently had a passport in that name. Before it could be sorted out Kimber and his 'wife' caught the Union Pacific train for Chicago, where he had yet more connections – this time in the form of Murray Humphreys.

The Humphreys and Kimber families both had Welsh ancestry. Humphreys, nicknamed Murray The Camel by the Press because of his natty camelhair overcoat – and no doubt a snide reference to the 'hump' in Humphreys – owned a laundry on North Clark Street. He was part of Al Capone's gang, one of the few who were not Italian or Jewish. When Kimber arrived, Humphreys had troubles of his own. The City was reeling from the shock of the St Valentine's Day massacre, which took place in the same street as his laundry. One of the victims was the owner of a rival laundry, considered to be very convenient to Humphreys: apparently the man, Alf Weinshank, who was not a regular member of the targeted Bugs Moran Gang, had been lured there to receive the same fate as one garage mechanic and five of Moran's gangsters. Kimber, perhaps with the help of Humphreys, managed to return to Britain in August 1929. He seems to have lived out a quiet life after that.

In 1928 Spenser, Wag, Bert and Harry Palmer held up a casino. Although they 'made some money', they had to use their guns to escape. It was not an occupation Wag liked. He persuaded Bert there were less risky ways of making money. Spenser, who was a versatile operator, but too eager to make a name for himself, was gaoled for beating up a crooked cop. He was later deported to England.

Wag took over as master of a yacht belonging to silent screen actress Colleen Moore. At the time Colleen's marriage to film producer Johnny McCormick was in trouble and Wag made some reference to keeping both the yacht and Colleen off the rocks. Her career had blossomed in the early '20s when she played the first scatty flapper in the movie *Flaming Youth*. At the time Wag worked for her she had just played the leading role in a big time movie, *Lilac Time*, which paired her with a new sensation called Gary Cooper, who was getting most of the Press attention.

Wag described Colleen as a sweet girl with a good business brain. He may have been some consolation to the superlative movie flapper. Certainly he escorted her about town between husbands, but as always with his women friends, he said very little. He did say the parties at Colleen's house in Angelo Drive were wild affairs.

Frequently he had to block gatecrashers and eject troublesome guests. On one occasion Tod Browning received a champagne bottle over his head and Wag drove a long way to Tod's house on Rodeo Drive. All the way Browning moaned and rambled on, at one time offering Wag a hundred dollars to go back and beat up the assailant. Instead Wag stayed at the house all night while a doctor patched Browning up. He never said if he ever earned the one hundred dollars.

Wag had established himself in the Los Angeles underworld and bought his automobile businesses from the proceeds earnt from protecting illicit beer joints. He also had a good round of friends. The crowd that Bert moved into included Vic McLaglen, Dick Baker, Reg Denny, Johnny Mack Brown, Colleen Moore and Barbara Kent. Johnny Mack Brown was an ex-football player and although he had limited acting talent he was in demand everywhere he went because women liked him. Wag loved being in his company because 'he attracted women like flies'. Dick Baker was the boss of a group of Canadian ex-servicemen who worked with Wag in an informal partnership of bodyguards, messengers and oddjobbers providing a range of services – from escort duties to clearing away evidence of nights of passion for stars feeling remorse, or calamitous bad publicity, in the morning.

Bert also took shares in a garage and prepared to carve his own piece of Los Angeles prosperity. He replaced Spenser as Licata's other bodyguard. Licata liked English people around him. 'They are more trustworthy,' he told Wag.

Trustworthy or not, the embarrassment for Wag was that he represented both sides. He managed to keep the thing going when Dragna decided to try to settle the differences between himself and Licata. Wag arranged a meeting in the Rose Room dance parlour on South Spring Street. Both sides turned up mob-handed and made a show of searching each other for weapons – although from the bulge in at least one coat it was clear that a less-than-efficient search had been made. Dragna's men filed through the door and lounged against the wall; Wag followed them in hoping that Licata would think he had got behind the enemy. Bert stood with Licata's men on the other side of the parlour. Dragna sat at the one table in the centre of the room and looked to Wag to join him, but Wag nudged Arnold Bruin into the chair next to Dragna who by now was giving Wag a wicked look. The negotiations were grim and strained. Dragna would not concede anything. He threatened attacks on Licata's clubs if Licata didn't stop meddling in his affairs.

Dragna kept looking to the door and appeared to be expecting reinforcements. Bert had seen this sort of thing before in his battles with the Sabinis, who were experts at stalling until help arrived. Finally, Licata had enough and got up. Bruin grabbed hold of his collar at which Bert rushed in and hit Bruin with a chair. Wag put the lights out and all hell broke loose. Some crashed through the doors to fight in the daylight. Inside, Wag caught glimpses of the enemy in the chinks of light coming through the curtains. He described the chaos, people scrambling to get out, the heaving and plunging of bodies, the screams and groans and then the flash of a gun which lit up the room. The lights came on and Wag found that most of Dragna's men, who were nearest the door, had gone outside. Licata's men appeared to have been mostly fighting among themselves. Outside, bodies lay on the sidewalk. One had a knife sticking in his cheek. The cars filled and everyone went, taking the injured with them.

Wag and Bert were now on opposite sides as far as everyone else was concerned. They contrived to have a new peace conference away from the heart of Los Angeles clubland. They chose a fish restaurant at Redondo Beach just south of the City. The meeting was to consist of Wag, Dragna, Bruin and Charlie Besant face-to-face with Bert, Licata, a huge man called 'House' (because he resembled one) and Licata's accountant Jake Lubick. The trouble was that both sides brought carloads of supporters. The meeting didn't stay peaceful very long. Bert got increasingly fed up with Licata's cockiness and started siding with Wag and Dragna. When Licata lost his temper Bert helped to eject him from the restaurant, while Wag jammed a revolver against the House's innards and forced him from the restaurant. Immediately a fight broke out between the opposing sides, most of it on the beach. Wag likened it to the Brighton beach fights with the Sabinis. Licata got the worst of the deal and scuttled back to the Windy City, leaving Dragna with a fingertip hold on the Los Angeles underworld.

In no time Bert had fitted into the Los Angeles scene. He acquired a limousine and a luxury apartment on Georgia Street. When he had joined Wag in America feelings of the war were still high. Tragedy struck when Bert, who was in the habit of letting it be known he was a British veteran for the kudos it brought him, visited a garage he had an interest in on South Spring Street. A lift operator, who was a German, brought the lift up behind him and crushed him against a wall, breaking his back. He died ten days later. Some speculated that Licata may have been at the back of it, as it happened soon after he left for Chicago. Wag buried his brother at a ceremony of British veterans in Inglewood Park Cemetery, Los Angeles. He then returned to the garage where he chased the German on to the flat roof and threw him into the liftshaft. Thinking he had killed him he went south to Mexico for the heat to die down. Bert's grave was found by his grandnephew, my son, in July 1996. Wag's diary makes no mention of Bert's death, but he closed his bank account and left town immediately following the funeral:

> I decided on a trip down into Mexico where I heard some officials of the large oil companies were recruiting Mexican labour for the oilfields down in South America. I arrived in Tijuana, just across the Mexican border 125 miles from Los Angeles, but on making enquiries I found they were not engaging any drillers at present, so I felt kind of disappointed at the prospects of seeing more of Mexico. My greatest thrill was to come later on. After looking around the town and buying a few curios I was amazed at the cosmopolitan nature of its people. There were Japs, chinks, half-breeds, beachcombers and some real tough guys. This is the hiding spot for all evil doers from the United States. The name Tijuana is pronounced 'tier wanna', what they term in the States as the Hell Hole of Mexico. From what I found about it after, its name fitted in well for its deeds. I made my way to the Post Office, just outside the town, which consisted of an antique fire brigade, police headquarters and an hospital and, of course, the jail.
>
> About 8 p.m. I saw it was getting dark and made my way back into town along a desolated lane which had a hedge on each side of it just high enough to cover a person from being seen walking along the road. At that moment my thoughts were miles away with the old folks back home, the country lanes of England. Suddenly I heard a shuffle behind me and on looking round I heard a very rough command in Spanish and at the same time a big .45 stuck in my ribs. I knew it was

a hold-up. I heard repeatedly the word 'Señor' and not understanding his language I knew his intentions were not good. I tried to explain to him in English and wait for my opportunity to knock his gun from his hand, but no sooner had I spoken another one came towards me from the other side of the road. I may mention they both wore bandannas (handkerchiefs) over a part of their faces to prevent identification in case of capture.

It seemed utterly useless to me for further argument and I was wondering whether these road agents were nervous on the trigger finger – if so I'm afraid this incident would never have been written – so all I could do in the face of that heavy artillery was to comply to their demands. My life was at stake. I was gently relieved of $211, plus my stage ticket back to Los Angeles which they were good enough to let me keep. I may mention that my thoughts at that moment were of a fiery nature. If I could have spoken to them I should certainly have said something polite after this style: 'Si Señor, or whoever you may be, my regards for you are of an honourable nature, but I seem filled by an all powerful hate towards you, I take this my only method of conveying to you the state of my feelings towards you and hope that we may meet again in the very near future, but under different circumstances, adios Señor.'

After that they seemed to pay some sort of compliment and with a sweeping bow and salutations they departed. Adios, I thought, that was little consolation to me with prospects of going 125 miles with empty pockets. I now began to view the matter in a more serious light. In the face of the recent reports given to me of these hold-ups, I tried to comfort myself with the hope that conditions were not fully as grave as they were and I felt thankful after that those hombres were not nervous on their trigger fingers.

I arrived back in Tijuana without reporting the affair to the police as hold-ups are of such frequent occurrence that they take little or no notice of such occurrences. I now set my course for San Diego, 25 miles away from the Mexican border, and reported the whole affair to the British consul there who took all particulars of the hold-up. It put me in high spirits with a feeling of patriotism when I saw the

ELEPHANT BOYS

Union Jack floating in the breeze on that building. To me a symbol of protection and safety.

For myself, I think the greatest task of courage on earth on such occasions as these is to bear defeat without losing heart. How proud I felt at the sight of the old flag. It came to me so suddenly, to me, to think:

Be England what she will,

With all her faults;

She is my country still.

The consul assisted me to reach Los Angeles where I arrived once again from another adventure. I seemed rooted to Los Angeles.

The heat was still on, the German was brain damaged and not expected to recover. Wag decided he urgently wanted to see more of California. For a spell he worked for the California Highways Commission in the Mojave Desert, but his boss tipped him off that the police were enquiring for people without the proper papers working in the camps.

I was anxious to see Death Valley. The place I had heard so much about before I left. This place I believe is the hottest and the lowest spot in the whole of the United States. I again went by stage, arriving at sun-down, and made preparations for the morrow. Next day about 11 a.m. the heat was unbelievable, a temperature of 130 degrees being common at midday. From about October to May the climate is delightful, the average maximum temperature ranging from 68 to 80 degrees. The stage road through the valley goes through Lone Pine, a solitary pine tree standing all alone on a small hill.

On we go through Jaywalker Trail into Darwin, on through Pannamint Valley, over Townsend Pass into Stovepipe Wells and the Devil's Golf Course, named for the heat and the large quantities of borax and rock salt to be found around here. On this desert a modern bungalow city has been built, all so wonderful. One would imagine they were on the Sahara Desert with its ever shifting sand dunes. It is a winter climate unsurpassed, a land of beauty and romance.

I often wonder what people would say in London if they were taken out on some Californian desert, or should waken in the morning and find themselves on some hacienda (ranch) on the outskirts of Death Valley looking out over an overwhelming panorama of blue sky, desert flowers and towering magnificent mountain scenery. To be sure this is the desert, but how different from the desert explained to you in some books and as pictured in the minds of most people.

In this region there are many scenic spots that await those who love the beauties of nature. One can see the sun sink behind the rugged mountains, a real fairyland amidst green foliage alive with birds and the soft murmur of running water from the mountains, a lovely oasis where the desert and mountains meet. Who can describe enough of the desert with its velvet starlit nights, the grandeur of the scenery in this vast waste? Mere words are not enough to convey a true impression of that irresistible allure which the desert has for those who know and love it. Those who come within its magic spell find that they have a yearning to return forever after. Fogs are unknown in the desert and I know a few friends who wish they were unknown in London. Of course we take them accordingly to our taste.

Out in this desert land you do not have to dodge motor cars, no waiting for your tram or bus, no crowding in the stores to do your shopping. Everything is there that you need. If you like, you may ride into the hills or across the mesa or around the many canyons, exploring. There is no other spot in America that has a more ideal winter climate or such unique surroundings. There is a real oasis in the desert. Palm tree groves in the canyons, clear, cool water running down from the slopes of these gorgeous snow-capped mountains. It is good water and good for you. A large part of the area is noted for its minerals; gold, silver, copper ore, etc.

One can cross the border here into old Mexico, also a land of magic. For all its wonders it is the desert magic which brings complete rest from one's business worries. Truly a marvel of nature.

The heat was so intense I decided to get back to cooler climes and after being two days on this wonderful desert I returned again to Los Angeles.

Wag's return to Los Angeles was not a happy one. The German had

ELEPHANT BOYS

gone to meet his Kaiser and the cops were enquiring for my uncle. He spent several weeks on Reg Denny's yacht, the *Cassion*. Denny also bankrolled him and conveyed him to Seattle. There he boarded the SS *Prince Rupert* and went on a cruise around Alaska:

We are now Alaska bound. The morning is fresh and clear with the mountain forests of Vancouver Island to our port, and off to starboard in the distance we see the snow-capped peaks of the Cascade Mountains glittering like diamonds against the sky. Alert Bay is passed with its rows of Indian totem poles in front of squalid-looking Indian huts.

I am very interested in the wilderness of the country viewed from a liner. Most of the passengers are too busy with deck games to notice when Putney Light and the blunt northern snout of Vancouver Island fade away on the port quarter. On our starboard the high coast of the mainland dips itself in the calm sea. On our port is a boundless expanse of blue sea flashing in the sun without one white crest to break its smooth surface. What a fine trip.

By looking at the ship's chart, we are now in Queen Charlotte Sound. How I remember you on my last journey south. Once again the land closes in and with it clouds rolling in beautiful grey and purple masses from the mountains. The wooded shores take on a deeper tone in colour, the smell of the pine and fir, the purity of the atmosphere, the snowy mantle on the mountains, make a beautiful picture.

Numerous islands are passed, their black sentinels of pines mirrored on a calm and shining sea. A spit of rain drives some passengers from the decks to the warm comfort of the glass enclosed forward observation saloon where one can view an unfolding panorama of ever changing beauty.

Ahead of us, where Fisher Channel narrows and thrusts between towering wooded crags, we can see a witches' cauldron of boiling vapour and rose-tinted mist, wonderful in its grandeur and held by cataracts that seem to thunder out of the clouds, mighty mountains that seem to plunge sheer into the sea, their wooded surface scarred and mown down with the paths of ancient avalanches, their frosty heads lost in swirling mist.

The hoarse roar of the ship's siren echoes in these narrow

ELEPHANT BOYS

canyons. Again the siren booms. The ship swings sharp in her course around the shoulder of some mighty mountain where we enter Ocean Falls.

A beautiful sunset dyes the mountain tops and struggles to lay a path of gold and crimson on the smooth surface of the sea as we turn seawards once more. Glancing at the chart of our course I become aware of the places we are near. Lorna Passage. Bella Bella, an old Indian village, showing a few scattered lights to our port. New Bella Bella on the opposite shore, the lights of its canneries twinkling in the fast gathering darkness. Seaforth Channel. Millbank Sound with its twang and faint heave of the outer ocean. Princess Royal Islands arise like a mighty mountain on our port side. Here we enter Finlayson's Channel and come to the famous Skeena River dotted with fishing boats which compels skilful navigation of a large liner of this draught.

In the morning the seamen of the forward deck prepare for our arrival in Prince Rupert harbour. A few hours ashore and we are off again. Prince Rupert fades away in the blue mist astern and after a long starlight night sweeps down on us from a sky that is clear and cold. More noticeable now are the lengthening of the hours of daylight. For we are now approaching the land of the midnight sun.

Here is the real outpost of the north where even in these small populated centres you feel the raw hardiness of frontier life. Ketchikan, for instance: how I know that place on my last homeward trip. We are simply besieged by bootleggers. Ketchikan with its boarded sidewalks, sourdoughs, the old timers of the gold rush days, papoose-laden Indians with their impressive faces and black beady eyes, big giants of lumbermen, fishermen and trappers, white men and breeds, lounge about the waterfront at their leisure.

Behind the town rise mighty forests so silent and majestic which seem to bid defiance to the northern lights which shine a silvery glare through its glades. Ketchikan in the Indian language means Town Under The Eagle.

A fellow passenger informs me that 30 miles from here is the famous Salt Chuck Mine, the largest producer of gold, silver, copper and platinum in the United States.

A thousand mountain echoes respond to the powerful

roar of the ship's siren as the ship leaves Ketchikan and makes a northeasterly course between Gravina and Revillagigedo Islands. The sun shines down upon a world of dazzling beauty with a fresh bracing wind blowing down from tier after tier of snow capped mountains, each range thick with forests and gemmed with cold sparkling blue-green glaciers. The numerous colours of the whole scene is too hard for me to express.

Here we come on to Wrangell Narrows between a cleft in the mountains through which the tide rushes in a smooth, powerful flood. The islands ahead of us, Mirkoff and Kupreanof, were once the possession of Russia when all this land was part of the late Czar's domains.

Settlers' homes dot the shores of the narrows, trappers and Indians live side by side, no race prejudice here. These narrows have earnt their name. The channel here is barely wide enough to allow our ship to pass through. After half an hour's steaming the narrows open out and we can see the town of Petersburg on our starboard and, far ahead, icebergs glittering and bobbing in Frederick Sound. A long swing to port, beneath towering cliffs that seem to rise up to the clouds, we enter Taku Inlet and see that wonderful glacier, Taku Glacier: one mountain of ice, about one and a half miles long, about two hundred feet high and no one knows how far back it runs. One of the crew informs me that from local information they say it runs back fifteen miles or more.

The setting sun throws its rays on this mountain of ice, it sparkles like diamonds with its blue, green and white lustrous beauty. The sea boils in snowy beauty at its base. There is a deafening roar and thousands of tons of ice shiver off the glacier face and splash into the sea to appear in a mass of swirling waves and join its cruising brethren in the deep waters of the sound, thence to find their way out into the ocean; and, dear reader, as far as I know that is how an iceberg is formed and let loose.

Onward we go and come to Juneau, the capital of Alaska. Through lovely Gastineau Channel, near the city and high up on the steep mountainside, is another gold mine. We can hear the rattle and crash of machinery. The clang of modern machinery echoes strangely in the silence of these northern wilds.

We stay here for a few hours and passengers take a trip ashore to visit the numerous places of interest. Off again to Skagway which is set at the end of an arm of blue salt water where a brawling river fed by the snow of the surrounding mountains falls into the sea with a mighty roar. This is one of the towns of the good old days of '98 where gunplay was amusing for those who handled them. One can visit the haunts of Soapy Smith, the notorious bandit, who was killed in a gun fight with Sheriff Reid. Savage-looking guys still roam the streets to this day on the lookout for greenhorns.

Skagway was the starting point of the gold rush trail through which so many men toiled in the great gold rush of 1898, many to die of cold and hardships over the frozen White Pass, many to succeed and reach the scene of the strike.

The White Pass and Yukon railway now crosses and recrosses the pass which seems to have been beaten hard by thousands of struggling feet. The trail winds zigzag among rocks and shale, around cold frozen lakes, across deep rivers and along the edge of deep ravines that were to claim so many lives of the many bold adventurers who passed that way.

Here the railway crosses Dead Horse Gulch and then comes on to the international boundary line between Alaska and British Columbia then breaks out on to Lake Bennett. The Yukon, with its views of mountain, sea and glacier, is of breathtaking grandeur. As we left Skagway in the early morning it was marvellously beautiful, but in a cold and glittering way. Now the sun lies astern, the surface of the water is a mass of molten gold broken only by the ship's wake and the silver splash of the porpoises at play.

There is only one port new to me around here: Wrangell, famous for its spruce timber and canneries. Today all the difficulties of a trip to Dawson have vanished. Only the thrills remain. One can go by rail to Dawson City, White Horse, Miles Canyon and the White Horse Rapids. The trip from White Horse to Dawson and into the real Klondike country is one which is becoming popular every year.

Between Selkirk and Dawson, the caribou herds in their migration from the arctic slope may be seen in thousands.

ELEPHANT BOYS

One of the most beautiful spots here is Five Finger Rapids, about 175 miles from Dawson. The entire country around here is lined with the names familiar in the story of the Klondike, but Dawson today is a most desirable place to live in. It is a real town with cosy homes and beautiful gardens, comfortable hotels and good roads to the surrounding creeks where so many fortunes were made. It is Dawson as it was, save for the many tough guys who strutted along the streets and frequented its dance halls.

I have often read the poem 'The Shooting Of Dan McGrew', but gone now are the dangerous Dan McGrews, the Swiftwater Bills, the Laudes, the Carmacles, the Harpers and the Hendersons, all gunmen of the gold rush days who would shoot it out with any sheriff, and all of whom came to an untimely end. But what a tale this place could tell. The real Klondike, the glamour of the old days when the few women of the camps wore diamonds as big as peanuts and the men threw their gold dust and nuggets around like sawdust. Yes, that spirit still remains, for the old-timers have not all gone, and the endless stories they can tell still make the Klondike a gold mine for the writer as well as the miner.

One can see a miner now and again scraping dirt from under an old hut where gold had been hidden before the banks got there, hidden by someone who never came back for the treasure. I was invited to go on an exploring expedition for some of this hidden treasure, but after a few hours' scratching and scraping I am sorry to say I never made a fortune. But there are still thrills there now when one finds some hidden treasure.

I saw all I wanted to see of this romantic country. Away past Dawson one comes into a volcanic region, a valley of subterranean volcanoes called by the Indians the Valley of a Thousand Smokes. It resembled to me an army camp with all their camp fires lit up. The view from our hilltop at dusk was an imposing sight.

Back to the ship again, where we turn around for our homeward trip. Just the same routine with music and laughter aboard amidst beautiful scenery *en route*. This trip seems a dream to me. Here I am on the top of the world, up into the outer regions of the arctic, thinking of England,

Phoebe (Grandma Mac) McDonald and son Fred, 1914.

Young Billy Kimber. Born in Waterloo, he was a force on the streets of the Elephant and Castle. He was also the first to organise the racecourse gangs in an attempt to hold down violence and provide a fair share for all.

Detective Tom Divall kept order in the dives around Waterloo Road and the Elephant and Castle, and on the racecourses.

Contemporary sketch of East End terror Henry (Alf) Solomon, implacable enemy of the Elephant Boys.

Neva Gerber, c. 1917.
Photo in Wag's possession.
[Copyright unknown.]

A curious photo taken in Los Angeles, 1928. Wag is back right. Bert is front right. Next to him is said to be Kate Meyrick. Ada also insisted that the man at back left is ex-detective and nemesis of the racecourse gangs, Tom Divall.

Wag's wheels.

Sergeant Dick Baker, Canadian Light Horse. Vic McLaglen is standing behind Canadian movie actress Barbara Kent. On the right is Miss Cannon, said to be Miss America; although records do not bear this out, most likely she was a contender.

Wag and Vic McLaglen, Hollywood, 1929.

Wag (second from right) and a bunch of scallywags selling plots of land in California. Wag owned a piece himself.

The heavy mob in happier times, c.1919, believed to have been taken in Stratford, East London. Ada insisted it was not a wedding photo despite the carnations. Most likely they were off to the races in their charabanc.

Ada identified them as: (1) Claud Fraser, (2) George Hatfield, (3) Joe Sabini?, (4) ?, (5) ?, (6) John Gilbert, (7) Harryboy Sabini, (8) Al Scasini, (9) Billy Kimber, (10) Bert McDonald, (11) ?, (12) ?, (13) George Sage, (14) Wal McDonald, (15) Billy Endelson, (16) Jim McDonald, (17) Tom McDonald?, (18) Harry (Frenchie) Cortesi, (19) ?, (20) ?, (21) Billy Banks, (22) ?, (23) Bert Banks, (24) Charles (Wag) McDonald, (25) Charles (Darby) Sabini, (26) ?

Wag with his 30–30
Winchester on a salmon
trap in Alaska.

Billy Burnup killed himself
rather than go to prison.

The inscription on the back of this postcard from Wag to Ada reads:
'Excuse hurry, just rushing through the town (Ketchikan, Alaska).'

Balin House, fronting on to Long Lane, Southwark.

The electricity sub-station between the 'squares'of Balin House, scene of much iniquity (but the graffiti is today's). We were sitting on the ledge, puffing our pipe cigarettes, when the Chapman gang came upon us.

Dave Morbin and Sally.

Stan McDonald, aged 17.

LEFT: Me at the time of the Jack Spot/Albert Dimes affair.

Junction of Frith Street and Old Compton Street, Soho. The shop on the corner was the Continental Delicatessen where Spot and Dimes had the 'fight that never was' (11 August 1955). In the street outside I danced a tango with Johnny Rocca.

Tommy Carroll in the passenger seat.
Movie actor and director Leslie Fenton
behind the wheel.

Ferguson's Alley, Chinatown,
Los Angeles. Wag and Tommy
Carroll fought their way back to
their car parked at the entrance
to the alley.

The Ambassador Hotel, Wilshire Boulevard, advertised itself as a
'22-acre playground in the Heart of a Great City', eight minutes from
the financial centre of Los Angeles. Golf, tennis, crystal pool,
cabaña-studded sun-tan beach, specialty shops, coffee-shop,
theatre . . . and the world famous Cocoanut Grove, the night choice of
stars of stage, screen and society. It didn't mention that Jack Dragna
had a suite on the top floor. Wag had the rooms next door.

London, its crowded streets, its motor fumes; and here, pure air, clean and rarefied. What a contrast.

I arrived back in Seattle full of life after such a splendid trip. There I decided on my trip down into California again and I was seriously thinking of taking the homeward trip to England if things had not improved since I left there.

Wag seem to have chosen his travels with possible escape in mind should he be detected. His routes gave an opportunity to skip either into Mexico or Canada if necessary.

Arriving back in Seattle, Wag intended to get back to Los Angeles, where Dragna could square the cops, but the writing was on the wall for Dragna's operation and he decided not to return to his service. Dragna had muscled in on Hollywood to extort money from producers who paid to avoid trouble on their sets. It was a brilliant idea that later would attract the interest of mobs from the east coast. However, he was not strong enough to withstand the constant challenges of more ruthless gangsters and the eventual encroachment of New York mobsters who envied the rich pickings. Dragna was pushed aside in the 1930s by Bugsy Siegal, assisted by Mickey Cohen who became the boss of Los Angeles.

By then Wag had moved south from Seattle to San Francisco and joined Joe Parente as a driver and bodyguard. In 1932, when it was clear prohibition was to be repealed, Parente's bootlegging business took a serious downturn. Wag therefore found that demand for his services had lapsed. His businesses were gone and he had the choice of the breadline during the Depression or trying something else. He returned to Los Angeles and took up his occupation as a bouncer and bodyguard.

Wag had a part in *The Trail of '98*, a film about the Alaska gold rush filmed around California and Colorado. Wag used his experience of his travels in Alaska as an opportunity to 'advise' on the film in exchange for a small part. He was feeling the bite of the Depression and was persuaded to join up with George Nelson who had been a machinegun guard for Parente's booze convoys.

Nelson had a gang which at times comprised Homer Van Meter, John Paul Chase and Wag's old friend Tommy Carroll, who by now was on parole from Iowa state prison. Tommy was not as Wag remembered him: he had lost much of his devil-may-care style and become a hard professional criminal. They decided to take on a

ELEPHANT BOYS

bank, something Nelson's gang had done before. Arch-schemer Van Meter was in prison; in his place the cocky Nelson led a botched raid on a bank in Stockton, California, which resulted in two being captured and Wag, Nelson and Tommy Carroll going on the run. At this point Wag, who was a young fifty-five, severed his connection with Nelson and took off for Los Angeles – where he renewed his career as an extra appearing in *The Big Trail*, starring John Wayne in his breakthrough role.

Nelson and Carroll later became members of the notorious Dillinger Gang, raiding banks throughout the Midwest. Tommy was Dillinger's getaway driver and 'outside man'. Newspaper reports of the time describe his chatting to bystanders as he lined them up at the end of his tommy-gun while waiting for the gang to come crashing out of a bank.

Interestingly, in one raid on the bank in Mason City, Iowa – where Tommy lined up the local police force and entertained the crowd with wisecracks – he drove the getaway car, which was reported as having been stolen from none other than Ann Harding. He was almost trapped when the gang was traced to a lodge in the wilds of Wisconsin; Tommy clambered over the roof, exchanging tommy-gun fire with FBI agents and police. The FBI killed an innocent bystander and wounded two others, but did manage to capture the 'Dillinger women' – one of whom was Tommy's common-law wife, Jean Delaney.

The gang got away. Dillinger's gang was hunted down one by one. Tommy was shot to death by police in Waterloo, Iowa, of all places, in June 1934 in front of Jean (on being given bail, she had scampered back to him), at the age of thirty-eight. His tommy-gun was under a blanket on the back seat of his car, but he'd been given no chance to use it. Baby Face Nelson – as George had now been branded by the Press – was the worst of Dillinger's gang. He killed three FBI men but was so badly wounded in the last shoot-out that he died of his wounds.

Wag, meanwhile, made up his mind that he would leave California:

A few days' look round and then I decided that my time had come to leave this beautiful state for ever. I informed my many friends of my intentions, who were ever so sorry I was

leaving them, and I made preparations for the homeward journey and Old England. After getting my passport, steamship and rail ticket all fixed up I bid farewell to this city I loved so well – El Pueblo de Nuestra Señora La Reina de Los Angeles, translated from Spanish, meaning The City of Our Lady the Queen of the Angels. Farewells to my numerous friends, and I was aboard the Golden State Limited, bound for New York and all places east.

ELEPHANT BOYS

6. A WANDERER'S RETURN

Wag had had enough and intended making his way to India to live with Anne – only to hear that she was about to return to England. She and her husband Bill Burnup, a crafty businessman who had a partnership with a major British company in India, had got into some trouble and were urgently departing. So Wag set out on his journey across the States:

> Leaving by the Southern Pacific Railway I passed through Pasadena, a city of memories to me on my desert travels. On through to Redlands with its orange groves, into Yuma, Arizona, through New Mexico into Texas, the land of the long-horned steer with its picturesque cowboys, out on the range singing to the cattle to pass away their weary and lonesome time.

Wag travelled through Oklahoma and Kansas to Illinois, where he made a short stop-over in Chicago to visit 'friends'. Perhaps he contacted Murray Humphreys to see if he could do for him what he did for Billy Kimber; then again, Neva Gerber came originally from Chicago! Curiously he notes in his diary a sample of Chicago underworld slang. Much of it is recognisable from American books and movies, but some of it is new to me and worth recording (see the glossary on page 134).

He notes that his short visit was disturbed by 'shady characters', perhaps agents of Licata, and that his friends urged him to get on

GLOSSARY OF CHICAGO UNDERWORLD SLANG

ELEPHANT BOYS

Ace or buck one dollar
Ankay prison, the jail
B of I Bureau of Identification at the detective bureau
Big house or pen penitentiary
Big shot a success, something good, a reliable gangster
Boots to give a man the boots is to kick him when he's down
Brew beer
Broad, Jane, dame or sweetie a girl
Brown stuff whisky
Bump off to kill
A buy when a Federal Agent purchases liquor for evidence
Buzz telephone call
C one hundred dollars
Chap to use a machine gun
Cinch something easy, simple to do
Cold sausage a heartless killer, a fiend
Come off the result of something good
Con a convict, also a confidence man
Cover up any means used to mask a real purpose
Croak to kill
Croaker a physician
Cross to betray
Cut to tamper with whisky in such a way as to increase the quantity without losing its strength
Cutter one who cuts whisky
Deal a transaction
Deuce two dollars
Dick a detective
Dip a pickpocket
Dope sometimes means information, also refers to drugs, or news of any description

Draw to cover with a revolver
Dust cocaine
Fry to be electrocuted
The G the Federal Government
gallery, the photograph files at the detective bureau, the same as our rogues' gallery
Gat a gun or revolver
Give the arm to attack one from the rear holding the head in the bend of the elbow, a method used by gangsters without the aid of a gun
Giving it to kill
Glimmer on ice a diamond
Goldfish room the room in the detective bureau where suspected persons are questioned, none too gently, the third-degree method
Grand one thousand dollars
Heat or hot a city or locality unsafe for lawbreakers
Heater a cigar
Heavy man a bully or official killer in a gang
Hoist hold-up
Hot wanted by the police
Jagaboo a coloured man
Jam in difficulty
Job illegal business
John Law a cop
Lay low to hide
Lookout a watchout or spy
Lunch hook hand
Money man one who finances an illegal enterprise
Nitro or soup nitroglycerine
Nose trouble someone who is a nosy Parker
Put on the nose bag have something to eat

his way. He took the New York Central Railroad from La Salle station and travelled through Indiana, Ohio, into Wheeling, West Virginia. He then went on to Baltimore, Philadelphia and New York. He was at this time purely a tourist doing the rounds of the sights in New York City. The Empire State Building was only just being completed.

> To attempt a description of this wonderful City in my short stay is all but impossible. The immense height of some of its buildings, the throngs of people on the 'Great White Way', the sky signs, 42nd Street, the Rosey Cinema which holds 6,000 people, Times Square with its cheapjack stores, Coney Island . . .

He walked the length of Broadway, from Bowling Green to Battery Park, and took a boat trip to the Statue of Liberty and Ellis Island, where thousands of immigrants were being screened before being allowed entry to the United States. After a few days he boarded Red Star Line's *Lapland* for a fairly rough crossing of the Atlantic. Steaming time from New York to the Eddystone Lighthouse was logged as seven days, two hours, eighteen minutes, at an average speed of 17.67 knots; total distance 3,026 miles. Port of arrival was Plymouth where he took the boat train for London to be met at Waterloo by a crowd of family and friends. Whether his journey from Chicago to England was the same as the illicit exit of Billy Kimber has never been established.

Bill Burnup and Anne had commuted between India and England, making as many as seventeen trips. They also owned a house in Hayter Road, off Brixton Hill. It was here that Jim moved with his new wife, my mother Grace, whom he had met when they both worked for Badger's Sweet Company in Poplar, east London. Anne nagged poor Bill to exhaustion. To gain some respite he frequently visited the upstairs rooms of Jim and Grace.

Grace was one of six sisters and a brother from a respectable family living in Poplar, east London. Her father was a lighterman on the Thames in the days when they rowed barges and had to cut icicles from ropes they were handling. When Grace met Jim there was a gulf of eighteen years between them. Mum said dad always looked younger and she got a shock when he told her his age. It made no difference: they married at Brixton Registry Office in 1932.

Life was hard in the Depression. Jim was finally driven to go and seek assistance at the dole office. On being told by somebody there that he should have 'put something aside when times were good', he almost cracked and set about the fellow. But a policeman there, on duty to prevent such anticipated behaviour, warned: 'There's nothing you can do about it, mate. Walk away or I'll have to run you in.'

Jim remembered that all his life.

The troubles with the Sabinis had been continuing. Wal and Jim, although not at the heart of Kimber's organisation, were considered by other gangs to be rivals. Neither of them had any remaining interest in bookmaking but their presence on racecourses – where they earned a few bob by running messages and errands – was seen as a challenge.

Jim had a falling-out with Sid Baxter, a Hoxton tearaway who associated with the Sabinis. Jim was earning a day's wages at Sandown when Baxter asked him for a tenner. This was typical blackmailing behaviour – pay up or be cut up. Jim was not violent by nature. Nevertheless he was very strong and he gave Baxter a right-hander that put his lights out. Baxter let it be known that he would get Jim and that he had on his team George Sewell. Ex-boxer and current thug, who terrorised Bethnal Green and lent his strongarm talent to various mobs including the Sabinis and Aldgate Jews, Sewell was considered an enforcer. Probably he accepted commissions for his handiwork. Wal knew the dangers and asked Kimber to intervene. Kimber had business interests that no longer included warfare, so he asked two associates to talk to Sewell.

Those associates were John Phillips (who had once been slashed by Jim Ford) and his brother Arty, who had both been acquitted of the gun affray in the Gray's Inn Road. But they misunderstood the request and got a team together from the Elephant and Castle to go looking for Sewell. They found him and Baxter in the Admiral Duncan pub in Old Compton Street, Soho. What followed finished Sewell as a force and got the Phillips brothers long prison sentences. Six men took the pub apart, with Sewell and Baxter being cut to ribbons. The viciousness of the attack brought John Phillips five years and Arty three; others received lesser sentences.

Sewell retired to Brighton and never fully recovered from his drubbing. The message was clear: even with Wag away there were plenty willing to take up his cause, especially if they could do Billy Kimber a favour at the same time. There is a story that, soon after Darby Sabini's death in 1951, Sewell beat up Alfie Solomon because he had deserted Darby. If so, both must have been pushing sixty and should have been planning their pensions instead of swapping punches.

Windmill Street in Soho was soon the scene of another major fracas. The Italians favoured a number of Italian and Greek restaurants and coffee-shops in that area – all of which were exempt from paying money to the Sabinis. However, they were not considered to be exempt by the Elephant Boys. In a night of savagery in June 1931, the Elephant Boys wrecked seven Italian and Cypriot establishments in Carlisle and Bennett Streets, Rathbone Place and – most serious of all – the café of Zacharias Panagi in Windmill Street. Police rounded up scores of suspects in police tenders and held them at Tottenham Court Road police station. The guilty, as always, merged with the innocent and nothing much came of police charges.

Jim was desperate enough to consider a scam offered to him and Wal by an old Hoxton villain, Eddie Guerin, who hung around bookie joints and dog tracks. Guerin's *claim* to celebrity status was that he once escaped from Devil's Island in French Guiana after being sentenced in France to ten years in that hellhole. In fact, he did not escape from the island itself but from the mainland; however, this didn't prevent him from telling colourful stories about himself. Jim was almost sucked into a scheme to forge travellers' cheques but Wal, who had taken Guerin's measure, suspected that he and Jim would end up the losers.

Guerin was now seventy years old, with a life of crime behind him. He had operated on the Continent and in the United States where he met persistent criminal May Churchill (better known as Chicago May). She became his companion until she fell out with him and shot him in the foot outside a Bloomsbury hotel. He boasted of being connected to American mobs, but it looked to Wal as though he was now into petty, small-time stuff. Anyway they pulled out.

Guerin was arrested soon afterwards for forgery and stealing travellers' cheques from a widow. In his defence he allowed his counsel to tell the jury of his colourful past, claiming the police

ELEPHANT BOYS

were expecting a conviction because he was notorious. The judge said he had hardly heard of him. Apparently the jury hadn't either, but they were both grateful for the tales of his eventful past. He got three years' penal servitude and he couldn't escape from that. Out in two years, after displaying impeccable behaviour, he stooped to his lowest when he stole five pounds from a handbag – for which he received twelve months. Generally believed to be an American, he was in fact Irish. He died, impoverished, in 1940.

Wag arrived home in 1932 and moved in with his sister Ada at Bedford Street, Walworth. One of Wag's new deals involved the selling of worthless shares. It was a comedown from his colourful Los Angeles life but he was short of money. Through Billy Kimber he met Jake Factor, a Yorkshireman who had spent most of his time in Chicago – some of it in partnership with Murray Humphreys. Factor, known in Chicago as Jake The Barber because he once earned his living by being personal barber to gangsters like Al Capone and Murray Humphreys, learned valuable lessons while lathering the cream of swindlers. He also impressed his clientele with his business brain by adding to their ideas. While shaving the world's con men he learned their tricks of the trade, eventually being allowed to invest in crooked schemes.

Factor became a genius at coming up with money-making scams, usually through selling dodgy shares in worthless schemes. He gratefully became aware that some people will do anything to make a lot of money without risking much capital. The State of Illinois had suffered enough crooked share deals at just about the time Jake was moving into the trade. His solution was easy. He was still a British citizen, so he moved to London. His opening scheme was buying up worthless land in Kent and Sussex, dividing it into lots and then selling it – through high-pressure sales techniques – to gullible investors who believed that in Britain there was nothing to fear from such schemes. (After all this wasn't America.)

Investors, starved of the high life in depression-hit Britain, revelled in being chauffeured about in limousines and treated to expensive lunches as they attempted to recover their wealth. In return they scraped money together, singly and in groups, to get in on land deals in Britain and the States. To snare them, Factor needed backers willing to put money into his schemes for a percentage of the profits. Billy Kimber, through his connection to

Murray Humphreys, became his recruitment agent. Wag had not much money to invest, so he roped in Anne's husband Billy Burnup. Billy's return from India had been hurried. He had been involved in illegal exporting to Britain, where there was a huge market for exquisite silk products, to avoid paying taxes on his profits. Somewhere it had gone wrong and he scurried home to cover his tracks. The chance to get in on a share-pushing deal appealed to him and he put up money to help Factor set up trusts, on which he became a board member. They circulated prospectuses and published financial journals with a flourish: it all gave the company, British Allied Estates, which Factor had incorporated in Canada, an air of respectable professionalism.

Responses to the company's literature were followed up by intense salesmanship. Factor imported con men from Chicago to push shares over the telephone and through investors' meetings. Wag and Wal made easy money by setting up premises and ferrying potential investors to sites. Factor offered deals at low cost, just enough to suck people in, then he pressured them to buy more lots in which all investors would get a share of the profits if oil or minerals were found on any one lot. The lot owner would get the lion's share, but everyone else would get something. This worried investors – who feared they might miss out if they didn't invest in more lots – and gradually they paid over more and more money. Factor and his associates actually paid out dividends to keep their scam going, but it was beginning to get hot.

It went wrong when Factor lost control over his imported team once they got a sniff of how easy it was to make money in Britain. They began schemes of their own and brought Press attention on their activities – particularly after a punch-up between British and American factions on the steps of their Kingsway headquarters, when Wag took exception to the intrusion of one American import named Red Cohen. Factor scooted back to the States, leaving Billy Burnup holding the baby. As Billy juggled the books in Britain, Factor moved into Canada where he began much the same sort of caper. Then he returned to London to launch even more schemes.

He lived in the best hotels, openly displaying contempt for the Stock Exchange. He created new companies, switched funds, and set up syndicates with bewildering speed. As complaints rolled in from unhappy investors, the Stock Exchange finally launched an investigation. Factor simply moved back to Chicago. As the scandal

ELEPHANT BOYS

unravelled, Billy Burnup was arrested, along with others, and bailed. It was too much. Before Billy came to trial he waited one evening for Anne to go to the Trocadero cinema at the Elephant and Castle; then he lay on the bed, fastened one end of a bootlace to the bedpost and the other around his neck, then rolled off the bed. That's how Anne found him. Jimboy, who was now grown up, slept in the bed that same night.

Attempts were made to extradite Factor before eight weeks had passed, after which time the process would lapse. His lawyers pulled every trick in the American courts to delay his return. Even so he came dangerously close to extradition. He was finally nailed down for a court appearance where he would be ordered back to Britain. Even then he wasn't finished. He played his last-resort card when he arranged his disappearance. He was kidnapped. With the help of Murray Humphreys he disappeared for twelve days until a ransom of $70,000 was paid.

Humphreys, now leader of the Chicago crime syndicate while Al Capone was in prison, was being challenged by some troublesome rivals. One of them, Roger 'The Terrible' Touhy, was framed for Factor's kidnapping and gaoled for ninety-nine years. A sweet move: Factor was happy, Humphreys was happy and they didn't care about the rest.

Factor never again returned to Britain. In 1959 Touhy was released from prison and almost immediately gunned down. Evidence points to Factor paying Humphreys, through some contrived share deal, to have him killed in case he took revenge for those twenty-four years spent in gaol for nothing. Some say Humphreys himself pulled the triggers on the double-barrelled shotgun. Certainly Humphreys had as much to fear and may have considered it a matter of personal safety.

The manner of the passing of Billy Burnup was too much for Mum, dad and Jimboy. They moved to Lorrimore Square, Walworth, and soon after Jimboy married. Jim and Grace then moved to Frederick Road, Kennington, which is where they were living when Stan and I were born (but I was actually born in Charing Cross Hospital).

Anne moved to Josephine Road, Brixton, where she let rooms to theatrical folk appearing at the Brixton Empire. On one occasion, she returned home to find a couple had completely stripped the house of its furniture and done a moonlight. She could not bear to remain in the house alone and moved in with sister Alice – now Hayman – in Tulse Hill where both eventually died. The only uncle I really knew was my dad's younger brother Fred, who lived at Watford and died in the 1960s. My half-brother Jimboy, who was more than twenty years older than me, was always regarded as uncle Jim.

Another of Wag's attempted deals was the handling of forged bonds. He and Wal had somehow connected with Isek Najmark, who needed Wag's new-found knowledge to shift over a half million pounds worth of dodgy bonds. The bonds were printed in Poland and shipped all over Europe and the United States. Wal went with Najmark, the 'Moriarty' of his time, to Poland to collect the forgeries and to see what else could be done. On their return, Detective Sergeant Greeno pounced, arresting Wal and Najmark at Liverpool Street Station. In the baggage of two Poles travelling with them was a selection of printing plates and specimen forgeries of British national health and unemployment insurance stamps. The two Poles were returned for trial in Poland; Najmark got five years in an English gaol; Wal did not answer his bail and went into hiding.

Wal had lived in a peace with the Sabinis that lasted until Wag's return. Wag, who had not been charged over the bonds, was now back with the Elephant Boys and badly in need of money. His remedy was to restart the trouble by dissolving arrangements with the detested Sabinis. To avoid trouble for Ada he moved out and set up headquarters in the Trinity Mansion Hotel in Eastbourne – an ideal location for the south-of-England racecourses, from where he presided over an assortment of racing toughs. On his team was some of the Hoxton mob who had never really settled their differences with the Italians and Jews. To regain the upper hand he led them in a pitched battle against the Jews in Shoreditch. Darby Sabini and Alf White, now deserted by Alf Solomon, were humiliated into handing over their leadership to heir apparent Harryboy Sabini. Harryboy continued to resist Wag. In one fight, Mickey McCausland – brother of Billy Kimber's old enemy, Matt – was killed.

Periodic scuffles occurred as both gangs struggled to control the racecourses. Ada said Wag was the target for Harryboy and had several altercations in pubs around south London and on the

ELEPHANT BOYS

courses. On one occasion he was approached by East End villain Dodger Mullins, who said he had been offered fifty quid to have him 'done up'. Jim described Dodger to me:

> He was always scruffy. I once saw him in a tailored suit but he had let the trousers slip so much that they were dragging on the ground and looked as though he had stolen a clown's baggy pants. He always had food hanging from his mouth and talked with his mouth full, making a conversation with him a dangerous affair. He wore a neckerchief, never a tie, and looked and talked like something out of *Oliver Twist* – Bill Sikes more than the Artful Dodger – where his name came from. He was totally bad, the sort who would steal anything whether he had a use for it or not. If you had something he would want it. He had a gang which terrorised East End shopkeepers, mostly for free meals, smokes and booze. He never paid for anything. His uncouth presence on racecourses had been curtailed by Billy Kimber, because he openly threatened bookies and punters and ran pickpocketing binges where so many people were robbed that on one occasion it led to a riot. He would not fight if he could help it and tried to blag a few bob from Wag for information given. It was entirely natural for him to stir up trouble to see what came of it. He once put someone on to some sort of scam Alf Solomon was running, but Alf got to know about it and they had their own war going on. Even so, Wag put a few bob his way.

One incident Ada witnessed close up. It was classic Wag:

> They came looking for Wag at my house in Bedford Street, Walworth, and – sorry for them – found him in. He saw them pull up from the first-floor front window and sent me down to answer the knock at the door. Only one man came to the front door and asked for Tom Jones, all the time looking past me into the house. I think he wasn't sure if he had the right place. I answered the obvious that no such person lived here and that he should try further down the street, as someone named Jones lived there.
>
> The man, who was big, had a scrap of paper in his hand

and said he had number three written down. The other man, a short fat Italian-looking rough, got out of a small Austin Swallow, I think it was – one of those with a soft top and only two proper seats. The big man called him over to the door and I thought they were going to rush past me into the house. At that, Wag opened the upstairs window and pointed a big army revolver at them. You've never seen such fright, I thought the big man was about to collapse. The small fat one started to back towards the car and I stepped back through my street door.

Wag came rushing down the stairs and caught the big fellow before he had hardly moved. He hit him twice over the head breaking the gun open, then threw it into the house, and got stuck into the big one with his fists. Wag was a terror when his temper was up. He knocked the man unconscious, then went to the car to get the other one. The short chap was pulling on the door handle to hold it shut as Wag was pulling the other way with his foot against the car to get better leverage. The little fellow was blubbering and wailing and let go of the door to get out while covering his head and face with his arms and hat. Wag was so wild I thought he would kill him. Instead he dragged him over to the other man and made him pick him up. Picture it, the tall gangly one being dragged up by the short ugly one and Wag beating the two of them with the little fellow's hat, talk about Laurel and Hardy. He booted both of them back to their car and they struggled in. The big fellow was the driver and it took ages to start the car. When it did go it lurched and spluttered as Wag threw one of my nice flower pots at it. Then it went round the corner.

I had thrown a mat over the gun as people had gathered to watch the fuss. Wag came in and shut the front door, then told me the gun was already broken and was not safe to fire. I won't repeat what I said to him about the whole affair.

The strife culminated in 1936 when a gang of Italians and Jews raided the Elephant Boys at the Wellington pub in the Waterloo Road. Dad said Wag, who was now the firm boss of all the gangs opposing Harryboy, was in the thick of the fight which spilled out into the street with scores of people involved.

The fighting broke out again at Lewes Racecourse when the Elephant Boys joined with the Hoxton Mob in an attack on the Sabinis and cut up four bookies. Wag personally 'did' Alf Solomon, the man who shot Billy Kimber. Jimmy Spinks, uncle of bareknuckled fighter Lennie McLean and leader of the Hoxton Mob, also had a grudge against Alf Solomon who had previously paid some heavies to attack him. They did a good enough job to put him in hospital in fear of his life after they had set about him in Hackney with iron bars. Jim said Spinks was a huge fellow, unable to keep up with Wag who overtook the fleeing Solomon and gave him a going-over with a piece of iron railing in a car park. So Spinks 'did' Solomon's pal Mark Frater for just being there. He went to prison for it. It was the last of the pitched battles until troubles broke out again with the next generation of villainy in the late 1940s and '50s.

In 1936 Ann Harding came to England to relaunch her fading career. In 1937 (the year I was born) Wag took Ada to meet her on the set of *Love from a Stranger*, co-starring, of all people, Basil Rathbone. By this time Ann had divorced Harry Bannister, but Wag's day had gone. He was now fifty-nine and showing signs of his hectic life. He was unpopular in my Mum's household because, in hard times, he dragged dad out to the pub too often. Times were tough. Mum, who would not accept money from Wag, told me she couldn't afford to put bread and jam on the table only to watch a boozy Wag scoff the lot.

Constantly he planned new deals. His last, during the Second World War, involved recycling army scrap with his new friend George Dawson. After the war Dawson made a fortune by selling surplus army hardware and dealing in second-hand cars. He became an expert with the bribe: demand was such that he often carried money around in suitcases. It was too late for Wag, who lived with Ada until his death in 1943. I was only five or six years old but I remember him dying from a stroke on the steps of the Deep shelter in the Borough High Street.

Family stories carried his memory on. My aunt Ada, who was a great source of stories on Wag, considered I was very much like him. She also described him as Britain's contribution to American criminality. Wal, still being sought by the police, took up with a widow and her three children and seems to have wanted to put his past behind him. The last that dad saw of his brother was in 1947 when he and Grace bumped into him and his woman friend in a Piccadilly pub. We have never been able to trace him since.

It is possible that Harryboy Sabini, who now led the Sabini–White alliance and had been humiliated by Wal, may have been responsible for Wal's disappearance. It was a time when Alf White and Darby Sabini had practically retired and Harryboy had difficulty holding things together – a point at which Jack Spot would step in. Somewhere along the way Billy Kimber, who had also been investigated for his part in the Jake Factor swindles, also dropped from view.

Ada was a tough old bird. I once remember her witnessing a coalman being cruel to his horse in Browning Street, Walworth. She ran into her house, grabbed a broom and came out again to give him a fair old clout. She must have been tough to live with. Her husband Dan Johnston, when I knew him, was a quiet, total introvert. The poor blighter would do anything for a quiet life. He hated kids and went into another room when people visited. He showed signs of the constant bullying by wilful Ada which had slowed him down to not much more than a cucumber. One morning in the late 1950s, Ada awoke to find him stone cold beside her; not much difference, I thought, to when he was alive – the poor devil even went out with a whimper, a far cry from the man who once fought the Sabinis. I remember Ada's tears when she stayed with us for a while and I thought 'You cunning old so-and-so'.

His must have been a business arrangement with Ada. When she returned from India she became a merchant of women's fashionable clothes from her Walworth home. Purchases were made in the magnificent trade-only Houndsditch warehouse, near Fenchurch Street, in the East End. Fashion shows took place at house parties, guest dinners and family gatherings. She did very well and although she could be a hard woman she was very good to my Mum and saw that she was always well clad.

At times Anne and Alice lived with her, but they couldn't get on. Wag, of course, could look after himself and poor Dan withdrew ever further into his shell. Ada would visit us on Sunday and my mother would traipse down to the Walworth Road every other Sunday to walk through Browning and Brandon Streets to Stead

ELEPHANT BOYS

Street, where she now lived, just a short distance from East Lane. The house is now gone although other similar ones still stand in East Lane. In early days dad, Stan and myself were dragged along. Gradually dad and Stan managed to evade the trip, leaving me to sit precious Sunday afternoons in what became a gloomy, cheerless house. I sat fascinated as Ada told and retold family stories. Come the time that she began to ramble, I shamefully managed to pass all of the responsibility to my Mum, usually having arranged something else for days when Ada visited us (although my Mum was always firm that we should be there to greet Ada when she arrived or come back for tea, as a matter of politeness).

When Ada died in 1963 she left a house full of trinkets and garments. My Mum's visits had been confined to a single room, so it came as a shock to find other rooms crammed with racks of clothes – most of them faded and frayed, so that when expensive dresses were touched they came apart in our hands. Cobwebs abounded: it was Miss Havisham's world of fashion. Drawers were stuffed with costume jewellery, belts and braids. Edwardian and Victorian necklaces, the sort which became very fashionable in the '60s, hung everywhere. Pots were full of junk.

Ada did not trust banks. When she went into hospital, a week before she died, dad went into her bedroom and took up the floorboards to retrieve her cash hoard for safekeeping. After she died, he noticed that the boards had once again been removed. The next-door neighbour, who had a key for emergencies, expressed his surprise. Dad thought it was nothing like his surprise must have been when he found the stash empty.

Disposal of the goods became a problem and was placed in the hands of Jimboy. Systematically we searched drawers and cupboards, uncovering boxes and tins of junk. In among them, surprise finds of half sovereigns wrapped in cottonwool pushed to the back of a drawer, pink ruby, sapphire and diamond rings gradually emerged – not all tremendously valuable, but it was fun discovering the treasure. We cannot know if we found it all. Jewellery, except for a diamond ring given to my mother, was auctioned at Christie's; the coins went to Spinks. Furniture, some, in the style of Sheraton, was sold to Chiesman's store in Lewisham.

The rest was offered to house-clearance operators. These wide boys pick out the plums and sell them from your property, leaving behind anything they can't shift. Jimboy had arranged for some to come in, but when I visited and realised what was going on, I turfed them out. They had placed a linage ad in the *South London Press* inviting punters to call at the house on which we had only a short-rent holiday. One of them got stroppy and told me all about his connections around the Elephant and Castle. I then told him mine. He departed on affable terms.

As usual, everyone who visited the house identified the clock Ada had promised would be theirs when she was gone. Jimboy's philosophy was to sell the lot with the exception of the diamond ring. Dad then divided the proceeds between close members of the family.

I liked Ada. She was a fighter and a real south Londoner.

Jimboy, the son of Jim and his first wife Janie Hobart, was born in 1913. He married in 1936 and had a daughter, making me an uncle at the age of seven. He had joined the RAF during the Second World War and towards the end of the war became a paratrooper trainer. He told me stories of humour and tragedy during training sessions. The parachutist whose chute didn't open and who came down on the shoulders of a sergeant: both survived. The jumper whose chute caught in the undercarriage of the plane and they couldn't get him back in: they kept flying over a lake inviting him to release himself into the water but he would not, or could not, do it, and finally they had to land with him dragging behind. Jim told all of this in colourful anecdotes.

He was a keen amateur sportsman who won every athletic gold medal in Boots staff sports day. A good amateur boxer, he used to coach in Brixton, where he trained one of the boxers for the England team who whitewashed the United States 10–0 in the 1960s and brought Britain's Heavyweight Billy Walker to fame. Earlier he had attended Morley College, then gained a place at Loughborough College. After the war he was a physical training instructor working for various London authorities. Eventually he managed Coldharbour Sports Grounds at Sidcup and trained glider pilots in Kent. He died suddenly from a burst aneurysm in 1982.

From Frederick Road we moved to Flat 29 of a building which still stands in Evans Road, Catford. Stan nearly drowned in an Anderson shelter in the back gardens there – these shelters were death traps because they were prone to flooding. He had a toy bass

ELEPHANT BOYS

drum that somehow ended up in the water and he fell in trying to retrieve it. I remember the commotion when some adult came running to pull him out. After the onset of the Second World War dad bought a house in Lant Street, off the Borough High Street, near where he worked since taking on the job of foreman packer at the British Trolley Track near Union Street (now being remodelled as Sainsbury's new headquarters). My mother, Stan and I had been evacuated from London. We went first to Folkestone, which was also a target, then to Bishop's Waltham, near Southampton, again a prime Nazi target. When dad acquired the house we all moved back.

My Mum hated it because it was next door to a horse yard which smelled of manure and swarmed with bluebottles. Exactly two weeks later Mum, Jimboy, Stan and myself were sheltering in the Deep from an air-raid attack. We returned home to find smouldering rubble. My vague memory is of my dad and Jimboy, who had gone on ahead, struggling with a man who was trying to walk off with a mattress. Dad had been in the house when the bomb came through the roof and two floors. Fortunately it didn't explode until he had run from the building. When dad returned to the house later in the evening he found people digging in the rubble; asked what they were doing, they said they were searching for a man who lived there. Dad explained it was him.

From there it was a rest centre in Laxton Street School and into newly built Balin House. Mum thought this was a very satisfactory outcome. Lant Street still exists (a paper recycling plant stands about where our house once stood). I remember it as a narrow, dingy lane. Charles Dickens lived there for a short spell; it also has the dubious claim to fame that arch-villain Freddie Foreman was once landlord of one of the street's pubs, the Prince of Wales. Freddie played both sides of the water. He was an associate of Tony Reuter and later the Krays, becoming one of the inner firm. In 1967 he received ten years for disposing of the body of Jack 'The Hat' McVitie, who had been stabbed by Reggie Kray. (It is said that the body of Jack The Hat rested in a car in Lant Street before both he and the car disappeared into the depths of Kent.) There was another charge, that Freddie had been the gunman who murdered 'Mad Axeman' Frank Mitchell, but that resulted in a not guilty verdict.

My brother Stan, three years my senior, had his own group of friends. They knew the same sort of people I did and went to the same sort of places for entertainment. They were one of a number of smaller groups on the fringe of the gang, basically having a good time – interrupted of course by two years' compulsory National Service. They were more interested in parties and girls than fighting and had their own jazz band in which Stan played the trumpet. He was also a very good athlete and became a first-rate distance runner with Deptford Park Athletic Club, coming close to England honours when added to the England squad at the White City. He and my half-brother Jimboy both won many athletics medals. Stan's group were sometimes involved in minor scuffles – it was inevitable in our area. Stan himself was a good enough fighter, adequately demonstrated one day when we visited Eynsford on a bicycle ride. Among our group was Dicky Mitchell, a loudmouthed bully and barrow-boy, who for some reason singled out Stan and dived at his back. Stan ducked and Dicky went over the top; when he got up, Stan knocked him out.

Tragedy befell Stan's group on Clapham Common one summer's night in 1953 while Stan was away at army camp. They were strolling across the common when they were approached by a Brixton gang who mistook them for some others. A fight broke out in which one of Stan's friends gave the attackers a hard time. After the initial exchange the group became separated and Johnny Beckley, who looked like a smaller version of the one who had fought back, was surrounded and stabbed to death. Matt Chandler tried to help and received a severe stab wound in the stomach: he only escaped by jumping on a passing bus, and later recovered.

Johnny Beckley, admittedly a bit cocky, was well-liked nonetheless and he received a south London funeral with a large turnout of friends. Reprisals were taken by the Elephant Boys who believed they knew who was responsible. Eventually a boy named Michael Davies was gaoled for murder and there followed a long campaign by his friends and family to get him out. He was released seven years after being reprieved from a death sentence. Nobody thought the police had got the right man. I was in one of the hunting parties which went after Johnny's killer: we had not been looking for Davies.

PART TWO

7. NUDGING THE BOUNDARIES

Our local patch had centred on Balin House and the back streets off Long Lane and the Borough High Street. Fogarty's merchant store in Long Lane had an array of open sacks and aromas. I believe it was there that I used to see rabbits hanging in the window. The bootmender's, who also supplied horse oils and liniments, had a foul-smelling cat's-meat counter. Above the shop lived the Rose family. I first watched television with them, on a twelve-inch darkened screen surrounded by goggle-eyed friends of the family. Everything was watched in bewildered silence.

Further along Long Lane, past Staple Street, was Frank's Fish and Chip shop, a baker's and the accumulator shop – where unwilling youngsters lugged this heavy apparatus to be recharged to keep the family radio going. Beyond, near Wilds Rents, was the Cider Shop that sold every conceivable brand of the beverage: local lads would partake of the more potent varieties and sprawl in paralytic bliss inside nearby doorways. Further on was the shellfish stall, destination of small boys with short legs who would trudge the long walk from Balin House for seafood, measured in a pint or quart pewter pot, for dad's tea.

Dad loved his Sunday seafood tea and it was mandatory for Stan or me to undergo the tortuous journey. The alternative was worse: if dad had become dissatisfied with the Long Lane supply, it meant a 35 bus ride to the Elephant and Castle and a walk up the Newington Butts to White's shellfish shop – a famous enough location that it named the area which was the gateway to

Kennington. Fortunately for me Stan, being the oldest, had his protestations swept aside and had to give up his leisure time for the benefit of seeing dad unwinding winkles from their shells with his pin (a pinch of pepper and down they went).

I hated that stuff. I could manage shrimps and prawns, nipping only the backs. Cockles were tastier, but gritty. Once I attempted to eat a whelk, which was like chewing a rubber band. Apparently you are supposed to swallow them. If that is true, how can you taste them? And if you can't taste them, what is the point of eating them? Eels are a delicacy for south Londoners. Except for me. Seeing them wriggling in trays on an East Lane market stall, waiting for their heads to be cut off and bodies to be sliced into sections, was too bloodthirsty even for an Elephant Boy.

Nearby Pilgrimage Street led to Tabard Gardens with its park and enclosed football pitch. Much of the park was studded with the slanting roofs of air-raid shelters, reminding us of the short passage of time since the end of the Second World War. Its playground had one of those long swings on which a group could sit while two stood at the end, swaying the thing into motion. Frequently it was swung with such reckless velocity that it would travel to its extremity and only the mechanism would prevent it from completing a somersault. A stomach-churning delight. Chaucer's Canterbury pilgrims had assembled near here at the Tabard Inn, where Tabard Street meets Great Dover Street. A public library occupied the building standing on the site.

Kipling Street also had a park with swings, roundabouts and a tennis court which we used often. In that area the pigeon man could be seen peppering the treetops with his shotgun and popping his bounty into a sack carried over his shoulder. Near here, on waste ground, some boys found a sack which they paraded about, saying it contained the remains of a monkey. This alarmed local parents, especially when the remains turned out to be those of a baby. Another relic of the time was the street lamplighter, cycling with one hand on the handlebars and the other supporting a long pole resting on his shoulder.

Also in the vicinity were Jail Park – named, I believe, after the old Horsemonger Gaol – and Bedlam Park which was named after the infamous asylum. They were outside our patch, but we visited in defiance of local hooligans to strut our stuff, as tough guys do.

Third Division South Millwall Football Club was located at the

ELEPHANT BOYS

old Den, off New Cross Road, just up from the Old Kent Road. From an early age my father took me to home matches. In those days a wooden rattle provided the means of salutation and a blue-and-white scarf confirmed allegiance. When able to travel with my mates I shared my loyalties with Tottenham Hotspur and a taste for First Division games. Spurs were always championship class, pulling off the Double in 1961. White Hart Lane was so packed in those days, especially if Arsenal were being entertained, that to get from the back for a good view we would be picked up by men and rolled over the heads and shoulders of the crowd all the way to the front. The experienced kept a tight grip on their pocket-money. Charlton Athletic had the best goalkeeper in the country, Sam Bartram – an example of how one player can pull in a crowd.

At Millwall the Lions supporters developed a reputation for crowd trouble and the lowest elements revelled in their notoriety as the worst behaved fans in the country. True club supporters looked with disdain on the hooligans. Eventually their irksome behaviour drove us away, for we loathed the oafs who swore and flung coins at the opposition. The only fun was what the marines would nowadays call yomping. We didn't have a name for it then, but it worked like this: we would start the first half behind the opponents' goal; then at half-time the whole of our end would stamp sideways, barging the crowd before us until we finished up behind the other goal.

Cricket was exclusively Surrey, who took the championship seven years in a row. They were a glorious side, with such stars as the Bedser twins, Tony Lock and Jim Laker. To see them took only a short underground journey on the Northern Line from the Borough to Kennington Oval. Middlesex were the favourite opposition, especially if Dennis Compton was playing: he had the same allure as Ian Botham was to develop years later. The difference is that Compton played with controlled aggression and was a legitimate batsman. Botham, who was predominantly a bowler, could sadly disappoint with the bat when he walked out to the middle in the glare of expectancy, took one big swish, launched a divot into the air and walked back to the pavilion.

I read somewhere that there are some London kids who have never seen a cow or visited the countryside. It seems to me that people are generally better off today than they were in the '40s and '50s, yet we were not strangers to the countryside. Abbey Wood was a No. 12 tram ride from the Old Kent Road. It was great for jungle games and for emulating our childhood heroes – Robin Hood, Zorro, Jesse James – and cowboys and indians. Hidden ambushes were accompanied by 'Whoosh!', 'Swish!' and 'Bang! You're dead!' as we fought with imaginary bows and arrows, swords, spears and guns.

I first learned to ride a bicycle in the 'square' of Balin House. I rode my brother Stan's BSA bike and fell off so many times on to the hard surface that my arms and knees were covered with grazes. I was so determined to master it, I just got up and tried again.

My first bicycle was a gleaming red Hercules with a Sturmey Archer three-speed gear operated from a lever on the handlebar. My mates Johnny Rose and Dave Parker had gold bikes of the same make. They liked to be trendy; I suppose I liked to be different. Stanley Pell outdid us all with his lightweight Dayton Ohio which outpaced our heavier bikes. It was common to go for long bicycle rides. As many as a dozen of us, or more, would cycle to places like Hastings or Virginia Water. Round trips of over a hundred miles were commonplace. For a shorter journey, of about fourteen miles or so, our favourite place was Farnborough in Kent. The route took us from the Borough, down the Old Kent Road to New Cross, on to Lewisham, Catford and up Bromley Hill, where we always rested by the horse trough close to the milestone which reads 'Nine miles to London'. Further rests were taken at roadside cafés. That was all part of the day out.

Farnborough was a beautiful spot and we got to know it very well. One area we named 'rodeo woods' because of the bumpy terrain. We could zoom in and out of the trees and jolt over the humps in the pathways. Some kids would pick bunches of bluebells or go blackberrying to take something home with them. Bluebells, however, did not keep very well. It was in a field near here that Dave managed to sit in a very large, very wet and very smelly cowpat. He cycled home alone.

(This did not quite emulate Teddy Meakins who previously had managed to soil his short trousers during Church service at Charterhouse Boys' Club. He went home with legs wrapped in brown paper.)

The hop fields of Kent were a popular cycling excursion: from the Borough, through Swanley, out on to what used to be called Death Hill to Wrotham Hill, and on to Seven Mile Lane, which took us deep into Kent. Whole families loaded their furniture and home comforts on to the back of lorries and headed for Horsmonden, Wateringbury, Goudhurst or Eynsford to pick hops during a six-week summer period. At weekends and during the annual fortnight summer holidays working husbands would join them. Most lived in wooden huts with straw-covered ground. I would cycle to the fields with my friends and stay overnight, or for a few days, sleeping on a pile of straw. My mates knew the hop fields much better than me. My family did not go 'hopping'. Dad was working and Mum was not disposed to sleeping in a straw-lined hut. Picking hops was back-breaking, finger-splitting hard labour. I sampled it on one occasion and decided it was something you would do only if you had to. I would tolerate staying overnight among the creepy crawlies – and, let's face it, lice, for they were pretty verminous places – but hardened hop-pickers were not put off by a few flea bites.

Fishing in the Serpentine in Hyde Park or out in the country at Leatherhead, Surrey, was another pastime. I had not the patience for long bouts of fishing, preferring to swing from branches and splash about in the river, or better still scrump apples. I narrowly avoided a farmer's boot by scrambling over a fence and jumping into a stream at Leatherhead. The countryside afforded an opportunity to use our Diana air pistols. These were primed by pushing the barrel against the ground to compress the air; they were wildly inaccurate and fortunately fairly weak. In a game I accidentally shot a boy in the eye as he popped his head around a tree. I didn't realise I had hit him until he remained lying on the ground weeping. The slug had lodged in his eyelid and someone pulled it out – the slug, not his eye.

Stan was envied for his BSA air rifle. He had joined the army cadets in Union Street and had a desire for more accurate equipment. Prized above his BSA was his collection of army badges and buckles which, if kept, would have been worth a small fortune in today's market. Briefly I joined the scouts, but couldn't be bothered to learn my tenderfoot. My flirtation with the sea cadets at Rotherhithe was longer, and would have been longer still if only we hadn't had continually to tie those knots. After I left they managed to get the ex-war motor torpedo boat to France; on the way back it took on so much water it had to be abandoned. I think it sank in harbour.

Stan bought himself a pre-war boneshaker, an Austin. It was off the road as often as it was on it, but having wheels brought considerable status. Mum and dad were extremely proud, on the few occasions they allowed themselves to be transported by Stan. His driving can politely be described as slightly reckless. He was always messing about with the thing. Eventually he decided to freshen up the red leather upholstery with a coat of paint. First he cleaned it with Gumption, then before it had dried got to work with his brush. The paint never dried. He kept rubbing it with cloth to no avail, the cloth was covered with the stuff, but it still remained on the leather. You would see him and his passengers travelling by, wrapped in blankets.

I was fascinated by the history of my own 'historic Southwark' as the council signposted it. We knew our own backyard very well. From the Borough we tended to roam in the direction of London Bridge, where we might be lucky and see American servicemen – to whom the request of 'Got any gum, chum?' usually produced a slab of this novel delicacy. As we grew older we patronised a selection of pubs. The George Inn had one of the oldest galleries in the country and formed an important part of historic Southwark together with Southwark Cathedral, just along the road. The Inn was, and is, very touristy. It also had an unfortunate collection of medical students from Guy's Hospital, as did the Miller's in Snowsfields. Noisy, scarf-adorned students were best avoided, especially during rag week when they got falling-down drunk and became highly obnoxious to cool dudes like us. They would perform stunts in and out of the pubs. One climbed the Guy's tower to exhibit a bra or some such trophy; tragically he fell and broke his back.

The Cider Shop at the Bermondsey end of Long Lane sold every variety of the stuff from the weakest to the hardest. It was prohibited to under-eighteens, although we could always get an older boy to buy for us. Some boys drank pints of the stuff and made themselves sick. We tried it for a while before deciding it was not for us.

Our locals became the Mitre in Duke Hill Street, the Whitesmith's Arms in Crosby Row and a cellar free house, called The Dive, in Southwark Street, close to the Borough Market. The owners, Johnny and his wife, were a boozy pair, constantly baiting each other. But they entertained us greatly, keeping up a constant patter with the most insulting remarks about each other. Johnny and I discussed business over our stingos, and he made me believe I had a good business brain, for which I thank him. My mates had a looser outlook on life. The thought of saving or investing money, or enquiring how to go about purchasing a house, were of little interest to them. Even then I knew I did not intend to remain in the Borough for much more of my life. After a break from The Dive we returned to find it closed. We never knew why.

Bankside is not far beyond The Dive and we enjoyed walking around the back of the Borough Market where the Clink prison once stood. In our time Clink Street was dusted with white powder, probably lime, and had a smell similar to burnt rope. The Anchor pub looks across the Thames to St Paul's Cathedral. It is said Wren stayed at the Anchor, from where he watched the construction of his masterpiece. The old power station, with its myriad of small bricks that look odd in such a large building, is a fascinating construction – now transformed into the New Tate Gallery. The whole of Bankside is now a trendy retreat for City yuppies and tourists. The rebuilding of the Globe Theatre has made it more so. I wonder if anyone will rebuild the Blackfriars Ring and the Bear Gardens to complete the restoration of one of London's playgrounds.

In the other direction is Tower Bridge Road. A Manzes pie and mash shop is still there with its narrow marbled tables and wooden pews. Close by used to be the Sausage and Onion Shop. In their window, trays of sizzling sausages, bacon, eggs and onions looked and smelled delicious. It was too expensive for us to indulge, though: we patronised a self-service cafeteria, an Express Dairy I believe, in which we enjoyed milkshakes and a delicious variety of fruit pie, the taste of which I have never again found.

The Old Kent Road gave access to the back end of East Street. From there we would walk through to East Lane market, which stretched to the Walworth Road, on the corner of which stood the A1 Stores where we would play the latest records before deciding to buy them. The shop and the Lane are still there. Also in the Old Kent Road was the Old Kent cinema. Here I saw the very first X-rated film, *Detective Story*, starring Kirk Douglas. I bunked off school. On Wednesday afternoons it was the practice to call the form register, then send us on a walk to the centre where we learned woodwork and metalwork. After answering my name I made my own way . . . to the cinema.

ELEPHANT BOYS

We also spread our own local boundaries. The Borough is nicely placed for visiting the City of London. A walk over London Bridge, or a short bus or underground journey, took us to the fascinating financial centre of London and those marvellous old churches. Petticoat Lane at Whitechapel – for a visit to the doughnut shop or a little further on to Club Row which specialised in pets – was an easy journey. Near to us at Lambeth was the Imperial War Museum, which had particular appeal so soon after the war. A close-up view of a Spitfire was many a boy's dream.

We travelled to the Science and Natural History Museums at South Kensington. I also enjoyed the display of minerals and gemstones in the Geological Museum. For some reason we did not visit the nearby Victoria and Albert. In the basement of the Science Museum was a series of push-button experiments and other paraphernalia, one of which was a silver ball that sat in the centre of a circular dish: when you stretched your arm across to grab the ball your movement triggered something that caused the ball to drop before it could be grabbed. One after another, a queue of kids and adults would attempt it. After a number of tries I approached it in a quiet moment, shot out my hand and to my surprise held the ball – then slunk away, wrapped in my own gratification.

A visit to St Paul's Cathedral; a climb up Wren's Monument to the Great Fire of London; a tour of the Tower of London; a look around Billingsgate fish market; all were easy to do. One favourite journey was to stroll over London Bridge and up Cannon Street to St Paul's, pop into a nearby ABC cafeteria for egg or beans on toast and a milk with a dash of coffee, then continue on to Holborn. At Holborn Circus, close to Hatton Garden, was the mysterious and immensely satisfying Gamages Department Store. It was brilliant, a labyrinth of passages and interconnecting departments full of surprises. You could wander around and suddenly come into the sports room where they sold guns, fishing rods and all the paraphernalia for huntin', fishin' and ridin'; or you would find yourself in the tropical aquarium; or best of all the magic and joke shop where you could buy itching powder, whoopee cushions, a nail through the head or hand, a gadget which enabled you to throw your voice, card tricks and all sorts of magic tricks and kits. Gamages had an atmosphere like no other store. It was a terrible tragedy when it closed. Further down the road was Ellinson's joke shop, which we always visited to the despair of our families, who suffered all the stink bombs, sweets-that-turn-your-tongue-black and other darkly humorous devices.

An underground journey would take us to the annual Food Exhibition at Olympia. We came away bearing shopping bags filled with free samples of milkshake powders; pots of jam, marmalade and honey; milk tablets which were delicious to suck; stock cubes, soups, and all sorts of cooking aids for our Mums. We went to every stand and collected as much as we could get away with, making repeated visits to our favourites. The exhibitors seemed to find it amusing to see scruffy kids trundling around with three or four shopping bags filled to overflowing with packets and pots of free samples. Rene Rose had a disaster when one of her bags split as we rushed to change trains at Bank underground station: her booty crashed from her bag and deposited a sticky mess of broken bottles and pots all over the platform.

I thrilled at the advent of the Festival of Britain in 1951. Primarily designed to celebrate the anniversary of the 1851 Great Exhibition, it was to be a scientific marvel. It was expensive to visit. I went once with my family and managed to afford another visit on my own. The Dome of Discovery bewitched young visitors who would have loved an opportunity to become a scientist. The Skylon provided a puzzle and the building of the Festival Hall was to provide a much-needed venue which I visited on many future occasions. Battersea Pleasure Gardens had been meant to provide a lasting memory of the festival and a pleasure park for Londoners. It did last many years, but sadly profit became its only motivation; enjoying a good day out was deemed insufficient to keep the fair open.

At fifteen years of age I was at work as an apprentice compositor at William Jones Clifton, a firm of rubber-stamp makers and engravers located in Hanson Street, Marylebone. We weren't far from Warren Street, with its sly car-dealers ostentatiously flashing their wads of notes as they bought second-hand cars among themselves and sold them to any mug taken in by their charade. I conjectured that the wad was all they had: they flashed that bundle in simpering camaraderie, they were a shifty harmony of the quick and the quicker, and I knew my first car would not be coming from them.

I had been selected as one of two apprentices from a hundred applicants – such was the effectiveness of my English, developed through reading all those word comics my Mum bought from her hard-earned wages. The other plus was my physical height: you had to reach the typecase on the case rack, and the spacebarge above it. The job involved picking lead type characters and the spaces to go between the words, and tightening the lines in a 'stick' (a metal contraption which clamped the justified lines of characters together). I loved it – even the boring beginning, when all I was allowed to do was use my first pair of tweezers to pick out lead spaces that had fallen among the type characters and redeposit them in the spacebarge. In this way I learned the layout of typecases and began to set lines of type when foreman Fred Tipple thought I was ready.

The first time I was allowed to set up a real job, I diligently chose my favourite typeface – Cheltenham italic – composed it in my stick, spaced the words and meticulously placed the leads between the lines until everything was perfect. Then along came Fred, took my stick, turned it upside down and gave it a shake. As I watched, a few characters dropped into his open hand, and I had learnt something about tight accuracy. I swept the floor in turn with fellow apprentice, Cliff, and filled the bucket with hot water for washing-up time, strictly limited to a maximum ten minutes before finishing time. To the bucket first went Nick, past foreman and now reader: he was the oldest and longest-serving and therefore first in the pecking order. Following him would be Fred, and others in strict order in fours, surrounding the bucket. When it was our turn to dip our hands in we would find the soap beneath a layer of scum that was sloshing on the top. It would not go today, but I didn't mind! I was learning a trade, a profession some called it.

Pay was fair. At fifteen I received £2 4s 6d a week and this went up in scale according to time served. A bonus could be added: a target of two hundred three-inch lines per week had been set and after that it was 2d in old money for each three-inch line. All was worked out by proofing the work and initialling the lines set, for a bonus clerk to count up. As soon as we were allowed on bonus, Cliff and I outpaced the journeymen 'comps', much to the annoyance of those who didn't like boys earning more bonus than them. Through my increased earnings I bought shares in a car. And on the advice of Eric, another comp who was buying his own house – something almost unheard of where I came from – I took

ELEPHANT BOYS

out an endowment policy with the Prudential, to be borrowed against later for a mortgage.

Cliff and I were constantly in trouble with the long-suffering Fred. We used to climb out of a window and clamber up on to the roof during a sunny lunchtime. There, one day, we realised that the roof was mostly covered in lead. Once we started peeling it back, it took hold and we rolled up great lumps of it – not to steal, just for something to do. Our department was located on the top floor and when it rained it came pouring through the ceiling. Fred and a senior apprentice climbed on to the roof and trod the lead back into place. Fred said nothing, but he had a way of looking at you that said it all.

The two flights leading down to the passageway where the clocking-off machine was located became a racecourse. Employees assembled near the top of the stairs, waiting for the finishing bell. Last down the stairs had to wait in the queue to clock out. At the bell we made a mad gallop down our first flight to beat the floor below to the bottom flight; they developed a habit of standing back for the 'flight of the mad apprentices'.

Thin pieces of lead spacing could be folded to make ammunition for elastic bands. These made a goodly sting when fired into your buttocks. We carried our endeavours into the street, making targets of windows against which the lightweight metal clattered and brought people to their windows. Somewhere in Hanson Street a man came up behind us, banged our heads together and, while we were reeling, gave us a good shaking up. He was a burly greengrocer from the shop on the corner of the street. When passers-by intervened he said we had fired at a motorcyclist. Stung by all of this, we planned our revenge. In commando style, we slunk out of the composing room, down the two flights of stairs into the old cobbled yard, and crawled below the downstairs office windows into Hanson Street. Once opposite his shop we let fly with heavyweight lead pellets, causing a crack right across his big plate glass window. We were back in the cosiness of our comp room when the police called. They couldn't shake us. We had been there all the time! When they had gone, Fred went into the plastics storeroom next door, rummaged through racks of empty cardboard boxes and pulled out the two that stored our ammunition. We mumbled something unconvincing and that was the end of it. We got that wicked look and no explanation of how he knew our hidden store.

Fred was a great fellow. He had been a fireman during the Second World War and walked with a permanent limp. One day he felt unwell and sat down on a long narrow bench in our room. I got him a glass of water. On my return he was lying on the bench, obviously very ill. An ambulance took him to hospital. I was standing near the phone when the call came to say he was dead. He was forty-seven. He was greatly missed.

When I worked for William Jones Clifton the firm also made plastic signs. In the manufacture of one batch thin pieces of Bakelite were punched out, leaving a hole the size of a sixpence. I gathered the pieces up and with Cliff tried them out on the ticket machine at London Bridge underground station. The lightweight 'coin' stuck in the mechanism. We got a sixpenny ticket all right, then another, and another as they spurted out in rapid succession. We legged it across the roadway and down the stairs to St Thomas Street with a station man in hot pursuit. We lost him in the grounds of Guy's Hospital. Cliff had numerous talents, one of which was the ability to tap out a code into a telephone receiver to dial a number free of charge; he would never tell anyone how he was able to do it.

The bonus clerk, who was not of our department, was a real creep and we were always playing tricks on him. The best of these was in the canteen one lunchtime. He always sat on the same bench to devour his food in a most unwholesome manner. Cliff and I got to the canteen first and with others occupied his bench, leaving only one unsupported end to sit on. While he was giving his lunch his full, eager attention, on my signal we all stood up, causing him to tip up the bench and slide on to the floor. He was a miserable bastard who would try to trim the bonus payments for the company. Given the choice, he would cheat employees rather than be fair. But he was game. In one incident he was beaten up by a dissatisfied engineer, and it has to be said he put up a plucky fight, although he made sure his opponent lost his job.

Mick, a journeyman comp, was a wild Irish rogue. He couldn't give a stuff about anything and was a constant thorn in the clerk's side. Mick had a home-made gun, a silver-coloured single-shot pistol that we persuaded him to demonstrate beneath the arch in the entrance to the firm's yard. An ear-splitting crack was followed by a ricochet that zinged past us, taking Mick's bootlace with it. The clerk came running up to Mick, who was kneeling down examining what remained of his lace. 'Sorry', said Mick, 'I farted when I bent down.' At this the clerk retreated to the accompaniment of our demented cackling. The clerk got his own back. When out of his time, Cliff had an arrangement with a new apprentice to clock him in when he knew he was going to be late. The clerk caught the lad, who was forced to admit the plot. In the words of Jack Straughan, the works manager, he had to 'let Cliff go'.

Straughan, or Straw, as he liked to be called, was often seen in the drinking dens of the Elephant and Castle, coming and going from places I wouldn't be seen dead in. Perhaps because I knew of his habit of haunting the dank places he was tolerant towards me. I used to give him a bad time as a barrack-room lawyer; he part cured me by once describing me as 'Exuberating in my own pomposity', a Churchillism I believe.

It was in the Tower Bridge Road that I bought, or rather my Mum bought, my first real suit. I was thirteen years old and in the true fashion of the day I adorned myself with a brown gabardine suit. It was off the peg, but it was special enough to make me feel dressed in style. My next suit was an American drape in true Alan Ladd style. An over-long herring-bone jacket with well-padded shoulders facilitated the customary bowl, that curious wide gait and thrusting of shoulders so humorously portrayed by George Cole's Flash Harry in the St Trinian's films. These were experimental times.

In our contrariness Johnny Rose, Dave Parker and myself purchased distinctive white packamacs in Petticoat Lane: the rainwear was a new invention and almost exclusively black. These passing phases developed our sense of style for when we could afford to pay off for a bespoke tailored suit. My first was a blue serge made by Montague's in Tabard Street, just close to the Old Kent Road. My mother proudly told me that some of her friends had said how nice it was to see the boys looking so smart. Such little angels.

Fashionable haircuts of the time varied from the DA (short for duck's arse) to the tidier Boston (which finished in a neat line just above the collar), the crop and the even shorter crew cut. Money spent at the barber was a prerequisite for mixing with those whose style we admired. Highly polished shoes, boned up with the back of a hot spoon or boot polish set alight and boned into the leather were tricks learnt from those subjected to National Service. Brown

ELEPHANT BOYS

suede shoes were an acceptable alternative, but scuffs had to be brushed clean with a quaint little wire brush. It was usual to be out most of the time – that was, until the emergence of television. Our first set, an Ecko black and white BBC only, kept us glued to that twelve-inch screen in a silent, darkened room, watching *Kaleidoscope*, a popular variety show.

Conscription for National Service was slowing down. Only grade one and two were being accepted. Poor Stan was assessed grade one and went into the Ordnance. He did his basic training at Catterick, Yorkshire, which was a miserable place. A few years later it became infamous when a conscripted soldier had his skin scrubbed from his back because the sergeant thought he wasn't clean enough. It is small wonder that sensible people ignored the cries of loyalty and did all they could to avoid conscription. After training, Stan used to get home some weekends. Then he would load heavy barrels on to lorries at Barclay's Brewery, near Bankside, to earn something to add to his miserly army pay.

Stan had to do a stint on guard duty at an ammunition store which was assessed as being a target for terrorists. To make sure no terrorist plot would succeed they armed Stan with a baton. Another time, Stan was assigned to escort a prisoner to Shepton Mallet military prison in Somerset. He was handcuffed to this hairy-arsed Scot for the train journey. Fortunately the fellow told him not to worry as he wasn't going to try to escape – he was only working his ticket to get out of the army.

The medical was your best shot to dodge call-up. I knew of a lad who attended it dressed as a tramp and answered every question in monosyllables; he was assessed as being mentally defective. But army surgeons were aware of many of the tricks. It was too obvious to pretend to be half blind or half deaf. They would leave coins on the floor and watch as a boy who had just squinted at a board stuck under his nose and 'failed' to see it, picked them up and pocketed them. Unexpected hand-claps would turn around deaf heads. I had to think of something different.

I was of a slim, wiry build and presented myself as of poor posture and feeble aspect. I wobbled when my ears were examined, flinched at the touch of that cold stethoscope and generally tried to be inadequate at everything I was asked to do. I didn't know how it was going. Then I had my final summing-up with a doctor.

He went through the questionnaire I had filled in and naturally asked why I had been convalescent. I told him about my suspected 'spot on the lung' and he seemed interested so I persisted; then, for good measure, I chucked in a comment vaguely suggesting I had suffered rheumatic fever. Furious scribbling in the pad followed and the doctor adopted an interested and kindly aspect towards me. I knew I had got him. The wait for the letter was agonising, then it came: Grade 3. A year before they would have taken me as a clerk or something, but I was not required in the foreseeable future. So long as Russia didn't invade I was all right.

I didn't feel the least unpatriotic. Conscription was a humiliation for all those I saw called up. They existed on penurious wages, were treated atrociously and cruelly punished for any misdemeanour. I wanted none of it. It may sound funny to some that conscripts bent double in pouring rain whitewashing stones outside an officer's residence while the rain washed it all away. They suffered a miserable life. What sort of people would make them do that sort of thing? To avoid conscription some went so far as to attack doctors at their medical – that seemed to me a sure way of getting selected.

Once in, there was one way out, namely a premature discharge. Freddie Bagroni headbutted a sergeant. It cost him a spell in Colchester before being thrown out. The Krays were both discharged for much the same sort of thing and so was Charlie Richardson.

We often witnessed violent acts around the Balin House area. A break-in took place on a small shop that formed part of the Borough underground station. Two young men from Red Cross Way hid a number of fountain pens in one of the shelter entrances on the debris. The loot was soon discovered: we had actually seen them hiding something and when they were gone we retrieved it. Within minutes they had returned and adopted an ominous, menacing attitude towards us littl'uns. Then from behind me, flung with ferocious velocity, came a brick which took off half the face of one of the thieves. Roydy, an older cousin of one of my mates, had settled the matter. There were some hardnuts around in those days.

It was natural to look for a fight when a dispute required settlement. I hated a runny-nosed little runt named Billy Mitchell. He would pinch his yellow nostrils and surreptitiously wipe the residue of his 'candle' on to anything within his reach, including other people's clothes. For some reason I threatened to belt him, but it was decided that because he was only thirteen and I was all of fourteen I had an unfair advantage. Therefore he was allowed to have Brian Howliss as a partner. The fight took place in Southall Place. We sparred and jabbed at each other until I cuffed Mitchell round an ear and made it bleed. Howliss didn't fancy the same and ran away, at which the fight was called off. Not quite in the Chapman league, but briefly it made my reputation. Memories, though are short: within a week, discussion had moved on to the straight fight between Jimmy Felstead and Harry Prosser. Harry was given the decision by a short margin.

Residents of the flats read avidly of local wrongdoers in the *South London Press*. Who had been fined fifty bob for being drunk and disorderly, or worse still, beating up his missus? Who'd been done for receiving, or for petty larceny? I remember the heartbreak of a parent whose son had been sentenced to be birched – a barbarous antidote to violent tendencies. The shame of appearing in a paper that was read by everyone was a potent force for good, although it didn't curtail our expeditions to Woolworths in the Walworth Road, where we systematically denuded their counters of all and sundry. Stan was once stopped by a policeman who examined his bag and found ten unlabelled cans of baked beans. Dad bemoaned his debut in the *SLP*. It was a relief to us all when Stan managed to come up with an innocent explanation. I wish I could remember what it was.

My earliest recollection of professional villainy is of the spivs who came about after the war. They sold nylons out of a suitcase or off a barrow in the markets and high streets. Black-market goods, ration books, scrapped military surplus or that sold through the back door made a thriving business. Lorries were an easy target: it was not difficult to jump on the back of a lorry and push a crate or a carton off. It sometimes was pot luck, but so much was needed that there was a good chance of finding something to sell. A lad could earn a bob or two commission on the right stuff. Cigarette and food vans were targeted. Sometimes an arrangement was made with the driver to allow his van or load to be filched. Dockers were a prolific source of supply: something out of every crate was part of the price for peace in the docks. Meanwhile, street bookies had their own thriving industry. Their enterprise paid off when they were allowed to become legitimate in the 1960s.

Then there was the underworld 'proper'. Billy Boy Harrison is a good example of a local hooligan. Not so much of a fighter (I once saw him hit someone and run away), he was a shrewd, manipulative, through-and-through dishonest crook who would thieve and con his way through London's underworld. He was completely untrustworthy. Those who joined him in various enterprises never received any of the proceeds once Billy Boy had taken the loot to fence it. He never paid up – excuses aplenty, cash none.

I learned the hard way when five of us decided to relieve the chemist shop in Long Lane of the cameras displayed in the window. After great deliberation, bricks were hurled through the window. Some of us moved in to grab the booty, cameras, clocks, shavers – anything that could be sold for a small profit. As I moved in I ducked into a jagged piece of window which tore a zigzag wound in my scalp. Blood spurted skywards as I reeled back. My mates continued grabbing up the loot and promptly legged it in the direction of Pilgrimage Street. I followed behind, calling them to come back and assist me. Every time I raised my hand to stem the flow of blood the pressure of my raised arm sent a stream of the red stuff spurting into the air. By the time I caught up with my mates in Trinity Square I was covered in blood. They took me all the way to Trafalgar Street, Walworth, to Al's home.

On opening the door, Al's mother collapsed. I could understand why when I looked in a mirror. My hair was caked and matted with blood and it was all over my face. After patching up, I made it back home in the early hours. In one of those quaint traditions of mothers, mine had a presentiment that something was wrong and had stayed up. Eventually I was persuaded to go to Guy's Hospital, where I received five stitches. The risk was obvious, but the doctor asked no questions and I did not receive the anticipated visit from the police.

Thieves, like we had become, did so out of devilment as much as anything else. Youngsters crave excitement. I have come to believe that when they have nothing constructive to do and the desire to do something comes upon them, they create the only thing they can: a mess. It is their way of achieving something, surely the explanation for much of today's vandalism.

ELEPHANT BOYS

Having got the goods, we really hadn't considered what to do with them. Receivers, usually small shopkeepers or market traders, would sell the goods on from 'under the counter' and return a small profit. Our problem was that the only one we knew told us to piss off. In stepped Billy Boy! Alby, who had held on to the goods, decided to trust the one person who could be relied upon to cheat everybody. And he did. Excuse after excuse added up to a lost cause.

Harrison came from a Bermondsey satellite of the Elephant Boys who all called themselves Boy. The most notorious had been Harry Boy Jenkins, who went against all advice and carried a shooter on a job. When escape was blocked after the robbery of a jeweller's in Charlotte Street in the West End, his mate panicked and shot dead motorcyclist Alec deAntiquis. Harry Boy went to the gallows with Boy Boy Geraghty. Terry (Boysy) Rolt was too young, at seventeen, to make the trip with them: he was the car driver and got released after nine years. The search for Harry was used for the plot of the film *The Blue Lamp*, which later gave rise to the television series *Dixon of Dock Green*. Harry's brother Tommy had been at the core of the Elephant Boys. He was one that bridged the wartime years and made it to 1944 when he, Ron Headley and another robbed a City of London jeweller's. During that raid retired captain Ralph Binney was run down and dragged over a mile beneath the car when he tried to wave it down. Tommy got eight years for manslaughter. Headley was reprieved from the death penalty. The City of London struck a medal for bravery, the Binney Medal, which is still awarded today.

A final word on Billy Boy Harrison. One late night he ran off from the Borough coffee-stall without paying for his meat pie and chips. The suspicious proprietor, ever vigilant for such bad behaviour, had opened the back door of the stall enabling him to get after Billy double quick. Grabbing the metal warning lamp from behind the door as he went, he caught up with Billy in Great Dover Street, where he did him good and proper.

The gangs of London made their reputations by fighting each other. Street gangs evolved from school mobs; best fighter in school was a sought-after reputation; and often these lads became 'top men' – the expression used to denote prominent gang members who were either leaders or among the best performers with fists and feet.

Brothers such as the Reyburns, Roffs, Richardsons, Carters, Garretts, and Rosas were top men. Individualists were Frankie Fraser, Boy Boy Stanford, Danny Irving, Charlie White, Puncher Hooper, Ginger Simmonds, Bonker Hammond and a host of others. In one incident, when a row developed, one hard man forced his antagonist's car off the road and into a ditch. The poor fellow had his leg sticking out of an open door and had it broken by being pounded with a brick. The pounder later fled abroad when wanted for questioning in a murder case. By comparison the Balin House Boys were, as a gang, more playful than vicious.

The monopoly on terror in our area was held by Frankie Chapman, who lived in Strood House, just inside the Bermondsey end of Long Lane. His brother Tony was a tough fighter, but it was Frankie whose name was used to frighten youngsters who showed signs of going off the rails. 'Frankie Chapman will get you', or 'Do you want to grow up like Frankie Chapman?', was oft on the lips of mothers who feared for the destination of their offspring. Frankie's right-hand man was Big Paddy, who once kicked someone so hard in the groin that he put him permanently in a wheelchair. Of course Frankie had the *de rigueur* scar on his cheek, said to have been given him by Tony (one of the Elephant Boys). The story goes that after Tony gave Frankie a stripe Frankie sneaked up on Tony as he stood at his stall in East Lane, leaned over and gave him the same. True or not, both had the crescent-shaped badge of rascality carved on their cheeks.

The Chapman Gang roamed all around our area. They were strictly Bermondsey Boys, with affiliations to the Brick Boys, and resented other gangs on their patch – uncomfortable for those of us with pretensions of grandeur. The last I heard of Frankie was when he made headline news in the nationals. A good-looking Italian boy named Izzillo had been chatting up a girl Frankie regarded as his own. When he saw them together in Newington Causeway he slashed Izzillo across the face with an open razor. The cut went from cheek to cheek across his nose, scarring the good-looking boy for life. Frankie got a two-and-a-half-year sentence, the recorder deploring that he was no longer able to prescribe the 'valuable treatment of a birching'.

8. APPRENTICESHIP IN VILLAINY

The Elephant and Castle junction is a crossroads between the old villages of Kennington, Walworth and Lambeth. It is also adjacent to the Borough, a description given to the ancient Borough of Southwark – the only one outside the walls of the old City of London.

In 1760 a tavern was built at the junction and was named the Elephant and Castle. The origin of the name is obscure. It could simply be a lift from heraldic devices that often depict an elephant with a castle on its back. Traditional chess sets also accommodate the castle in this fashion. But the romantic version is that the name is a corruption over the centuries of Eleanor the 'Infanta of Castille' who, while waiting to become the bride of King Edward I, resided somewhere in Lambeth.

The tavern became a well-established watering-place for coaches, inevitably attracting those endeavouring to live off the passing trade: smithies, farriers, itinerant caterers, ladies of ill repute, brigands and footpads. The area had many moments of notoriety. Nearby was St George's Fields, a swampy area used as a meeting-place for conspirators. The Gordon Riots started here, where Bedlam lunatic asylum would be built and where now stands the Imperial War Museum. Highwaymen prowled the dark grassland for carriages headed along the Clapham Road – later to become Kennington Lane and the Borough High Street. St George's Church, in the centre of the Borough High Street, was once a notorious gathering place for rabble-rousers.

1. Frederick Road. McDonalds
2. Frankie Fraser
3. Richardson's Addington Club
4. Richardson's family shop
5. Morbin's shop and Buster Edwards
6. Richardson Scrap Metal Yard
7. Surrey Canal (Johnny Carter jumped here to escape attack)
8. Roff Brothers
9. Windsor pub, scene of the attack on Charlie Woodbridge
10. Latona Road/Sydney Square, Harry and Johnny Carter
11. East Lane Market
12. Charlie Chaplin's birthplace
13. Ada (McDonald) and Dan Johnston
14. Ada McDonald, Grandma Mac, Charles (Wag) McDonald
15. Thomas à Becket pub
16. Tony Reuter
17. Bermondsey Secondary Central School
18. Toby's Gym Club
19. Manor Place Baths
20. Gurney Street (blown up after Second World War)
21. The George pub
22. Rowton House
23. Mason's Arms pub
24. Bell pub (David Brindle shot)
25. Temple Bar pub
26. Carter Street Police Station
27. Dicky (Dido) Frett
28. Bobby Brindle
29. Orange Café
30. Billy (Ginger) Dennis
31. Lennie Garrett

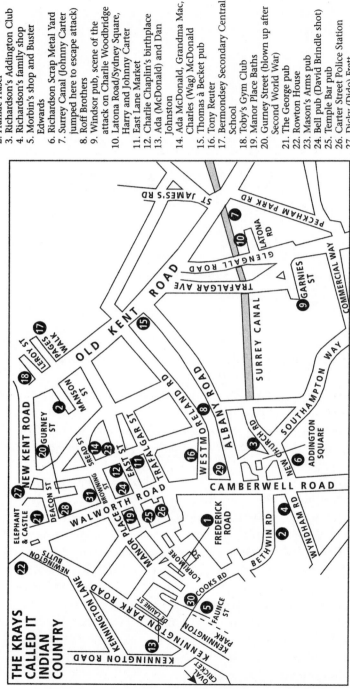

THE KRAYS
CALLED IT
INDIAN
COUNTRY

As the junction developed, tenements were built. As the years passed, these buildings transformed into rookeries for thieves and blackguards. In the mid-1800s the area attracted the attention of Henry Mayhew for his survey of poor London:

> Leaving the police-station at Stones End, along with a detective-officer, we went one afternoon to Gunn Street, a narrow by-street off the Borough Road, inhabited by costermongers, burglars, and pickpockets.
>
> Here one of the most daring gangs of burglars and pickpockets in London met our eye, most of them in the dress of costermongers. A professional pickpocket, a well-attired young man, was seated on a costermonger's barrow. He was clothed in a black cloth coat, vest and trousers, and shining silk hat, and was smoking a pipe, with two or three 'pals' by his side. It was then about seven o'clock p.m. and as clear as mid-day. About forty young men, ranging from seventeen to thirty-five years of age, were engaged around a game of 'pitch and toss', while others were lounging idle in the street . . .
>
> The south side of Newington Causeway, from Horsemonger Lane Gaol to the Elephant and Castle, is crowded with shops, the street being lit nearly as clear as day. There are several splendid gin-palaces in this locality, generally crowded with motley groups of people of various ranks and pursuits; and milliners' shops, with their windows gaily furnished with ladies' bonnets of every hue and style, and ribbons of every tint; and drapers' shops with cotton gown pieces, muslins, collars and gloves of every form and colour . . .
>
> There are some expert 'cracksmen' here, dressed in fashionable style, who indulge in potations of brandy and champagne, and the best of liquors. In their appearance there is little or no trace of their criminal character. They have the look of sharp business men. They commit burglaries at country houses, and sometimes at shops and warehouses, often extensive, and generally contrive to get safely away with their booty.
>
> These crack burglars generally live in streets adjoining the New Kent Road and Newington Causeway, and groups of

ELEPHANT BOYS

them are to be seen occasionally at the taverns beside the Elephant and Castle, where they regale themselves luxuriously on the choicest wines, and are lavish of their gold. From their superior manner and dress few could detect their real character. One might pass them daily in the street, and not be able to recognise them.

Mayhew paints a colourful picture of a rollicking low-life spiced with fashionable dilettantes. At the turn of the century the Elephant and Castle had established itself as a haunt for London's premier boosters (or shoplifters) and fences. By the 1920s the Elephant Gang was still thieving and had added to its reputation by supplying hard men to other gangs.

During the Second World War the Elephant and Castle's neighbour, the Borough, was a known haunt for deserters, swindlers, black-marketeers and the Hole in the Wall Gang of burglars. The spiv, who could supply just about anything, was born here. By the end of the war the Elephant Gang was pre-eminent in London. From its ranks came the tough families and individuals, including the likes of Lennie Garrett, Johnny Carter and Charlie Richardson. I sat on the edge growing, listening and observing . . . After its last fling in the 1950s and '60s, Southwark Council did what rival gangs never could do: they destroyed it, simply by pulling it down.

The Elephant and Castle, after the Second World War, was that area comprising the circus where once stood a police box from which a policeman controlled traffic flow around his little island. Roads leading to the circus included Newington Causeway, New Kent Road, Walworth Road, Newington Butts, St George's Road and London Road. On the wall on the corner of Newington Causeway and New Kent Road rested the Guinness clock, a large, luminescent rendezvous point where boy arranged to meet girl. Many a relationship began with a date beneath the Guinness clock.

Around the corner in the New Kent Road, past a pub, stood the Trocadero cinema, which had a magnificent interior and was also a concert hall. Cross Tarn Street on the same side and immediately you stepped on to the forecourt of the coffee-stall, a collection point where denizens of the underworld would lurk and plot. Opposite across the main road stood the Elephant and Castle cinema, behind which patrons queued in pens. More or less next to that was the pub bearing the famous name: on its roof stood the silver-coloured pachyderm which, now painted in a sickly pink, adorns the shopping centre. In spite of its name the pub was not a venue for us, as it was pure paddyland.

That short stretch of road saw many a colourful event. It was there that Black Eva, who would pee on a client for five bob, knocked out a buck navvy in the middle of the main road. There I first witnessed two Elephant Boys in full flowing action, when they redressed some insult from a couple of navvies by bludgeoning them to the pavement. One fell in front of my feet and I witnessed a boot slamming into the jaw of the victim, jarring him into unconsciousness. Buck navvies abounded: florid-faced rednecks with shocks of tousled hair, often transported to their places of work standing on the backs of open lorries like so many paintbrushes in a pot.

Newington Butts housed the George pub and leads the way to the Walworth Road and Kennington. Tucked away on the other side to the George was Rowton House, a hostel for itinerant workers, almost exclusively Gaelic. It was customary for the boys to clean it out every once in a while. St George's Road leads to the Imperial War Museum and Lambeth. Its only modern renown is in that pub-quiz question, 'Name the four cathedrals in London'.

On the corner of London Road, beneath Burton's Fifty Shilling Tailors, sat the Imperial Billiard Hall, a palace of disrepute and dark goings-on. Outside here I was nearly wiped off the pavement by an opened car door in someone's attempt to sweep me into the Imperial's doorway or the gateway to hell. London Road saw much action, not least of all outside the Shamrock dance hall just down a side street. It also leads to Waterloo and the gateway to the delights of Soho. Further round the circus Newington Causeway, more prosaically, led to Stones End police station and the ominous London Sessions House.

The Elephant Gang was the most celebrated in London. Its fame began before the First World War and continued between the wars. For some reason tough guys collected at the circus, which was the central point between Walworth Road, Lambeth, the Borough and Old Kent Road. After the war the surrounding areas developed their

ELEPHANT BOYS

own 'teams'. The Brick Boys were a tough gang from the Bricklayer's Arms area of the Old Kent Road. The Walworth Road Team occupied the East Lane area. The Borough Boys grew up around Long Lane, which linked Southwark to Bermondsey – Balin House produced the nucleus of this gang, which generally collected at the coffee-stall near St George's Church opposite the Borough underground station. Lambeth had its Lambeth Boys – another Lambeth denizen was Frankie Fraser – and from further afield there were similar gangs from Brixton, the Angel, Hoxton, Bethnal Green and Stepney.

Some of the gangs were named after their leaders. The Chapman Gang from the Long Lane/Tower Bridge Road area had a fierce reputation: Frankie Chapman, although still a teenager, was feared and respected by many district gangs. Ronnie and Reggie Kray were making a name for themselves in the East End. Johnny Diamond from the Angel was a prominent name. The Dumb-Dumb Boys, a gang of mostly deaf-and-dumb boys, were led by Pinkie, a real rough lad. And there were many others.

Satellite gangs of the Elephant were numerous. The Balin Boys, the grown-up variety of Balin House urchins, were definitely inferior to the Chapman Gang. Often we were at war with the Bermondsey Boys, a large crowd from around Bermondsey Street, Tower Bridge Road and Tooley Street. Some of them were boxers at the Lucas Tooth gym, which produced Bermondsey's best boxers. They outnumbered us greatly and it was only thanks to the presence of Reyburn's Boys – a subdivision of the Elephant Gang – that some of us Balin Boys escaped a going-over one day. We were surrounded outside the Borough underground station when Steve Reyburn, whom we hardly knew, came by with a few others: he offered to fight a boy named Hackett, but when it was clear he was on our side it settled the matter and the war was over.

The Walworth Road Team were from the East Lane area and headquartered at the Orange Café in Camberwell Road. They were a fun crowd and we spent some time with them. Tony Pastioni, a sometime member, was easily their best fighter. They occupied a youth club in the Walworth Road which was wrecked after they fell out with some of the Elephant Boys who upended a billiard table and somersaulted it through the window. Like many other teams they used the Mason's Arms in East Lane, taking a subordinate role to the Elephant Gang proper. With some of them I staged a second smash-and-grab, on a jeweller's in Walworth Road. This provided such little profit that I decided to withdraw from that particular pastime.

Not so the Brick Boys, a stand-alone gang that centred on the Bricklayer's Arms pub at the junction of New and Old Kent Roads, Great Dover Street and Tower Bridge Road. Some of them completely cleared out the front windows of Stone's electrical shop in the Old Kent Road: they carted the whole lot away, more a smash-and-removal. 'Puncher', who lived in Balin House, was their top fighter. Several of the Balin House Boys joined up with the Brick instead of the Elephant and both gangs knew each other well enough to maintain a truce. Puncher's brother was one of our Balin Boys who favoured the Elephant.

Many gang members belonged to more than one gang and often the Elephant Gang was strengthened by allies. The basis of the Elephant Gang was Reyburn's Boys. There were two groups really: one led by Barry Reyburn, in the age group nineteen to twenty-five, and the other by Steve Reyburn aged fifteen to eighteen. The Richardsons were becoming well known at the time. Charlie often joined forces with the older group and Eddie with the younger. Strictly speaking they were Camberwell boys, but like so many they were attracted to the magnet of the Elephant and Castle. Then there were the Carters, Brindles, Callahans, Roffs, Rosas and more. Joined together, they formed the premier gang of its time.

When I was aged fifteen we decided to take our little gang along to the Elephant and Castle. This was big league. We had outgrown the ambitions of the Balin Boys who always took a subordinate role in the shadow of their bigger rival. On our first visit, five of us walked the 'backway to the Elephant' from Balin House via Trinity Church Square to the coffee-stall located on the corner of Tarn Street and New Kent Road. It was the haunt of the Elephant Boys.

We drank coffee, nudging and whispering to each other as first Tony, then Terry, then Frankie, Ronnie and a mouthy little runt whom nobody argued with because he was one of the Pitts family, collected at the stall. It was a meeting-point and soon they were all gone to some mysterious place. We waited . . . Eddie Richardson appeared with Roy and we actually told them their friends had left. Lennie received the same service and we swelled with pride at having spoken to these celebrated members of the younger team.

As the evening wore on, various shady characters came and went

ELEPHANT BOYS

like carnivores visiting a watering-hole then slinking into the night for whatever nefarious activity they had in mind. It was several nights later that we repeated the exercise and saw for the first time Steve Reyburn. He was a big lad, only about seventeen years of age then, heavy set, with a bare-knuckle punch that could remove the head from a Belisha beacon, studs and all. I saw him do this on several occasions.

Stories about him were prolific. He could knock out a mule with one mighty punch, and is said to have done so. One time we paid a visit to Borstal to talk to Steve over the fence while he worked digging in the fields. We chided the guards and generally geed Steve up with comments about his confinement. In response Steve acted the fool, causing the guards to chastise him. Picking his time, he took a spadeful of dirt and flung it over his shoulder 'accidentally' showering a guard. His punishment was ten minutes of 'digging on the double'.

Steve's elder brother, Barry, was the acknowledged 'King of the Elephant'. He would stand at the Elephant with his camelhair coat unbuttoned, arms clasped behind his back and the coat flowing over them. He stooped forward and was accustomed to put a word in the ear of passers-by; I don't know what he remarked, but it generally had the effect of hurrying people on their way. His was a dominating presence, akin to a rooster commanding his territory, powerfully built with a punch so hard he rarely needed more than one or two. Both he and Steve had a peculiar fighting stance. They would circle their left in front of them, which had a mesmerising effect, then the right would come over . . . Bosh! and it was all finished.

Incidents could be brutal. Tony Reuter, an acknowledged puncher, took exception to the scrutiny of a young constable at the coffee-stall. After an exchange of words the young copper tried to take him in. Tony grabbed a coke bottle and laid him out, a blow so vicious that the young constable was invalided out of the force. The hunt was on. Although others went into Kennington police station and 'confessed' to the attack, judging they would likely receive a lighter sentence than the more notorious Tony, the coppers wouldn't buy it.

Tony eventually got five years for the attack. When he came out, a party was arranged to celebrate his release. A girl was provided. At some stage she declined his attentions and in the Kennington street outside it all got a bit nasty. Some men tried to intervene. In the mêlée the girl came flying over the top of the crowd and Tony decorated the pavement with a few partygoers. He was back inside in no time.

The coffee-stall just by the Trocadero cinema was the hub of southeast London. In all weathers, the year round, the lads would collect once the pubs and cinemas had turned out, or while waiting for friends before going off somewhere. It was a belief that because the forecourt was private land, the police had no authority unless called on to the land, or a crime was being committed. The police would patrol past the forecourt, which was about twenty-feet square. The chaps would line up around the edge with their toes to the pavement, being careful not to step off the square. Face-to-face confrontations with policemen snarling insults to arrogantly smiling villains enjoying their spoof could be humorous affairs; but they could turn nasty as was the case of Tony Reuter's tragic assault on the young constable.

The funniest episode occurred when two policemen with an alsatian dog 'crowded' the lads who were drinking their coffee and enjoying a meat pie. They were encouraging the dog to snap and strain to get at the boys. Mickey Roff, a character right out of Damon Runyon, was present. Mickey had a reputation as a tough guy, but he was also an artful rogue. On this occasion he looked snazzy in his wide-brimmed stetson and yellow camelhair overcoat. He was in playful mood. To great amusement he offered the alsatian a piece of his pie. The two policemen failed to see the funny side of it and came on to the square to have a go at him. Mickey ducked behind the coffee-stall and came out with the governor's alsatian, which was a real brute. The police dog did a hasty risk assessment and immediately sat down in submission, to roars of laughter. The policemen took one look at the beast and decided to call it an evening.

Soon afterwards Mickey, a Carter Gang member, was strolling in the West End when a car driver stopped beside him to ask directions. Being on guard against possible attack, Mickey promptly put in the car windscreen and ran off, straight into the arms of two constables who, with the aid of passers-by, struggled for fifteen minutes to subdue him. In court Mickey explained that he came from a rough area where if a car pulled up beside you it meant trouble. The magistrate felt that was not a good enough

ELEPHANT BOYS

reason for knocking police constables about and gave him three months. The name of Roff hit the headlines recently when Danny Roff, the man who shot Great Train Robber Charlie Wilson, was gunned down in a revenge killing in Bromley.

It was at the Elephant and Castle coffee-stall that I first met Kenny Lynch. Like me he was attracted to the Elephant and the characters who inhabited the place. He came all the way from east London and together we would get the late night No. 10 bus home. I got off at the Borough, he went on to Aldgate. He went on to become an excellent night-club singer and entertainer. I first heard him sing in the Locarno ballroom, Streatham, on one of those occasions when people were allowed to sing with the band. You had to be good to be allowed to do that. He sang a Frankie Laine song and was truly excellent. He was often persuaded to sing by popular request. From that start he developed a successful show and television career. He's still performing in night-clubs and occasionally on television.

Another of the inhabitants of the Elephant was Nosher Powell, who at one time had been rated as one of Britain's best heavyweight boxing prospects until he tired of hitting opponents, or the canvas, and took up acting and stunt work instead. He appeared as a heavy in numerous B films including a bout with Freddie Mills in *Emergency Call*. Twins Jim and Henry Cooper were occasional visitors to the Elephant: Henry trained over the Thomas à Becket pub on the corner of the Old Kent Road and Albany Street. He made good as our best heavyweight boxer, winning outright his Lonsdale Belt.

The boys, or the lads, or the chaps, as we were variously called, were not all serious villains. Some chose not to get involved and just sat on the fringes enjoying the good times. The younger team liked a good laugh, but inevitably trouble went with the territory. A prerequisite for being an Elephant Boy was the ability to fight. You could get away with not being terribly good, but you must have 'bottle'. Take the fight where we swapped punches with some unknown team until the police arrived. Frankie L fled with the rest of us and hid behind a lorry, only to find he was sharing his hiding-place with one of the other gang. Nervously they watched the police and each other, then slunk off in opposite directions. When somebody was asked if Frankie was a good fighter, the reply

came . . . 'He's the type that grabs hold of your bollocks and hangs on.' I always remembered that.

Mike S was called up for National Service. Being a big lad, he was trained for the Guards and had to do sentry duty in Whitehall. The boys would visit while he was on duty. He resented cameras being thrust in his face by rude tourists; when it happened while we were visiting, one of us dropped a Yank right at Mike's feet.

A great sport was car-bouncing. A couple of big lads would stand on the pavement and pull down on the side roof of a car, release it, then bounce it again, and again until it reared into the air, overstrained springs screaming, and turned over. It was an alarming sight to see a complete stranger's parked car disposed of in this way.

The lads could also fight among themselves. St Jude's youth club, Lambeth, was the scene of a scrap between Terry Britton and Tony Cummings. Terry was heavily built to Tony's lighter frame, but was peppered with punches which marked him up pretty badly. Tony bobbed, weaved and jabbed, and looked set to cut Terry to pieces. He had him stumbling about with blood in his eyes. Then Terry caught him with a big one and knocked him spark out. What's that saying about a good big'un always beating a good littl'un?

The Imperial Billiard Hall was located beneath Burton's Fifty Shilling Tailors on the edge of the circus. It was a large hall with a dozen or so billiard tables and, tucked away around the corner, a full-sized snooker table. It was packed with colourful characters. There was the clique who objected to a Teddy boy who strayed in, so they adorned the ceiling with his velvet collar. Then there was the manager behind the 'jump' who sold teas and soft drinks. He had been set upon so many times he kept a revolver in a locked drawer behind the jump. Frequently he was called on to break up fights, but he couldn't win: either he stopped a right-hander himself or had his till looted while he was away. I remember two big lads picking up the till and carrying it out to the stairs, where they broke it open while he was occupied with a set-up fight.

Snooker was as popular then as it is now and there were some really good players around. Much of the activity of the Elephant Boys centred on the Imperial Billiard Hall. From my early days at Charterhouse Boys' Club I had become a good player and I soon got to know the clientele and became established as part of that particular scene. The standard of play was usually high and there was the usual presence of hustlers, well known to us, who took a bob or two from the unwary. Handicaps of a black or several blacks starts were customary and most players knew their ability well enough to make a pretty even game. Betting on snooker was rarely for more than small amounts – often only for who would pay for the table and buy the teas at the bar. Of course you could lose your pocket cash if you played all evening and had a bad run. Young hangers-on, as I then was, were referred to as 'juveniles' and tolerated only as long as they were polite and respectful. I was cocky enough to play and beat some of the notable members of the gang at snooker. Gradually I became accepted as having 'bottle'.

In one of my best-remembered games I played Ronnie Dennis for ten bob. He got a good lead on me and started to act up to the boys watching us. He made a rash offer of 10–1 he'd beat me. At those odds there was a rush to get a bet on. Poor Ronnie watched as I gradually overhauled him. As I was lining up on the pink for a winning shot Steve Reyburn brushed up close to me and murmured, 'If you pot it I'll chin you.' I didn't give it any thought and cut the pink into the top right pocket.

Ronnie was immediately swamped and had a half-dozen outstretched hands demanding payment. He could only afford to pay me and Roy Hicks; the rest would have to wait. As Ronnie recovered from his nightmare I could see Steve, whom I hardly knew, eyeing me up. I turned to him and said, 'Sorry Steve, I had money on it myself. He never said a word, just walked away. I dare say he could not be seen to carry out his threat in front of the others, but then again he was such an unpredictable fellow I guess it was just my lucky day that he couldn't be bothered. One certain thing is that even though I had caused Ronnie to be cleaned out and owing even more, he would never have been a part of Steve's interference. As far as I know only Steve and myself were aware of what had occurred. If I'd given way I would have been finished with everyone. It emerged later that Steve was impressed by my nerve. Even Ronnie forgave me after the shock of losing all his money had passed, and I was in. There was a notable change of attitude towards me. I was no longer a 'juvenile', as I was soon to find out.

It was not always like that. On one reported occasion, Eddie Richardson played Steve Reyburn and Steve consistently took

Eddie's money until he had cleaned him out. Eddie was a good player and not one to complain. When the final game was over Steve went to the 'jump' and ordered a tea. Eddie looked a bit flushed and followed him over, saying, 'Buy me a tea now you've taken all my money.' Steve, who was not celebrated for his munificence, declined on the grounds that Eddie should be more careful with his money – all this put in Steve's own most delicate way. The situation simmered for a while. Steve could wallow in a situation like this and he made one or two asides to others at one of the tables. It took a brave man to bridle Eddie Richardson in this fashion.

Suddenly Eddie was on him. Both crashed on to the table and rolled over and off the other side. A real stand-up fight followed. Both were big lads and it was a tough punch-up with feet and fists flying. Steve was a strange character and when the battle spilled through the door, along the passage and on to the stairway – all avidly followed by spectators cramming the passageway – he decided he'd had enough and shouted, 'No more Eddie, I swallow, I swallow' (an accepted phrase for submission). Eddie stopped and the fight was over, until Eddie turned to walk back into the hall. Taking advantage of the short respite to get his second wind, Steve launched a new attack and they careered around the hall until both were punched-out. Exhaustion ended the fight with both pretty well marked up. A week later they'd forgotten all about it.

This was the fight that some authors have labelled the fight for 'King of the Teds', which is said to have taken place on a bombed site. But neither Steve nor Eddie were Teddy boys. The title has been ascribed to Tony Reuter, who took it on in exchange for a fee for a *People* newspaper story.

Steve Reyburn was heavily built, weighing about sixteen stones even at the age of eighteen. He was wily as well as strong. When one punch-up occurred in the Imperial Billiard Hall, in which he was not involved, he started throwing billiard balls about the place. At least a dozen men were fighting and, in amongst the mayhem, billiard balls flung full pelt were ricocheting off the walls. It was just Steve's way of saying 'you shouldn't be fighting in my manor'. At other times you would be playing snooker when, with a loud crack, a ball with a lot of stored momentum would rebound around the room. A glance at Steve identified the unmistakable smirk of

the billiard ball bandit. The proprietor had a stock of chipped billiard balls and broken cues that had dented his profits. The cue broken over a knee made a very effective cudgel.

One late evening when the hall had closed we went on one of our periodic hunts for buck navvies. Near the billiard hall was the Shamrock dance-hall and several pubs devoted to the inebriation of the London Irish. There were several hunting grounds. This particular night Steve was in full cry. I became involved in one of the skirmishes. Three of us were swapping punches with some game navvies; the battles were between groups strung out along both sides of London Road. Several pockets of men were fighting when suddenly, from the other side of the road, came empty milk bottles flung with ferocious strength one at a time, bursting off walls, going through windows. I looked across to see Steve with an armful of empties, chucking them about whilst being replenished by eager juveniles who were scouring shop doorways.

The Irish were always game and often outnumbered us. They had a celebrated navvy whom we nicknamed Samson. He was enormous, with a great shock of hair and a ruddy face coloured by weather and hard beverages. He always gave a good account of himself and had the measure of many of us. One night he went on a rampage along both sides of the part of the New Kent Road that located the Trocadero and Elephant and Castle cinemas. He settled a number of quite innocent people and a policeman. One of the boys decided to get involved. Ronnie was quite tough but was soon laid out by the giant Samson who lumbered off in the direction of the Old Kent Road. At this stage Steve arrived and took stock of the situation. He took a run at his back. Launching himself into a horizontal flying kick, he hit Samson in the small of the back with both feet and nearly sent him into orbit. Samson's rampage was over.

I hadn't known there was an initiation process into the gang. One night we were returning from St Jude's club in Lambeth where they held dances and the usual snooker and table tennis. There was a lot of suspicious muttering going on and a number of us were obviously being discussed. Suddenly I was grabbed and Eddie Richardson cut a large tuft of hair from the front of my head. Two others received the same fate. Another lad named Mason ran for it and appeared to have escaped. He was a good-looking boy with a fine head of smartly cut hair. He had fled a few hundred yards behind us, when a bus passed us going in his direction and Whippet jumped on. Unseen by Mason, Whippet got off when he had passed him and when a number of the gang chased Mason he ran straight into Whippet. In the mêlée he had a sizeable chunk of hair removed and a finger was almost severed in the struggle. Nobody admitted doing it, but I think we all knew. Mason was never accepted into the gang, it was a punishment, not an initiation.

More was to come. Rowton House was located just off Newington Butts, where the Elephant met Kennington. It housed itinerant labourers, most of them Irish. There was a sizeable Irish element in the community at that time. A number of raids had been made on Rowton House by the 'boys', who considered the Irish natural enemies. The place had been wrecked with beds pushed through windows, lights torn down and furniture destroyed. The Irish were hated and considered fair game. Some of them, known to us as 'bucks', were giants, with faces florid from weather and drink, great shocks of hair and usually a fair quantity of booze in them. After the haircutting I was taken to the back of Rowton House and we waited until an Irishman about my size came along and I had to fight him. This was part of the initiation: there was to be no help if I got the worst of it.

He was a gritty fellow and both of us were bloody when it was all over. I was chagrined when the fight was declared a draw. My opponent was patched up and helped back to Rowton House while I was left to tend my own wounds. This didn't stop him reporting the matter to the police. In the centre of the circus sat a policeman in a traffic control box. That night it was 'Bunny', so called for his protruding teeth. My adversary was seen talking to him and the familiar Black Maria was soon circling the streets and we faded from the scene. I was now a full gang member, invited to parties, punch-ups and those mysterious places where things were going on that you never got to hear about unless you were 'in'. Being 'in' was just like being a 'made' member of the Mafia.

Some of these elusive places were the pubs. The first great pub I enjoyed was the George in Newington Butts. On a Saturday night it was packed. There could always be found a substantial number of the boys. A piano player knocked out the old favourites and the new ones around. Johnny Ray was a current chart-topper with 'Little White Cloud' and 'Glad Rag Doll', and these were sung by

'turns' who went up to the 'mike'. Roy Hicks did a great impression of Johnny Ray. Inevitably there was trouble from time to time. A coming-out party was thrown for Danny, a real hardcase who was one of the older gang. As usual a girl was provided but she became terrified at the brutal demeanour of her escort. It was the first time I had seen him. He was a swarthy, thick-set tough with a white scar etched on his right cheek. He looked very alarming. I was at the all-comers party, together with Johnny and Dave, which was held in the George. In one of our more shameful episodes, in order to be some of the boys, we attempted to intervene to save Danny from the police. He was on waste ground between the George and the Elephant, dragging the terrified girl who was trying to escape. Police bells could be heard and we three ran on to the waste ground to warn Danny. As I yelled, 'Nitto, Danny, it's the law', he thought we were having a go at him. He pulled out the biggest clasp knife I have ever seen – to call it a flick-knife would not do justice to its size. The blade snapped open in my face. I kept on going, with Johnny and Dave trying to keep up with me.

One night Ronnie had an epileptic fit in the saloon bar of the George. Roy Hicks jumped on his back in a effort to control him. Other people, thinking there was a fight, cleared the area, knocking over tables as the pair pirouetted about the place. It was all within a tightly packed area, made worse as some people tried to separate them. It was a fierce, macabre affair with Roy clinging to Ronnie's back as he threshed about causing devastation. This was the final straw for the police, who naturally enough listed it as a fight. Pretty soon the music licence was taken away due to 'inadequate fire precautions' and the George ended its run as the 'in' pub. It was pulled down shortly after.

Loyalty was transferred to the Beehive around the back of the Carter Street area off the Walworth Road, which became the Saturday night pub. Sunday lunchtimes were spent in the Mason's Arms in East Lane, a thriving market-place. Drinking was sufficient to become merry. Getting drunk was less common than becoming 'woozy'. Lager and lime, bitter and light ale were popular; shorts came in the form of whisky and American and a gin and tonic for the girls. There were hot turkey rolls at Christmas, egg-and-bacon sandwiches, and hot pies (eaten the way south Londoners do, upside down sloshed with brown sauce and cut into from the bottom) – luvly grub. The pub sing-song added to a good time:

everyone joined in, particularly old dears who belted out 'You made me love you' in between putting away their gin and tonic. All the popular pubs had a 'mike' and regular pub singers – some of whom were very good, some laughable – who were encouraged to perform for the enjoyment of all. Queers, something of a novelty without the benefits of the Gay Liberation Movement, provided good entertainers. Many were talented musicians and singers.

The singing was often punctuated by entertainment of a different sort. One example was four fellows leaving the Mason's Arms one Sunday to be ambushed by two carloads of the Carter Gang, who went to work with car-starting handles and tyre levers. It was a bloody battle with severe injuries on both sides. The four were eventually taken to hospital, unconscious, to be revived and stitched.

Further afield was the St Helier pub in Middleton Road, Carshalton, which has recently suffered the fate of the George in that the locals managed to have it closed. In truth the police do not want closures: they like to know where villains congregate, for among them reside the informers and ear-flappers, fringe members and rumour-mongers who feed the grapevine aided by too-talkative amateurs. Plainclothes police sometimes mingle, but it is far more sensible and productive to listen to information from 'sources'. The Horseshoe in Tottenham Court Road became a meeting-place for the Richardson Gang after Toby's Club closed. There you could rub shoulders with the cream of southeast London's villainy.

Gang fights were a common activity for the Elephant Boys. Often the gang was augmented by a number of satellite gangs, so was never a constant size. Major fights occurred with all of the notable London gangs at one time or another. To maintain supremacy other territories were invaded. Camberwell, Brixton, the Angel, Hoxton, Bethnal Green, Peckham, Shepherd's Bush and the West End all received reminders of their inferiority.

Reasons for punch-ups were numerous. Girls, insults, or a reputation-building excursion just to prove who the guv'nors were – especially when a gang was making a name for itself – provided excuses for punitive expeditions. Second only to the Elephant Boys were the Angel Gang from Islington. They were a tough crew who sometimes teamed up with the Hoxton Mob. Word went out that the Elephant Gang was setting out to 'top them' and small units

began to collect at the Elephant. In a short time over two hundred had amassed near the circus to embark in a convoy of cars and vans (and at least one lorry) headed for the Angel. There were several pitched battles, the biggest being at Old Street near Hoxton Square. By this time the Elephant Gang had split into smaller groups and a pretty even battle of about forty apiece provided the best fight of the evening. Game as the Angel boys were, they were eventually 'topped'. During the brawl Johnny Diamond fought toe-to-toe with one of our top men and won great admiration. He took a terrible beating. He kept getting up, only to be put on the deck again. Eventually he was restrained by fighters from both sides. He was a horrible mess, but game as a pebble.

The follow-up was particularly frightening for me. Several weeks later I was walking towards the Guinness clock at the Elephant. As I reached the clock I paused, looking for the girl I had arranged to meet. A car pulled up and someone shouted, 'That's one of them.' I recognised the hostile faces of some of the Angel boys and fled. Where to go? Some of them were getting out of the car. I ran across the circus and the car came after me. As I mounted the pavement the car came up the kerb and the door was flung open in an attempt to wipe me off the pavement. I felt it go past as I dived into the Imperial Billiard Hall.

When I burst into the hall my blood ran cold, for it was almost empty – just a few old un's playing snooker and not the type to join in battles. The hall had no back door, so I made for the toilet, which was around the corner of the L-shaped room. When I turned the corner into the recess I came face-to-face with two of my pals, Eddie and Patsy, who were occupying the large table. Both were top-rate punchers. With some assistance from me, they drove the five who had followed me in back out into London Road. There they jumped in their car and took off. Billiard balls and cues, feet and fists saved me from a terrible kicking. I've been very fond of those two ever since.

On the downside the girl told me to get lost.

Greatest of the dance-hall fights was at the Locarno, Streatham. Seven of us, including two of our best fighters from the Elephant, had gone to the Locarno in response to a request from Eddie Richardson. He had had a difference of opinion with a boy named Joey Dowd, leader of the Brixton Boys. The crisis came when Joey arrived with Eddie's girlfriend. It was certain there was going to be trouble. Their side sensed it and sent a message to us that we had better not start anything because they had counted their twenty-six against our seven. Apart from me and Eddie Richardson there was Peter Reuter, Tony Cummings, Big Tipps and two New Cross boys, Johnny and Mickey. Tipps was a giant, both tall and broad, but very affable. I suppose, because of his size, Joey walked up to him and asked if he 'knew him' – a well-recognised statement to start a quarrel. He had hardly got the words out when Eddie knocked him out. He landed with his head at my feet. We had arranged to grab a chair each when the trouble started: they were wicker and light in weight. Dutifully I grabbed mine and looked in horror as it seemed the whole of the dance crowd came towards me. I threw the chair forward and some of them split off and came for me. Fortunately they also attacked the others. Immediately at the onset Johnny turned to Mickey, who was his particular mate, and said, 'Let's get out of here.' And they did.

A very tall, slim boy who knew us (and had the very descriptive nickname of Snake) tried to get involved on our side. He was immediately flattened. I got into a tangle with four of them and it was mainly a question of swinging chairs at each other. Eddie was out on the dance-floor, fighting with about six of them who were in a circle around him. Peter was also surrounded. Behind him I saw a big fellow rip a figurette off the end of a banister and try to reach over the crowd to hit Peter with it. At this time I had a heavy glass ashtray cupped in my hand. I managed to get to him and crack him on the head, knocking him down. About this time Tony was slashed at with a razor. He raised his arm to protect his face and received a deep slash across the side of his wrist. I was hit by a table (unlike the chairs, it was not made of wicker) and joined Tony on the floor, the only two on our side who went down. I was in agony and must have passed out for a while.

When I regained my senses I looked up and saw Tipps with his back to a wall. He had a table in one hand and a chair in the other and was covered in wicker chairs. They couldn't get near him, so they lobbed chair after chair until he was beneath a giant pyramid. Peter and Eddie had flattened many of our assailants. Some of them were carrying Joey Dowd from the hall. I saw Eddie walking alongside them, pummelling his rival as they tried to get their leader away. He was covered in blood and his ear appeared to be hanging off. Suddenly it was over.

ELEPHANT BOYS

Like an idiot, I had brought my overcoat (who takes their overcoat to a fight?!). I staggered to the cloakroom to get my coat, becoming separated from my mates. The cloakroom was halfway up a wide flight of stairs which had a brass handrail running down the centre. As I started up the second half of the stairway with my coat, still in agony from a badly bruised back, I saw the Locarno bouncer at the top of the stairs. He had not been in evidence during the fight but clearly fancied his chances against me alone. He was a tough guy who had just enhanced his reputation in a knife fight – it was at a time when Mecca was hiring some notorious villains as their bouncers. I ducked under the banister and ran up the other side and saw him go somersaulting past me after Peter, who had come back for me, had hit him with that great tree trunk he called an arm.

Peter and I jumped on a 96 bus and got back to the Elephant. There we compared wounds. Tony had a slashed wrist. Tipps's face was puffed up and he had a lump the size of a lemon on his forehead. Peter hardly had a scratch. I had a bruise the size of a dinner plate on my right shoulder blade which still troubles me. Eddie's fingers and nails were stripped and raw, where he had defended himself against the onslaught of chairs, and as he held his arms out I can remember his fingers shaking with pain. Johnny and Mickey were unmarked and Snake, who had turned up, had the biggest black eye I've ever seen.

The fight became quite famous because of the odds involved. We never claimed a victory, but for six to stand against twenty-six and come out at least equal was to us a considerable deed. Eddie and Peter were in an exceptional class and did most of the damage. I say six of us because we started with seven, two ran away, and Snake had a go. Johnny and Mickey were 'tried' by their peers and John explained he thought we were all running as we were outnumbered. He was banned from the Elephant. Mickey, who was considered to be game, said he followed John after being told we were all leaving. His story was accepted. Snake was 'recognised' for his gameness and could have joined the gang. However, he declined on the grounds that he was not a tough guy and couldn't fight anyway – he had just tried to help his pals. John always put his charm before taking a chance. He's now a Hollywood film producer.

If I had grown in reputation and confidence with the Locarno fight, I was soon brought down to earth by a following event. I had

CHARLIE CHAPLIN FILM COMPANY
1416 LA BREA AVENUE
LOS ANGELES, CALIFORNIA

LOS ANGELES CALIF.
OCT 22
7 30 PM
1924
ARCADE STA. 6

Mr. C. McDonald,
Maple Hotel,
226½ East 5th St.,
Los Angeles, California.

ABOVE: Westlake Park, Hollywood, late 1920s, where film producer Mack Sennett made comic pictures. Also the scene of some of Charlie Chaplin's escapades.

BELOW: Syd Chaplin's house. Brother Charlie once lived here and still had a studio round the back.

Charles (Wag) McDonald, Royal Field Artillery, on Woolwich Common, 1914. Master horseman, boxer, adventurer, traveller, entrepreneur and gangster.

Walter (Wal) McDonald and my half-brother Jimboy, c.1919.

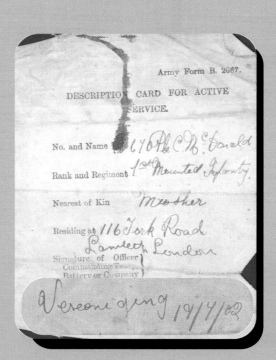

Army Form B. 2067.

DESCRIPTION CARD FOR ACTIVE SERVICE.

No. and Name 676 Pte C Mc Donald

Rank and Regiment 1st Mounted Infantry

Nearest of Kin Mother

Residing at 116 York Road Lambeth London

Signature of Officer
Commanding Troop
Battery or Company

Vereoniging 19/7/02

Wag's army pass, Vereeniging, South Africa, 1902, at the time of the Boer surrender, showing the York Road address where Stinie Morrison was arrested.

Ada Louise McDonald, suffragette and fashion buyer.

Arthur James (Jim) McDonald, my dad, Royal Field Artillery, Secunderabad, 1917.

Albert Edwin (Bert) McDonald.

Bert's wheels. The ad in the back offers to buy your teeth.

Trinity Mansion Hotel, Eastbourne, Sussex. Wag's headquarters during the 1930s where he plotted against Alf Solomon and the Sabinis. He also wrote articles for the *South London Press* and other newspapers about his travels in America. (By kind permission of Quality Hotel Mansion.)

Bert's burial in the British Empire veterans section of Inglewood Park Cemetery, Los Angeles, September 1929. A Canadian gives the salute. Bert's grave was found by his grand-nephew David in 1996.

Bert, pistol on hip, working in the Mojave Desert, waiting for Billy Kimber to move on to Los Angeles.

Wag (third from right), San Francisco, 1931, on the run hoping to return to Los Angeles. On his left is Arnold Bruin.

On the pavement outside the Southampton Arms in Mornington Crescent the guns came out when the Sabinis attacked George Sage and his Camden Town gang.

One in 20,000. The arrows [see facing page] indicate Wag's participation in the 'picture of the century'.

WORLD PR...
RAOUL W...

THE
BIG
TRAIL

FOX MOVIETONE PRODUCTION SHOWN ENTIRELY IN
GRANDEUR
CAST OF 20,000 FEATURING
JOHN WAYNE · MARGUERITE CHURCHILL
EL BRENDEL
TULLY MARSHALL · TYRONE POWER · DAVID ROLLINS
STORY BY HAL G. EVARTS

SY *Cassion*, Reg Denny's yacht, aboard which Wag hid after disposing of Bert's killer.

GRAUMAN'S
CHINESE
DIRECTION FOX WEST COAST THEATRES

HOLLYWOOD BLVD. AND ORANGE DRIVE

◆

A FEW HIGHLIGHTS OF THE PICTURE OF THE CENTURY

Produced Entirely in Grandeur	4000 Elk, Moose, etc.	227 Cowpunchers, Bull Whackers, etc.
Cast of 20,000	110 Mules	
93 Players with Speaking Roles	200 Chickens	Complete Medical Corps
725 Indians of Five Tribes	50 Pigs	14 Wardrobe Mistresses
485 Pioneer Wagons	500 Buffaloes	12 Indian Guides, Interpreters, etc.
1800 Head of Cattle	20 Wild Turkeys	123 Baggage Trains
1400 Horses	14 Colts	Filmed Entirely on Location

◆

"THE BIG TRAIL" is a thrilling, soul-stirring romance of those daring, hardy souls . . . The American Pioneers. It faithfully re-enacts the glorious never-to-be-forgotten scenes that marked the Westward movement one hundred years ago with the departure of the first pioneer wagon from the Missouri for the Oregon country. . . . A MIGHTY SURGING WAVE of humanity . . . land hungry . . . liberty hungry . . . home hungry . . . thousands of men, women and children heroically, unflinchingly facing the terrors of land, sea and sky . . . sloshing through heaven-bursting storms . . . thirsting through blinding, blistering deserts . . . crawling over trackless mountains . . . and through death-clinging mud and swamps . . . struggling with nature . . . battling savage Indians . . . fighting wild beasts . . . all their heartaches . . . heartbreaks . . . loves . . . youthful romances . . . dreams . . are yours . .they live again   brought miraculously to truer life by the Twentieth Century wonder of GRANDEUR!

SEATS NOW . . . FOR PREMIERE AND FOLLOWING PERFORMANCES AT . . . BOX OFFICE, GL. 5184—OWL DRUG, 6TH & BDWY—ANY AUTHORIZED TICKET AGENCY

Cameras and Projection Machines at GRANDEUR PICTURES by GENERAL THEATRES EQUIPMENT CO. SOUND by WESTERN ELECTRIC SYSTEM

Roy Chaplin (Luxey), me, Dave Morbin and Dave Parker, Jersey, 1956.

A night out at Toby's. Left: Dave Hooper and Jean.
Right: Dave Parker, Luxey and me.

been aware of a group of strangers at the coffee-stall at the Elephant. This was not unusual, as the stall was a popular meeting-place for many people, but these seemed to be 'eyeing me up'. I was alone and departed on my way home through Tarn Street and Bath Terrace. When I reached Trinity Church Square I suddenly realised I had been followed. Three of the group were close behind me and closing so fast I knew I was in trouble.

I ran into the Square, straight into two more of them who must have walked ahead of me on the other side of the road. I tried to burst through the pair in front, but they grabbed hold and in seconds they were all over me. I flung a few punches, but it was no good; I was floored by a rain of punches and took kicks to the head and body. All I could do was curl up into a ball and protect my head and vital parts. I don't think I lost consciousness because I remember them running off. People came out of the period houses and an ambulance was called. I lay there till it arrived. At Guy's I received yet more stitches, seven this time, and I had three broken ribs. I never knew who they were and I never saw them again.

One of the gangs that gathered at the Elephant, but was definitely not regarded as some of the boys, was the gang of queers. Mostly they had names which could be taken either way, male or female, such as Phil, Terry and Frankie. Occasionally they would fight among themselves which was a hair-pulling, face-scratching occurrence. They were about twelve strong and their favourite activity was soliciting servicemen outside the Union Jack Club at Waterloo. I had an embedded hostility to anything effeminate and even now flinch at the thought of anything homosexual. When I was a small boy I had a fight in the square with a boy bigger than me; when I came in crying, my dad promptly chucked me out again to have another go. I was encouraged to be manly and could not conceive of being anything other than that.

I never engaged the queers in conversation, perhaps because I feared being mistaken for one of them, or worse still, a client. I was present when one of them boasted loudly of his encounter with a visiting American film star (who is still alive). It was not pleasant listening. I confess a naivety, I must have been the only person on the planet who didn't know Rock Hudson was gay. To me he had been a movie hero who had everything: good looks, good physique, women loved him. How can you be on stage with

Dorothy Malone and not fancy her? I've never been able to watch a Rock Hudson film since.

There was a tendency to buy large American cars at that time. Many local villains could be seen wearing dark glasses and Italian-style suits cruising their Buicks, Ford V8 Pilots and Packards. Spotlights were fitted to the side, principally to be 'flash'. They could be used to good effect picking out potential prey hiding in a doorway after a gangfight. Most cars at that time were black, one exception being Bobby Ramsey's bright yellow Packard. If you could afford one of these gleaming leviathans you could create quite an impression. It was beyond my pocket. One solution was to buy cars in partnership. I had a fifth share of a Packard before I held a driving licence.

Taking cars for joy-rides was a popular pursuit. Before I had obtained my driving licence I learned how to drive in friends' cars and 'borrowed' ones. The knack was to collect together a bunch of keys by pinching or buying them one at a time. Many cars in those days had the car key number stamped into the door lock and on the ignition socket. It was simply a matter of 'casing' a car, selecting a key from your bunch, or even buying it from a local garage, and going for a ride. One night friends and I 'borrowed' an Austin from the car park at the back of the Trocadero and went on a joy-ride to the Welling Embassy Dance Hall. There we got involved in a scuffle. The police were called and we were searched as we left the hall. I deposited a very large bunch of keys behind the curtains on the bandstand and we had to bus it home. I remember one lad nicking a bus from New Cross Garage. He took it on a mad jaunt around Peckham before being apprehended. He got off with a fine of four pounds after pleading that he had always aspired to be a bus driver like his dad.

There were some mad characters around. One wide boy known as Lennie limped along with the aid of a walking stick. Because of a war wound he was able to draw benefit without being sent for a job by the Labour Exchange. One night there was an incident in the Walworth Road in which he used his stick to good effect over the heads of a couple of antagonists. Police arrived and we had to flee. I well remember limping Lennie overtaking me, stick flailing in the air, as we passed the bottom of East Lane. He was in his forties, I was about twenty.

East Street, known locally as East Lane, provided many

characters among the traders. You could buy white sand as corn cure, ballpoint pens with no filling, honeycomb made up in someone's kitchen that could lay the unwary low for a week. A favourite stall was the sarsaparilla stand which was still there when I visited the Lane recently – run I believe, by a relative of the former trader.

Policemen were not so often seen in pairs in those days. Frequently they were quite heavy individuals given to handing out a thick ear as an instant remedy for minor infringements. One evening some of us were messing about, jumping on and off buses in the New Kent Road and making a general nuisance of ourselves. Running and jumping on buses was commonplace. The technique, for the fit, was to run hard to overtake the bus, then slacken speed as it caught up and judge the pace so that you could leap on the platform when its speed was equal to yours. On this occasion we were jumping off again. It was a considerable skill to jump off a fast-moving bus and maintain your feet by running until the speed of your exit was absorbed into your legs. A policeman known as 'Olly', due to his resemblance to the well-known comedy actor, intervened and Danny gave him a bit of lip. Olly poked Danny in the stomach with his truncheon. Danny instantly doubled up, screaming that his non-existent ulcer had burst. The following edition of the *South London Press* carried a report that a police constable had been attacked in the New Kent Road and had defended himself against hooligans. It wasn't only the lads who were crafty.

The lads were always out to make a few bob. Tony Reuter and some others collected a nice fee from the *People* newspaper for sitting as reformed characters on a bench at Billy Graham's first evangelist meeting in London. They were simply rounded up by the paper and taken to the meeting. I don't believe Billy Graham had anything to do with it. The Sunday papers often ran series on London gangsters. *The People* was the most productive. Over the years the Sundays provided stories on the West End villains Jack Spot and Billy Hill, who were contesting control of the London underworld. Both drew their support from the tough areas of London and the papers serialised the underworld scene including a number of south London boys, Johnny Carter and Frankie Fraser, who were gaining in reputation as the power behind the thrones.

Tony Reuter, who was married to Johnny Carter's sister, was on

ELEPHANT BOYS

the run at that time for his attack on the constable at the Elephant. *The People* published a story entitled 'A Teddy Boy Confesses', a colourful description of the 'King of the Teddy Boys', by Tony Reuter, which followed his contrived appearance at Billy Graham's evangelist event at Wembley Stadium. Tony never was a Teddy boy – he held that overdressed fraternity in contempt – but he is reputed to have earned £500 for his story. The serial, presenting him as a reformed character, only ran two editions: when he went to collect his money from the *People* offices, the police were waiting for him and arrested him for the attack on PC Anthony Stills. The following week a notice appeared in the paper saying that due to legal reasons the episode would not appear. They never did finish it. Incredibly he got bail, which he didn't answer to, costing his Mum and one of the Dennis's £100 forfeit. When the police caught up with him again he went away for five years.

All of the Elephant Gang were snappy dressers. Suits cost roughly the equivalent of two weeks' wages or more. They were made-to-measure by excellent tailors on the basis of a deposit and some of the balance paid at each of two fittings with the remainder paid on collection. The style varied but was never outlandish. The Italian style had a fairly short two-buttoned jacket with 'sloop shoulders'. When the Edwardian fashion came in it became a three- or four-buttoned three-piece suit without velvet collar, although this sometimes appeared on overcoats. Fashionable materials at that time were mohair, or a twenty-two ounce worsted in, say, clerical grey. Just try to buy that quality material nowadays. Among the notable tailors were Harris and Hymies, both in the Cut near Blackfriars; Diamond Brothers at Shaftesbury Avenue; Sam Arkus in Berwick Street, Soho; and Charkham's of Oxford Street.

Every generation has its choice of music and whatever we choose it is certain not to be understood by our parents. The earliest record I remember my brother Stan buying was 'The Flight of the Bumble Bee', followed by such 'greats' as 'The Sabre Dance', 'Ghost Riders in the Sky' by Bing Crosby and a song by Phil Harris about a card game with a one-eyed player wherein he trolled, 'I'll close that other eye'. We had an old wind-up gramophone and any record was a pleasure. When record players began to change, so did our tastes. I and my mates would sit in each other's bedrooms playing cards and repeating records over and over. For some reason

Johnny Rose was particularly taken with my record of 'Blacksmith Blues', which went: 'Down in old Kentucky, where horseshoes are lucky, stands the village blacksmith under the chestnut tree . . .' We couldn't get him to play anything else.

My dad bought us a brand new Decca cabinet record player which I christened on the first day with the first long-playing record I ever bought (or he bought for me) – Ella Fitzgerald singing the Cole Porter Song Book. It was played over and over again. Although my parents tolerated it I'm sure they thought Ella's style was akin to caterwauling, especially that scat singing she did so well.

It was at this time I discovered jazz. Stan was part of a traditional jazz band and played his trumpet with gusto. I had a go on a borrowed trombone and decided I was better at listening than playing. Popular groups were Kenny Baker's Dozen, Chris Barber, the Dixielanders and Humphrey Lyttleton before he became more progressive and gave up the baggy trousers and brassy sound. He often played in the 100 Club in Oxford Street to galloping scruffs with bulging jumpers and brown cords.

This was too unsophisticated for us. We had discovered be-bop in the early 1950s. Charlie Parker had brought jazz up to date with a jolt. The more subtle sounds and blood-tingling improvisations in what came generally to be called modern jazz were performed by Lester Young, Sonny Stitt, Clifford Brown and our favourites Dave Brubeck, with his east coast contention style, and Gerry Mulligan and his west coast variety. Both Brubeck and Mulligan could lift you out of your seat with that amazing step-by-step build-up to a crescendo where Brubeck would seem to go higher and higher – he had a habit of dropping back the volume and picking it up again so it sounded as though it was ever increasing in power. Mulligan had that quality of bouncing away with his baritone sax after a quiet passage and catching you by surprise, although you may have heard the piece over and over. If you don't believe me, try Brubeck's 'Two Part Contention', featuring Paul Desmond on alto sax, and Mulligan's 'Carioca' with Chet Baker on trumpet.

We could hear good live music. Oscar Rabin's orchestra played exclusively in the Lyceum ballroom at the Aldwych. This was the most popular of the dance-halls, mainly because of Rabin's musicians. They had a Sunday afternoon jazz club featuring resident jazz musicians and those who were guesting just for the Sunday club. Groups from within the band would assemble in

front and play popular American standards: 'Take The A Train', 'Hawk Talks', 'Seven Eleven', 'The Chase' and many more. Tommy Whittle, Don Rendell, Ken Ray and Kenny Clare on drums, who brought the place to a standstill with his solo of 'Skin Deep', were top professionals.

Records were bought at Foyles in Charing Cross Road. The top floor had a marvellous selection of jazz and blues which made them very popular. Another reason for their popularity was their purchasing system. Records were actually displayed in their sleeves. The method was to play a record in a booth; decide you wanted to buy it; take it to a counter for it to be bagged and a bill to be issued; take the bill to the cash desk to pay; bring back the receipt; and collect the record. On exit a security guard would check your purchase. But if you had a receipt from a previous purchase you could rub out the handwritten instructions and substitute your own. The receipt was only stamped 'received with thanks', and the date was handwritten, so you filled out your own receipt, collected your record in the Foyles bag and went on your merry way cheered on by the security guard. They must have lost thousands of pounds. Seller beware!

The West End is only a short bus ride from the Elephant and we soon knew our way around the streets and clubs of Soho. Modern jazz clubs gave us an opportunity to combine the 'modern' fashion in clothing with our leaning towards modern jazz that could be enjoyed at a number of venues. The Florida, near a corner of Leicester Square, usually housed drummer Tony Kinsey and his group featuring Bill Le Sage on vibes and piano with, perhaps, Bert Courtney on trumpet and a bass player. It was a civilised atmosphere catering for those who wanted to listen rather than jive. For a more adventurous and vigorous style the place to visit was the Fifty-one Club in Newport Court, off Charing Cross Road. It featured Tubby Hayes, Ronnie Scott, Bert Courtney, Jo Harriet, Bob Efford, Vic Ash and many other top liners. It had a dark, smoky atmosphere and was perfect for a good drink and a mellifluous evening. Phil Seamen was the best British drummer of his day. Unfortunately he was given to taking an injection of the hard stuff every now and again and could not maintain employment in any of the big bands of the time, owing to his unreliability and tendency to doze off. A story goes that he managed to get a job with a pit orchestra at a West End theatre.

Promptly he dozed off, only to awake and crash a cymbal at the wrong point in the show: he stood, announced dinner was served, and got the sack.

Club M on the corner of Leicester Square, the Tavistock Rooms in Charing Cross Road and a Brewer Street club provided transitory venues. As they came and went, the Flamingo in Wardour Street went on and on, and attracted the very best luminaries from home and abroad. Vic Feldman, an ex-pat British drummer, gave an enthralling performance, as did George Shearing, Oscar Petersen and the MJQ. Absolute bliss was an appearance by Carmen McRae, the natural successor to Billie Holliday, although their styles were distinct. Carmen had a crystal-clear voice which could cut glass, and a delivery which was precise and melodious. Her sense of lyrics and interpretation was immaculate. Sadly, she never received full recognition in this country. When she appeared at the Flamingo she had in tow a group of British B film actors who had met her at the airport and had been dogging her ever since. They were led by Richard Wattis, a thin guffawing twit and Peter Reynolds, a poof, who played ridiculous tough guy roles, trench coat and all. Between numbers they kept urging her to finish and go to a party they had arranged. She was embarrassed and we were getting very fed up. I think it was Steve who strolled over and put a word in Wattis's ear. I don't know what was said, but it brought about that startled look he was famous for and no further interruptions.

The Lyceum's Sunday Afternoon Club was a popular venue for the young Elephant Boys and rival gangs from north, east and west London who were usually in evidence. A shaky truce existed for most of the time. Most fights were over girls and usually with American servicemen. Jiving was the popular form of dancing at the Sunday Club. On Saturday nights the atmosphere was different. Entertainment was directed at the more general public with jiving allowed only for certain dances with the odd couple breaking the rules. In between sessions youths visited the bar to indulge in the delights of a black and tan, or the lethal mixture of stout and champagne called a black velvet. On one occasion, when the Rabin band wasn't available, it was replaced by the orchestra of Billy Tennant who refused to allow jiving to his music. Attendance flagged until Oscar returned.

Big bands were popular. The Trocadero at the Elephant and Castle was on the big band circuit where Ted Heath, Johnny

Dankworth, Ronnie Scott and others made popular appearances. Ted Heath was the best of the British bands, recognised in America and all over the world; he featured singers Dickie Valentine, Denis Lotis and Lita Roza. Trombonist Don Usher featured in the stirring 'Night Train' and went on to lead the band after Ted Heath's death. Often fifty or sixty of us would occupy one section of the Trocadero's stalls and create a terrific atmosphere by setting up a steady banter with the bandleaders and by joining in with the music – sometimes even appearing on stage. I well remember being sung to by Lita Roza as she ruffled my hair. What a beautiful girl. The fact that a whole section of the stalls was taken over by our group was a source of entertainment for other patrons. They were not annoyed at the noise of stamping feet, clapping of hands, and loud repartee between gang members and those on stage. The whole thing was good humoured and enjoyable.

I can only recall two incidents of real trouble. One was when a man sat next to one of the lads and put his hand on his leg. The lad indicated to his larger friend sitting next to him what was going on and he got up, squeezed past his friend's seat towards the aisle and, as he came face-to-face with the man, punched him. There followed a great commotion when the man ran on to the stage of the Trocadero pursued by two indignant youths who were punching him as he screamed, 'I didn't do anything, I'm waiting for my sister.' This carried over the microphone, to the amusement of the audience.

The other incident was when Jimmy Rose was recognised in the audience. He was the leader of a small team from Rotherhithe who in some way had offended some of the boys from the Elephant. He was sitting in the front row of the second stalls and two of the lads were laying into him. Quite sensibly he did not retaliate but dropped his head down covered by his arms and took a beating. Some of us, shamefaced by a two-to-one situation, intervened. He was game and not badly hurt and thereafter had the respect of the gang and became one of its fringe members.

9. HEADS YOU WIN, TAILS I LOSE

Dice was the blight of my life. All the lads played it. When the Imperial Billiard Hall closed at night for the public it could be arranged for one of the employees to open the place and let the boys in. These 'schools', as they were known, occupied the full-size snooker table with sometimes ancillary games played on the smaller billiard tables. The schools were usually croupiered by established tough guys who knew the vernacular and kept a tight control on the game. Their word was final, their reward was a kick-back from the pot and they were the only guaranteed winners.

Some schools were arranged in private houses when an entrance fee was charged (usually five shillings). A sandwich and a pickled onion might be provided. The sandwich could be the biggest gamble of the night. Bobby Brindle had a floating crap game that cost five shillings to buy in to. He also got a share of the pot. When I knew him he sported the terrible white scar Johnny Carter had given him. It ran all down his right cheek and into his chin, the worst one I've seen. At times fights would break out, but as long as they didn't interfere with the game the fighters were left to sort it out.

Dice is totally absorbing. I can remember many a wedding reception ruined when the groom and his guests crammed into the gents and rolled spots. In the big schools hundreds of pounds would change hands. Money could be won or lost in two ways. The thrower would put up a stake that was covered as an even bet by one or a number of gamblers; the dice were then thrown and that

became the mark. The thrower lost immediately if he threw double six, double one (snake eyes) or two and one – these are difficult to repeat and are called craps. If the mark is four, five, six, eight, nine or ten the thrower continues until he throws either a seven – in which case he loses – or before he throws a seven he repeats the mark. In that case he wins and either takes the pot and retires, giving the croupier a part of the money, or he takes something out of the pot and throws again for the remainder. He continues taking out money or letting it ride until he loses or retires. If successful he will keep taking money from the pot, 'seeing the croop', all the time playing with other people's money. If at any time he throws seven or eleven as his mark he automatically wins.

The second method of betting is after the mark has been set. Then, side bets are placed by anyone in the school with the thrower or anyone else willing to make a bet. Odds are given of 2–1 against repeating four or ten before a seven is thrown; 5–2 against five or nine; evens for six or eight. These odds are not strictly accurate, but were uncomplicated enough to be universally accepted in illegal dice games. The croupier took a percentage of a winning pot or relied on tips; it worked well on most occasions. A tough, skilled or popular croupier could do very well, a less recognised one wouldn't be given, or elect to take, too much from the pot. Games were played in secluded corners, car parks, alleyways, parks and toilets, even churchyards. The billiard hall was favoured for its green baize. Games were thoroughly illegal and a fine was the penalty if caught. In one instance Danny Staples paid his ten shilling fine in pennies, one hundred and twenty of them, to a bemused clerk of the court.

On the subject of gambling, there is a certain slang that was commonplace. Some of it has obvious origins, some is a mystery to me now as it was then:

Tanner, sprassey	sixpence (6d)
Bob	one shilling (1s)
Kybosh, one and a kick	one shilling and sixpence (1s 6d)
Two bob	two shillings (2s)
Tosheroon (abbreviated to 'roon'), two and a kick	half crown (2s 6d)

Dollar, Oxford, scholar, Oxford scholar (dollar)	five shillings (5s)
Half a nicker, half a note, half a quid, ten bob	ten shillings (10s)
Nicker, note, quid	twenty shillings (one pound)
Deuce	two pounds
Carpet	three pounds
Fiver	five pounds
Tenner	ten pounds
Score	twenty pounds
Pony	twenty-five pounds
Half a ton, half a wedge	fifty pounds
Ton, wedge	one hundred pounds
Monkey	five hundred pound
Grand	one thousand pounds

This was familiar language in horseracing and naturally flowed over into all forms of gambling.

Other forms of gambling abounded. There were horse and dog tracks. There was point-to-point, where if you knew the right people you also knew the winner: as long as you didn't put down a lot of money and 'take a liberty' bookies would give the in-crowd the result in advance of the race. Then there was crown and anchor, played on a foldaway board balanced on a crate to catch the crowds as they left New Cross dog track: the game was and still is illegal, lookouts being placed to watch for the Old Bill. It was something to see how fast a crown and anchor set-up could be stowed away when an unbent copper was seen approaching. The same could be said for find the lady, the difference being that operators were unpopular because they were too greedy (the result of a game could be an unprofitable altercation).

Pitch and toss was, I believe, an import from the north played by schools over a hundred strong. Up there it embroiled itself in the Sheffield gang wars of the 1920s, which ended in murder and a trip to the gallows for the Fowler brothers. In London it was played by small boys pitching pennies against a wall, simply to see who was the nearest. (This version was called pitch and toss because in one variation the winner would get to toss all the coins in the game and call heads or tails. He kept the coins he called right and the

ELEPHANT BOYS

remainder were shared by the other players.) There were many variations. The biggest school I ever saw comprised printers from the *Daily Mirror* at the back of Red Lion Court, off Fleet Street, gambling their wages. Johnny's dad indulged a full life as a machine minder on the *Mirror*, a dedicated zealot to booze and a night tossing his wages away. Some of these old-timers lived life to the full, usually succumbing to cirrhosis of the liver.

Johnny's dad's 'other half' was known for slipping home late at night, removing her stilettos in the passageway leading to her flat and creeping in while the old man was flat out on the settee. She was also adept at giving an interfering neighbour a crack on the head with one of her shoes to set the two of them rolling on the ground with handfuls of each other's hair – their own form of pitch and toss. Women's fights were horrible affairs and fortunately quite rare.

Hypnotic one-armed bandits could steal your money as quickly as anything and there was great competition to gain the local 'franchise'. Terms were often a guarantee that your club or betting shop wouldn't be taken apart. The betting shop came about in 1960 and bred its own form of warfare. Many early entrepreneurs were the old street bookies, who were more adept at wielding a razor or a cosh than recording figures in the correct columns. Street bookies worked hard for their living. They were a target for the police, small-time crooks and professional villains. Off-course booking was illegal. To operate required an understanding with the police, either by giving information or bribes.

Our local bookie, Sid, worked by a bomb site close to Newcomen Street, a turning off the Borough High Street, and near the 'Carbolic' (the pub so named because it always reeked of the stuff). He was close to Balin House and had a good all-round view to see who was approaching from any direction. As a young lad I once earned sixpence from Sid by standing in for one of his lookouts whose special duty it was to pay Sid's 'licence' to operate. I simply walked up behind a police constable who had his arms folded behind him and dropped a half-crown into his cupped hands. Later came the sergeant, who got five bob; and soon afterwards the 'tec', a plainclothes copper who received a one pound note in the same fashion. I would have willingly signed up for the weekly job, but its regular incumbent was bigger than me.

One theory held by petty robbers was that a bookie daren't

complain to the police. Bookies usually had to be very careful and also tough enough to fight off, or go after, thieves if they could identify them. Life and business was a constant hazard. Sid lived in Balin House on the first floor of the third block. He lived alone, although he had another property elsewhere. His Balin House flat was his office, conveniently provided by the council.

When we reached our teens three of us decided to relieve Sid of his Saturday morning takings. We knew he collected a fair wad in bets and returned to his office at about one o'clock. The plan was simple. Watch from the first-floor landing window to see him returning through the square. Then dart up one flight of stairs to hide until he put his key in the front door. Then rush down the stairs, knock him into his passageway, turn him over and scarper with his bag. Along he came. Up we went. Pulled down our balaclavas. He turned his key in the lock and down we charged. I tripped over one and brought down the other. Sid went in and slammed the door and we kept going downstairs. Whenever I saw Sid after that I wondered if he knew what had been going on. When betting shops were legalised he and his relatives did the honest thing and opened several shops. I believe they were later bought out by one of the big betting shop combos.

Welching on bets was always a possibility. Bookies always demanded money up front. Punters were at risk, mainly through getting others to place their bets. George Spain, an old-timer from Islington, once paid some of his friends at the Borough an unexpected visit. At closing time in the Hole in the Wall pub, near the Borough underground station, George was reluctant to leave his friends, finally pleading for a place to stay. It turned out that he had been given stakes to place at various bookies. He pocketed the lot, only to see a lot of winners come home. Unfortunately for George the punters included Albert Dimes, and he left for south of the river very quickly.

George had a café in Ridley Road market, Hackney, where gathered all the riffraff of the East End. Teas changed hands along with betting slips taken by George as an unofficial bookie. He always placed favourites with other bookies, but handled many other bets himself. The clientele didn't care so long as he paid off. Gradually George got to handling all the bets himself. Punters did not pay tax on his services and he began to get some large bets. Inevitably came the time he couldn't pay off so he went into

ELEPHANT BOYS

hiding, leaving his wife and daughters to run the café. In April 1952 a crowd looking for George, led by Albert Dimes, wrecked the place. Dimes took fourteen shillings from the till. Meanwhile George had got himself a job running a buffet stall on King's Cross Station. Too well known to remain anonymous for long, he received a visit from Dimes and his cousin Scarface Jock Russo. Too slow to lock himself in a nearby cellar bolthole, he threw the tea urn, drenching Dimes in scalding water. Russo dragged the screaming Dimes's hands under a cold tap while George hopped it to his brother's house in Canonbury before visiting us. The last we heard of him he was heading north to Tyneside.

I was only turned over once. A man who had a reputation as a spieler (a man who could draw a crowd around him and sell almost anything) welched on a few pounds he owed me over a snooker bet. Word went out that I was looking for him, even though I had put the loss down to experience – it was my fault for betting with an obvious con man. He was a tasty villain from southwest London, so we didn't meet up for a while. Tony Cummings, who didn't particularly like me, was putting around a story that I was going to get this hardnut who was twice my size. When we did meet up some time afterwards he blustered out some apology and then tried to borrow some more money from me. I settled for calling him a few names in front of his mates. In 1963 I heard his name again. He was part of a team which descended on a mail train at Sears Crossing and carried out the Great Train Robbery.

In its own way the Great Train Robbery was a gamble that went wrong. It was put together by Buster Edwards, who recruited from two south London gangs to exploit a small gang's success in stealing small packets of Post Office mail. Buster was a well-known clubber and thief from Faunce Street, Kennington, next-door-neighbour to friends of mine, the Morbins (who knew him as Ronnie). His nickname came from some amateur bouts and service as a night-club and clip joint bouncer. Not much more than a petty thief, he was nevertheless quick to take advantage of an opportunity. When word was that the mail could be robbed without too much trouble, he decided to put together a team of like rogues. Old Dave Morbin said he was asked to take part but he declined, believing it to be one of Buster's fantasies. Dave reckoned Buster was very talkative and was openly recruiting the likes of

Charlie Wilson and Gordon Goody, both well known to the police. Frank Fraser says he was approached, but turned it down.

When the first team saw the size of the job they brought in a heavier crowd: Jimmy Hussey, Tommy Wisbey and Bruce Reynolds who quickly took charge of the operation. By this time, oddballs like Ronnie Biggs and Roy James had been signed up and were about as reliable as snow on a summer's day. Biggs was a petty thief in the same class as Billy Boy Harrison and should not have been included. By rights Reynolds should have called it off – perhaps he thought that if he did, Buster would go on with it anyway. The raid, in the style of a Jesse James robbery, followed and became part of world criminal folklore.

The police had some initial difficulty in tracing the gang's operational base at Leatherslade Farm, but they had so many names to go on that they knew virtually all the perpetrators. Leatherslade yielded enough clues to make it certain. Biggs should have cleaned off the prints, but with his irresponsible approach to everything he couldn't be bothered to wipe the window frames and feeding implements. Government pressure sent the police into a frenzy of activity. It was as well they knew who some of the culprits were, or they would have rounded up half of south London and charged them as accessories.

I, along with others from the Borough, was asked to fill out a questionnaire on my activities after two sacks containing some of the robbery money was found in a telephone box in Great Dover Street, close to where we lived. The use of such questionnaires may seem strange: surely guilty people would simply lie, but just try later on to deny dates and times which have been put in writing. The police were just being 'busy' – they hadn't a clue at that time who had put the money there, and still they don't know.

It appears that the money in the phone box was Scottish bank notes and considered to be worthless, so whoever found it had phoned the police to say where they could find it. No doubt this was someone who, feeling the police were getting close to him, was preparing for a deal by giving them something to claim a success. Imagine stumbling on that cash before the police got there! A holiday in Scotland, I think.

The Great Train Robbery myth grows by stories of South African and German financial backers who eventually consumed the profits from the raid. Believe me, it was just a crazy gang of south

Londoners getting too playful for their own good and suffering the judicial and political recriminations.

Card schools took many forms. Pub cribbage games, played for pennies, and family-and-friends sessions on a Sunday afternoon around the living-room table were social affairs played for amounts just enough to make the games interesting. Solo, nap, poker and pontoon were the favourites to while away pleasant hours. When only young men played, games could also include 'shoot', which was the fastest way to lose money ever invented. Games put on by local entrepreneurs were risky and best left alone: there were too many ways for games to be rigged for the 'guest', especially a novice.

Horseracing was mainly for adults who would book on to a coach for a day out at Epsom, Hurst Park, Kempton Park, Goodwood, Sandown or even Ascot. On-course betting was safer and the Tote above reproach. Where there is money the criminal fraternity invent ways to obtain a share. Specialists can fix races, but the cleverest con is from the horse owners who influence results when profit motivates them. It stands to reason that a good horse put out early in its career cannot sensibly win all its races – this would shorten the odds every time it ran, but of course if horses are being held it makes the whole business of understanding form irrelevant, unless that is, you can use your knowledge and contacts to judge the intricacies of the game. But that is for experts. At best, horseracing should be treated just as a good day out.

Strongarm presence was always about, in the form of unlicensed protection given to pitch bookies. In the early 1950s Jack Spot was very much in control; towards the end of the '50s Albert Dimes had taken advantage of Spot's troubles to grab the major market share. One of Spot's henchmen, Johnny Carter, held pitches at numerous tracks and regulated who could or could not hold down a pitch. One of a large family, he and brother Harry had influence at south London dog stadiums. They headquartered at New Cross and had a presence at Catford and Crayford. Johnny was in his thirties, that age when villains are held in esteem for their ability and willingness to break an arm by smashing it over a bended knee – or for the deft wielding of an open razor, sometimes followed by the helpful advice to 'sew that up'.

Johnny was at war with everyone, but in his prime he was the dominant organised villain as distinct from singular assorted characters like Frankie Chapman, who practised with equal dexterity for recreational purposes. The Carters battled anyone they supposed to be a threat: the Brindles, Frank Fraser, the Harris brothers, all of them or some of them, it just went on and on. Great fist and furniture fights erupted spontaneously in Elephant and Castle and Old Kent Road pubs. Ambushes with the liberal use of car-starting handles and lead pipes wrapped in socks to bludgeon incautious offenders leaving a known venue were legendary.

There is a story that Johnny had a specially constructed sword which, when mechanically triggered, propelled itself to a prodigious length – a bit like Wyatt Earp's Buntline Special, and of the same dubious authenticity. In his interview in one of the Sundays at the height of the race gang wars he claimed to have made and lost a six-figure fortune. I have to say that he followed an opulent lifestyle with his big black Buick, Savile Row suits and smart trilby. He splashed his money around and of course spent sundry amounts of time in prison, which held back expectations of becoming London's number-one gang boss. He asked me why I sometimes called him Wyatt. When I described the heroic proportions of the western hero he glowed with pride. I'm quite sure he thought he was alone against the world. At least he didn't think I was taking the piss.

Toby's Club was situated in Leroy Street, off the Tower Bridge Road. The premises was an old warehouse which had been turned into a better-than-average drinking club. Saturday and Sunday drinkers enjoyed good entertainment and in later years there was a casino. The atmosphere was excellent for that sort of club and many people came down simply to have a decent evening in relaxed surroundings; but you could also rub shoulders here with the cream of south London villainy. Owner Toby Noble had a string of grocery and general stores. He had pretensions to be recognised as an ex-prizefighter and numerous pictures of Toby stripped to the waist in manful poses decorated the stairway to the club and the upstairs bar in the midst of the more celebrated professionals. The trouble is, nobody could recall Toby's career; but we liked his club, so we said nothing. On the door was Tommy Daly who had been boxer and trainer and, when well past his best, was allowed to carry

the bucket and sponge as part of the train following a boxer into the ring.

The only fights I ever saw in Toby's were in the training ring put up on Sunday lunchtimes for exhibitions. What a time: a beer, handful of peanuts and a pro working out with a sparring partner. Sparring partners could earn good money by being knocked about for training purposes. Both boxer and partner wore protective headgear. When Kid Gavilan, the American World Welterweight Champion who had invented the bolo punch (an uppercut which came up under the opponent's heart) and caused a sensation in the boxing world, came over to defend his title, Toby arranged for him to train in the club. One sparring partner, egged on by his mates, began taking Gavilan on in rough-house style. The Kid's manager jumped in and stopped it to everyone's amusement. The Kid pulled out of training in the club. The boys were taking a liberty, really, to be fair to the world champ: he couldn't afford a cut eye. He went on to keep his title.

The pulling quality of pubs and clubs is in their atmosphere. Toby's atmosphere included plenty of style, entertainment, comradeship, and a gallery of crooks, con men and sharp business individuals – most of whom seemed to trade in the commodity of the day, toiletries. Long firm fraud was getting underway and was readily exploited by the shady wheeler-dealers, many of whom got a start with this activity. Another part of Toby's pulling power was that girls could not be members: their only way in was on the arm of a boy, an opportunity gratefully drawn upon.

ELEPHANT BOYS

10. PARTIES, HOLIDAYS, FUN, FRIENDS AND TRAGEDY

Family holidays soon after the war were usually two weeks by the sea at Margate, Clacton or the slightly more exotic Great Yarmouth. Margate, for me, was a disappointment. Barbed wire still guarded the beaches and it was a bleak and miserable place. The following year we visited further along the coast at Ramsgate. It had a cleaner, if less racy, attraction. We visited several successive years in the late '40s, staying at a boarding house in Grange Road. Stan and I could meet up with friends from other families and play the slot machines with money provided by dad, who saved his threepenny bits all year round – only to have us moan until we had squandered it away in the arcades and the Merrie England fair.

For a fortnight's holiday it was important to get theatre bookings for the second week: the first week was already booked by those already in their second week. I forget the theatre, but year after year we went to see Dickie Henderson and Roy Harper, a singing cowboy who blasted away with his silver six-guns punctuating 'Drifting Along with the Tumbling Tumbleweeds'. I loved it. Funniest man was Don Saunders, who had a comic walk. He was a disappointment when he attempted to make it on television, but for a seaside show he was hilarious. I developed a taste for subtle comedy. Subtle, in spite of the noise, it was. In later years Sid James couldn't make me laugh if he tickled me with a feather, but Tony Hancock only had to raise an eyebrow. It takes more than a dirty laugh to set me off.

Our parents expected we would behave correctly, as was the custom for a stay at a boarding house. Londoners were regarded as suspicious by seaside landladies and my mother was determined we would not disgrace ourselves: not too much noise; don't dare ask for more hot water once the jug placed in a bowl in your bedroom had been exhausted; be on time for meals; and never, never complain. Such was the pleasant nature of the surroundings, and our landlady, that we returned year after year. On our last visit Stan and I went off to see *Captain Horatio Hornblower, RN*, a spectacular naval epic starring Gregory Peck. It is a familiar repeat on today's television. We got back late for dinner. Mum's language was saltier than the film script. She embarrassed very easily, always worrying what others would think. I suspect our landlady didn't much mind, although I recall she didn't provide a meal. Anyway, our holiday finished as usual with a choice of a knickerbocker glory or a peach melba at a half-crown each at a café on the seafront. A great luxury.

When I ventured on holiday with my friends in the '50s it was first to Newquay, Cornwall, with Dave Parker, Terry Brereton and a new friend, Dave Morbin. Dave had in tow a strange lad named Roy Chaplin. On some occasion Roy had complained about the soap provided in a boarding house saying his mother always provided Lux. Dave Morbin promptly nicknamed him Luxey and it stuck. Two weeks of booze and birds was satisfying to young men away from parental scrutiny.

Next I 'borrowed' an old Austin and we drove to Clacton where we abandoned it for a chalet and teamed up with many of our friends for a two-week Butlin's binge. We had a marvellous time. The afternoon jazz club. Ray Winstone's band. The ice-cream vendor thrown into the pool struggling to get free from his tray as ice-cream tubs bobbed all around him, the evasion of camp guards as we opened up the perimeter fence to let our friends enter without passes. Dave Parker's new-found girlfriend who wore an off-the-shoulder blouse that had men standing on tiptoe for a glimpse . . . There's nothing like a holiday with your mates. Dave Morbin had been disappearing into a chalet with a girl, much to our annoyance, so we nicked a pair of knickers off a washing line and during the train journey home tucked them inside his handkerchief in his top pocket for Mum to find (and she did).

We followed up with a holiday in Jersey. Able only to afford one week in a boarding house on La Colomberie, we spent the first nights of our ten-day holiday sleeping on the beach near St Helier. Police combed the beaches trying to prevent this activity, but plenty of youths from the mainland accomplished it. I didn't dare nick a car on a strange island, so I took with me a driving licence borrowed from a friend and hired a car which I nearly drove off a cliff. Well, it was dark. Dave Parker looked down and saw the sea as I drove along a cliffside path which I thought was a bumpy road.

When we returned home I borrowed the licence again for an Easter weekend. I hired a Hillman California, picked up Dave Parker and then drove from New Cross to Marylebone, where Dave's dad worked as a boxing trainer in the Fitzroy Gym in Fitzroy Square. When we left I drove along Euston Road, and turning into Great Portland Street, collided with a van. We exchanged details – I had to use the other fellow's name, of course – then we drove to Kennington to pick up Dave Morbin and Luxey. I parked with the good side showing. Dave and his family came out to admire the beautiful two-tone saloon. As they walked around to the damaged side I bolted into Morbin's shop and hid under the stairs; even from there I could hear Dave M bollocking Dave P. We kept it for the weekend.

On one occasion a police car stopped us on the Thanet Way because I looked too young to drive. As they inspected my licence I developed an uncontrollable shake at which the copper told me not to worry and sent us on our way. When I returned it to the garage I parked the damaged side close to a wall, but the bloke tumbled to it. I think he must have known I wasn't licensed. He chuckled and made no fuss at all. The one who worried the most was the chap I had borrowed the licence from. He spent some weeks waiting on the postman's call. Strangely, he never again lent me his licence.

Getting away from home was a novelty for youngsters who had sheltered in their family homes during the war. Travelling abroad was not easy and often meant working to get the passage home. Digging potatoes in Jersey and picking tomatoes in Spain were two ways. A third was to join the Merchant Navy and jump ship in Australia, as two of my acquaintances did.

Dave Morbin lived with his parents above their grocer's shop in Faunce Street, Kennington. His dad, 'old Dave', was a genuine

underworld figure. He knew everybody including Buster Edwards, who had a club nearby and who was yet to find fame as a train robber. Lennie and Jimmy Garrett – who had a pedigree as arch-villains – were his wife's brothers. Lennie doted on his nephew, young Dave, and we got on well with him. He and old Dave told us stories well into the night. Len also took us to parties. At one I first met Frankie Fraser. Frank had a reputation even in those days. I remember the advice given by Lennie: 'Whatever you do don't stare at him or he'll think you're having a go at him.' Naturally enough we stared – you had to – but it passed off alright. Frank was a shortish, good-looking fellow who didn't look mad or terrible, but anyone who knew his reputation wasn't fooled by that. He was as game as a pebble, a real scrapper, and would use anything that came to hand. For years he was known to us, the underworld and the police as the most dangerous and dedicated gangster. Generally, he was unknown to the rest of the world. Now in his twilight years he is enjoying late recognition and has gained celebrity status. Forty of his seventy-odd years have been spent in prison, so I didn't really see much of him.

Through young Dave Morbin I had got to know Lennie Garrett very well. He was in his gangster prime during and just after the war. When I knew him I suppose he was in his thirties, although it is hard to judge someone who has done lots of bird and 'lived' life recklessly. He led the Green Van Gang which raided the London Docks just after the war. He was a typical sharp-witted con man and thief. Old Dave Morbin reckoned Lennie was number one on Scotland Yard's ten-most-wanted list. The gang broke into wharves to steal contraband goods to sell on the black market. The green van became a symbol. Many times they narrowly escaped capture. In those days police cars had two high-powered lamps on the roof. The idea was to throw the shadow of the car they were pursuing in front of them to make vision difficult. On the occasion they tried it on the green van they were surprised when the rear doors were thrown open and a battery-powered headlamp blinded them. Stories say the police car finished up in the Thames, but Lennie said it only ran into some gates of a Port of London warehouse.

Lennie was as tough as anyone I have known. He had been a professional boxer and was formidable in a stand-up fight. In addition to his green van forays, he snatched wage satchels from clerks ill equipped to resist. On business, he carried a pair of

Stillsons strapped to his wrist, and one night he gave a copper a belt with it when he attempted to arrest him during a noisy quarrel with his girlfriend near Waterloo. The copper was a big fat one who gave as good as he got. Len got away but his nose was a little more wonky than before. Later he was arrested and got five years for the assault. It was this incident that would lead to his split from Jack Spot's gang.

Len was a con man. Among his many routines was the glass eye trick. He had a friend with a glass eye who would sit alone in a pub and lose his eye. After a thorough search, when it didn't turn up (it was in his pocket), he would offer a reward of twenty pounds for the return of the eye, leave a false address and leave. Len would join the search, eventually 'finding' a piece of coloured glass made to look like a glass eye and say he was unable to claim the reward as he was catching a train to Glasgow that night. He would then offer to split the reward, and induce some 'mug' to part with a tenner for the fake eye. It struck me it was a lot of hard work for a tenner to split between two con men, but he assured me a tenner, or a fiver, was very welcome in those days. He had sold white sand as corn cure in East Lane and he knew dozens of cons – one of which me and Dave Morbin tried out.

We borrowed a barrow and put it up in Southwark Street just near the Borough Market. We then pinched some posters from Walworth Town Hall which warned of the dangers of flies as germ carriers, collected a cod's head and some meat bones from the cat's-meat shop in Long Lane, soaked them lightly in paraffin and displayed them on the barrow surrounded by some white pellets. We had hunted up some cockroaches and we tipped them just outside the circle of pellets which surrounded the meat. The cockroaches retreated from the paraffin and we sold the repellent tablets at 6d a packet. They were made by melting a penny candle in a frying pan and punching them out with a pea shooter. We didn't dare go back.

I remember when I was quite young, Lennie took me and Dave to the wall outside Wandsworth Prison. At a prearranged time we would throw weighted packets of cigarettes over the wall to Len's brother Jimmy, who was a tobacco baron. Lennie deliberately scattered them so that his brother and his mates had to scramble for them. We could only imagine the pandemonium on the other side.

Lennie was also a camping enthusiast; he enjoyed the open country and was clever at 'going to ground'. He played the equivalent of army games, tying trees down to make cover in the woods; no farmer could ever find him. He would take eggs and chickens and snare rabbits. Farmers would do well not to find him. On one campsite at All Hallowes, Kent, near to our hide there was a privy built over a fast-running stream. You sat on a box and dropped your waste directly into the flowing water, which carried it away. We used it to the annoyance of the site owner. He kept shooing us away, but we would sneak back, causing him to come puffing and wheezing from his caravan. His downfall was that he used the facility himself. We wondered what Lennie would do. Demolish the roofless hut around him? Chuck something over the top? No, the cunning bastard emptied the contents of a paraffin burner on to a rag, set light to it and floated it along the stream to pass under the owner as he sat in blissful solitude. When the flames licked his undercarriage he shot up in the air while we guffawed from the bushes. It was beautifully done.

One of my best memories of Lennie was a bunch of us walking from Leicester Square to Piccadilly Circus, when on the other side of the road he spotted the British Heavyweight Champion Johnny Williams. Lennie called out, 'Hello Johnny, what are you doing? Flogging your arse around Piccadilly Circus?' I smirked and then saw Williams advancing across the road. I looked to Lennie, only to find he and the others had disappeared like rats up a drainpipe the moment they smelled danger. I was across the Circus and halfway down Lower Regent Street before I caught up with them. 'Did you sort him?' wheezed Lennie. By the time I got my breath back it wasn't worth commenting, the others were falling about.

Young Dave Morbin was a respected member of the Elephant Boys. He also had well-off parents. The Kennington shop did very well, especially as old Dave would shift just about anything from anyone. Like many, young Dave came and went as he pleased, forming alliances with different members. For some reason he attached himself to our little team within the gang. He worked as a warehouseman at Wyman's newspaper distributor's near Blackfriars, where he made good money in that union-dominated paradise, spending as much time sleeping on stacks of papers as loading them on to vans for distribution to newsagents. Only Fleet Street linotype operators had it better. Young Dave boxed for the

Times Boxing Club at Blackfriars and he was good. I saw him in action during a less regulated battle.

Some fights were impromptu. One evening a number of us were talking at the Elephant coffee-stall when a lad of about fourteen asked for help. He and his pals were at a dance in Manor Place Baths, where they had been threatened with bottles by an older gang. One of his pals was known to us, so we marched on the baths about a half-mile away. The gang had planned on following the lads out on to the street and 'doing' them. Instead, they came upon us. A fierce battle followed. I got involved with one of them. We were having a fair old tussle and were both bloody; gradually I got the better of him and forced him against the railings of an area. As I was about to deliver the *coup de grâce* Dave Morbin stepped between us and knocked the poor fellow over the railings and into the area – a drop of about eight feet. Thanks, Dave. I remember another of them lying face down while Dave sat astride him punching him in the kidneys: every punch brought forth a shriek that punctuated the night air. I also remember Johnny showing everyone his dented shoe and complaining it was 'too soft for kicking'.

Dave Morbin bought a Standard 8 which invalidated the need to borrow other cars, or licences. We spread our patch to Chelsea, Hammersmith and Putney. Our favourite places were Chelsea clubs and pubs; the Star and Garter at Putney; and the Bull at Barnes just upriver from Hammersmith, that had a jazz club and would feature the best of British jazz in a packed Sunday lunchtime session on the banks of the Thames. You could also catch an occasional glimpse of Billy Hill, who had moved from Camden Town to Barnes. I impressed my friends by having a conversation with him on the pavement outside the Bull while they could only gawp. We chatted about my dad and uncles, particularly my uncle Wal whom Bill remembered as one of his role models – alas he never knew what became of him. For the rest of that lunchtime session everyone wanted to be seen talking to me as if some of Billy Hill would rub off on them. He had a sort of film-star status.

We also visited Cable Street in Tower Hamlets. It was argued that this was the most dangerous thoroughfare in the country. It had seen battles during Mosley's blackshirt marches, and it was here Jack Spot claims to have commanded the attacks on the fascist marchers. I dare say he was in the thick of it, but he was pretty

good at 'drawing the long bow' as to his own part in anything. We parked the Standard 8 and Johnny Rose, Dave Parker, Dave Morbin and I walked through the most desolate street I had ever seen. I am reminded of a line from a Mickey Spillane novel: 'Down these mean streets a man must go'. He had Mike Hammer and downtown Los Angeles in mind, but Cable Street did for us. We passed several groups of men and felt that eerie bristling of hairs on back of neck. I was glad when we left.

It was a good time of my life. Parties were plentiful, many of them at Luxey's council flat at Whites Grounds, Bermondsey, where he lived with his parents and older brother and wife. Parties would commence on Saturday, and if the booze held out, would be reconvened on Sunday, then adjourn until next Saturday, and so on until we or the drink were exhausted. Luxey's family were generous people and made everyone welcome at their parties. At one of these in walked some big lug, a real rocker – big, broad and noisy, not at all our style of fellow. His first mistake was trying to chat up every girl. His second mistake was chatting up Dave Morbin's girl. On it went, his voice sounding over Frank Sinatra's *Songs for Swinging Lovers* (a party favourite). I could see Dave Morbin getting peeved in his quiet way and muttering to Dave Parker. Then out went the lights. Thwack! Arghhrr! . . . A pause, and the lights came back on to reveal this fellow with a red-raw eye and nobody anywhere near him. Dave M was in the kitchen, everyone expressed concern and surprise and the poor chap acknowledged he didn't know who to blame. He was surprisingly contrite, a condition brought on, no doubt, by the efficiency of the operation and the weight of the punch – he wasn't looking for another. Dave M always denied the deed and Dave P, who I swear was nearest the light switch, of course had nothing to do with it. To all those who to this day believe it was me who turned out the lights or threw the punch, I can only refer them to the satisfied smiles on the faces of the two Daves. We always referred to Sinatra's record after that as *Songs for Swinging Punchers*.

In the 1950s music changed from the heroic propaganda songs of the war years. Pre-war music flourished briefly with Al Jolson and Frank Sinatra, but teenagers in search of something different to identify with listened to popular American singers such as Jo Stafford with her 'You Belong to Me'. Kay Starr and Billy Eckstein were good band singers, but although technically good they gave way to lively newcomers like Frankie Laine (he sang the theme song for the popular TV series *Rawhide*) who enjoyed enormous popular success. His records displaced those of Sinatra and Bing Crosby, although Sinatra would make a comeback in the 1960s to prove he was still the best male singer. Dean Martin split from silly Jerry Lewis and those ridiculous films which make the Carry Ons seem funny. He and others such as Perry Como, Al Martino and Eddie Fisher crooned to the top of the hit parade – only to be swept aside by the onset of Tony Bennett, Peggy Lee, Guy Mitchell and Johnny Ray. We were fortunate that television featured the Perry Como, Danny Kaye and Dinah Shore shows, which featured top entertainers. Unfortunately northern viewers complained that television was too Americanised to understand and they were taken off. Presumably the north wanted to go back to Gracie Fields, George Formby and Albert Modley. Such sophistication.

At the London Palladium we saw Al Martino, Frankie Laine and Johnny Ray. Johnny Ray had great appeal with his 'Glad Rag Doll' and 'Little White Cloud'. We went to many concerts and developed an interest in jazz – the modern variety which began when Charlie Parker developed be-bop out of the earlier New Orleans style. I never saw Yardbird Parker, who died in the 1950s, but we were blessed with visits by Jazz at the Philharmonic, which featured top American musicians like Dizzy Gillespie and Lester Young and class singers such as Ella Fitzgerald. There were also solo performances by stars such as Billy Eckstein and the amazing Sarah Vaughan. She once entranced an audience at the Royal Festival Hall with a cast on a broken leg, sitting throughout the concert, turning her chair around to entertain various sections. It was one of the most memorable performances I saw.

The very best was Mel Tormé at the State, Kilburn, the biggest cinema in Europe, which doubled as a concert hall. Tormé, nicknamed the 'velvet fog' because of his mellow voice, was enjoying success with his LP *Mel Tormé at the Crescendo* and he sang all of the favourites – 'Goody Goody, Mountain Greenery', 'Jeepers Creepers' – and showed off on piano and drums. He was a great showman and responded to a great audience. He went on so long after the final curtain that stage hands pushed the piano off stage to stop him playing. It was great stuff. Luxey, who I always regarded as Dave Morbin's friend, mortified the rest of us with a

ELEPHANT BOYS

'Go, go, go' in the middle of a song: something modern boys did not do. I was embarrassed to be seen with him. It was the sort of thing you had to apologise for to others who knew you.

Big bands and jazz groups did the rounds. Duke Ellington, Count Basie, Buddy Rich and Stan Kenton, who made spectacular band tours; Dave Brubeck on piano with the superb Paul Desmond on alto sax; Gerry Mulligan on baritone sax with the young luminary Chet Baker on trumpet; the MJQ (Modern Jazz Quartet); George Shearing; Oscar Petersen; Errol Garner and so many more. The like will never come again. We saw them all.

One of our favourite pubs became the Lilliput at Dockhead, near Rotherhithe Tunnel, which featured the best British modern jazz groups. It had two crowded parallel bars with the music played at the end across both bars. Wednesday and Saturday were jazz evenings. Further along towards Surrey Docks, now renamed Surrey Quays in an attempt to make it more salubrious, is the Gregorian Arms. Called the Greg, it was a quieter pub which had that indefinable atmosphere which made it popular with the 'boys'. I was there when a boy named Bates, who considered himself a tough guy, strutted and bragged too loudly of his derring-do. He foolishly upset one very tough Elephant Boy, who shoved a broken split bottle into his cheek and twisted it. It was a liberty, really: Bates was not in the same class as his attacker, but that was the way things sometimes happened.

One thing I did not have in common with Dave M was his occasional use of a queer. One night walking towards Kennington we came upon an unfortunate wretch known as 'Dolly'. To me he was grotesque and in spite of Dave's urgings I could not bring myself to follow them into the stairway of a block of flats. When Dave returned he complained he had lipstick around his flies. Ugh.

Later Dave Morbin took up with a seventeen-year-old girlfriend. Sally was a quiet, lovely girl who doted on Dave and occupied much of his time. We drifted apart as mates do when a serious girl comes along. Early in 1957 I received a telephone call from his mother to say he had been taken into St Thomas's Hospital after complaining to his doctor his gums bled while he brushed his teeth. His doctor whisked him straight away into hospital for tests, which sadly identified acute leukaemia. He rallied for a while and came home for a party. He had been supplied with an NHS wig to cover his hair loss caused by radiation treatment. When some silly girls giggled at his appearance he threw it away in disgust. Soon he relapsed and within four months of becoming ill he was dead. I visited him the night before and we discussed a break we were planning in Norfolk just so he could get away for a while. I phoned St Thomas's the following day and when they were non-communicative I guessed the worst.

The *Daily Express* took me to All Hallowes in Kent, because Dave had once complained of a burning sensation on his arms when he rinsed himself in a stream during a camping weekend. Although they tested for radiation with a Geiger counter they found nothing. To see a superbly fit, fun-loving twenty-three-year old go so quickly was heartbreaking. To add to the tragedy, one week after his funeral Sally put on a record Dave had given her, took a large dose of aspirin, drank deeply from a bottle of gin, then lay down and went to sleep. They are buried together in Streatham Cemetery.

ELEPHANT BOYS

11. GROWING PAINS

Sex and girls were not at all the same thing in the 1940s and '50s. Sex was that faintly obscure 'waves over the rocks' thing in the movies. Girls were flesh, although that was mostly forbidden.

My first girlfriend was Jeannie Lawrence. We played ball in the square of Balin House when we were aged about ten. Separation was triggered by the emergence of firm mates Johnny Rose and Dave Parker, who naturally gave the fisheye to female acquaintances who were not their own. Girls were always part of the scene, though they usually had their own games and cultures. Boys were not encouraged to take much interest in the opposite sex. There was little conversation about the difference between boys and girls. Boys in those days doggedly failed to discover the hidden pleasures.

It took a girl, Jean something-or-other, to decide I was having a physical relationship (the kissing variety). Everywhere I went she appeared. She came from, of all places, Red Cross Way. We were about fourteen years old and I was pulled and mauled whenever she took the fancy. Presently I heard that a boy from Red Cross Way thought he had the rights. He was said to be a bit on the big side and I spent some uncomfortable times looking out for a possible assault. I had glimpsed him once, but he probably never even knew who I was. The split with Jean came when she wrote me a love letter after she hadn't been able to find me for a while. She gave it to Stanley Pell, who gave it to my brother, who read it aloud to everyone. We had a fight. Jean didn't wait for my farewells. Immediately she transferred her affection to some other poor devil.

Games were a good way of fumbling our way around girls. I had

fun wrestling with Josie, only to find she had more fun wrestling with Dave Parker. After that disappointment I tackled Rene. Tackled is the word, for it was a question of blocking her path up the stairway to the flats, causing her to push past. It became so commonplace that my mates nicknamed her Rene the Grope, though to be fair she wasn't the one doing the groping. Another Rene caught my eye, but she found a boy outside the flats. I found that girls discovered boys when they decided it was time to do so; the boy had little say in it. Alas I was not Rene's choice.

As we grew older, groups of boys and girls associated in games of true and false with kissing forfeits. I can't remember the name of the girl who lived in Grange Road, Bermondsey – but she was startled when, to collect my forfeit, instead of stepping into the passage I in all innocence selected the bedroom. Afterwards I could hear her giggling to her friends that I had taken her into the bedroom. I wondered what all the fuss was about!

A clumsy hand inside an unbuttoned blouse in the back row of the cinema was the next step. This could be a satisfying achievement, but anything else was most unlikely. One girl, Maureen, was fairly accommodating in the stairway of the flats in Balin: she didn't mind when one after another we had a feel inside her blouse, but she wouldn't remove her white bra in case her mother discovered her in some dishevelled state. One of the boys became frustrated by this. It was a rainy day so he stepped outside, collected a handful of mud and left a handprint on that white bra for mother to see. She never played again.

The back row of the cinema was occupied by hot bodies reefing each other and girls would only occupy that area if they were willing to satisfy a little fiddling about. It sometimes happened in the main body of the cinema, too, when it became the object of keen observation from several rows behind. I remember, on leaving the Astoria, Canal Bridge, mentioning to my brother the activity going on in the seats in front of me. He was very unimpressed with my failure to communicate the goings-on, which he had completely missed.

I had the misfortune to sit with a rather buxom young lady on a coach beano to Southend. She was so vigorous in her kissing that I felt quite sick afterwards. My mate Rod Keech had covered himself and his partner with a coat and was being much more intimate; then some boozy old duck came dancing up the aisle and proceeded to pull the coat away. Talk about pandemonium! She tugged, he pulled it back, the girl made frantic adjustments to her clothing and the rest of us cried with laughter. Rod thought he was on such a good thing on the return journey that he disembarked near where the girl lived at Surrey Docks. But while they were in a doorway her boyfriend walked by and Rod made a hasty getaway. Unfortunately it was two in the morning and he lived at Chalk Farm, Hampstead, easily ten miles away.

Rod, who was a reader at William Jones Clifton, had a knack for pulling birds. At times it seemed I could use all of my tenderfoot technique on some attractive female to no avail, and all he had to do was look at them. They could be walking by on the other side of the road, still their heads would turn. There is no explaining what chemistry goes on at such times: whatever it is, if someone ever manages to bottle it they are guaranteed a fortune. I always ended up with the odd sorts – like the one who heehawed like a donkey every time she laughed, wore make-up resembling Cleopatra and wrote notes that she delivered to me through the firm's compressed-air tube communications system. (They read 'I have got so much loving for you, have you got some loving for me?' I read them aloud for fear someone would think I was taking her seriously.) Still, beggars can't be choosers.

I managed to pull one girl at the firm. We went to the pictures at a cinema in Tottenham Court Road. I have a recollection that the film was called *A Bullet For Joey*, not that I saw much of it. Activity became so intense that we adjourned to an alley near the cinema. I was much gratified by my success until I found out she had been with just about every other teenager in the firm. When later she became pregnant you couldn't find anyone who could remember having been out with her.

A bunch of us were hanging about near the Borough Market one day when a girl came up and spoke to us. She was, I suppose, sixteen or seventeen years old, pretty and very direct and much more mature than us. She had run away from home, having arrived on the train from Nottingham that morning and been picked up by a man seeing his opportunity. She'd been to his flat, after which he had walked her round the streets and then run off. She now had nowhere to stay. At sixteen we were full of curiosity, and of course willing to help, so we took her to Balin and into Johnny's flat while his parents were out.

Johnny, Dave and myself were looking forward to a memorable experience when we heard a key in the front door. We dragged the girl to the bathroom off the passageway. Fortunately Johnny's dad walked by into the front room and we were able to smuggle her out. Down in the square we met Dicky Mitchell, who soon 'sussed' what was going on and invited us all up to his family's flat. Once the girl was inside, he shut the door on the rest of us. We hung around for a while until they came out. Generously, Dicky offered each one of us to go into the flat with the girl. Our bravado had melted away. Perhaps we didn't dare be with the girl alone, even though nothing daunted her. Anyway, Dicky took off and we were again walking the streets with the girl who was absolutely pliable to whatever situation she was in. At the Elephant we bumped into some of the older boys who took her off our hands and we retired gracefully.

The next day was Sunday and in the afternoon we went to the Lyceum. Lo and behold, there she was: she'd been passed around to whoever would take her. She had just accommodated one of the boys in one of the passages behind the old theatre boxes. She left with Danny, not the kind to offer charity. On the pavement outside she knelt down and unbuttoned his flies. After she had finished – all of this in daylight in front of all sorts: the lads, taxi drivers, American servicemen, women, even a constable observing from the corner of the Strand – Danny for his and others' amusement twisted her ears back to make sure she didn't miss anything. It was a sordid act and, I think, even too much for her. She went off crying. I suppose she must have ended up on the game.

Picking up girls could be random. The best operator undoubtedly was Ronnie Dennis. While novices like us stood outside the Elephant and Castle underground station blurting out 'Carry yer bag, miss', to some amused young lady who blithely continued on her way without taking up the offer, Ronnie would walk alongside them engaging in clever conversation. Often he could be seen disappearing in the direction of the New Kent Road chatting away to some bemused female. We always wondered how he got on. One of the gang was reputed to hit girls who did not want to go as far as he desired, but this was unusual. But success could also be embarrassing. I can remember Frankie being constantly waylaid and pestered by a girl he scored with: she appeared everywhere he went, even hanging around close to the coffee-stall waiting for him to leave, while we all took the mickey.

The dance-hall was the place where one was most likely to 'pull a bird'. As well as the Lyceum and Locarno, there was the Hammersmith Palais, Catford Savoy, Welling Embassy and Ilford Palais. If you were doing well an early question was, 'Where do you live?' – essential knowledge in order to weigh whether the effort was worth a long journey seeing the girl home, possibly to get nothing more than a kiss and a date. Girls were pretty adept at getting fares paid by the unwary.

Strange things sometimes happened. Stan was once dancing with a girl in the Locarno, when suddenly she clutched him tight and manoeuvred him to the edge of the floor; as he bristled with anticipation she let go, clutched her chest and took off for the cloakroom. Later she explained that her bra strap had broken. Then there was George, a friend of Stan's, who would manoeuvre an unsuspecting girl in front of a mirror; there he would stand behind her and, with his mates looking on, he would jerk up her jumper while they all glared in the mirror. Another lad, Dave Parker, took a terrible pride in arranging two dates for the same time in the same place. We could only imagine two girls standing side-by-side under the Guinness clock until it dawned on them. He never had much trouble arranging appointments. It was down to the fact that he had the good fortune to look a bit like Dean Martin.

Professional women were quite frightening. I was never comfortable being accosted in Soho streets during evening excursions to clubs, bars and dives by 'ladies of the night'. There seemed to be quite a lot of them. I always hurried on with embarrassed haste. Mostly it was all amateurish fun. How times have changed.

The culture of southeast London just after the war depended upon close family ties. We would fight amongst ourselves, or with our neighbours, but it was settled between us. Rarely were the police called. If they did turn up they received little co-operation: right or wrong, it was perceived that the police acted exclusively for the ruling classes. Police protected property of the rich, they were not interested in the problems of people living life on the line. Courts had little sympathy with such people. Magistrate Mrs Sybil Campbell at Tower Bridge Road court was both feared and hated.

She could be counted on to berate some poor wretch who had stolen a coat to put on his child. Of course then as now, excuses could be found for the same behaviour in better-off people.

This attitude from the 'upper classes' was sure to polarise its victims. From that followed the culture of silence and of sorting things out among ourselves. Gang culture is not far removed from this. Cliques come together for mutual satisfaction and protection. These cliques are fluid within their own set boundaries, people move from one to the other, loyalties change, but the traditional culture remains. Group behaviour has its animal instincts for dominance, submission and challenge. Boys take up positions, best fighters become leaders, quick thinkers have a respected niche. Both qualities of fighting and thinking in one individual often lead to the arch criminal.

No better evidence of strata is needed than the school dinner. Head of the queue would quickly give way to the boy with most muscle. He would be followed by his minions, who held their place on the back of his prowess. Seating arrangements would enable toughs to sit together, displacing submissive diners at will. The dreadful eating habits of some would drive out those whose stomachs were easily turned. The communal salad bowl sampled by the tough end of the table was severely diminished before others had a dip, and by then unwanted bits had been returned to the bowl by fork or by being dribbled back in. The same thing happened in Borstals and prisons. At least at school you could opt to go home and eat.

Violence could be turned against the public. Mugging was not a term familiar to me, but there was the peculiar phenomenon of the 'cosh boy'. These nasties would wait in dark places (of which there were many) for anyone to pass by, then bash them over the head with a variety of cosh. The cosh could be anything from a sock filled with sand to a lead pipe, or a loaded wooden stick filled with metal or stone. These terrors mostly acted alone, almost always carried a knife and knuckleduster, and were considered cowards. Citizens and police loathed them and at the police station they could expect a good kicking. They were the best argument for corporal punishment. Unfortunately floggings with the birch and cat-o'-nine-tails were not confined to them, but were handed out indiscriminately by some courts as a reward for living in hard circumstances.

Just after the Second World War parents had a tough time with their offspring and with each other. Kids could hide for hours in bomb-damaged houses and factories or in hideaways, in the debris strewn all around. Ill-afforded clothing was scrubbed clean for immediate use again and again. Patches on trouser seats and elbows, and darns in socks and stockings were commonplace – as were the unrepaired tear in a boy's short trousers and the ladder in a woman's stocking. Shoes were repaired by dad hammering on a last, the sort of thing which is nowadays a trendy door stopper.

Hats for boys and men were rare. Gone were the pre-war days of the cloth cap when every male seemed to own one. School caps were invariably stuffed into pockets: to wear one would be to invite some tough to grab it and skim it over the broken-glass-topped wall of a bombed-out building or into a water tank. The occasional balaclava helmets, some made out of old woollen socks, kept the cold from little ears. Men sometimes wore trilbys, the titfer for racing men, but they were expensive. Those with a few bob chose the Homburg to go with the Fifty Shilling Tailor's suit and the tie with the V-knot. There was a short spell when tearaways wore the 'cheesecutter', a cap narrow at the peak and perched forward on the head – very much in the style of Del boy.

With the ladies, high-heeled shoes balanced precarious nylon-clad legs and a skirt at least six inches below the knees. Anything else would be considered rude. Women who turned up the hem to a dangerous four inches would be targets for gossip. This was partially offset by the arrival of the 'new look' which rescued the adventurous from wicked tongues. Gossip could be enjoyed on balconies and stairways, in the square and on the street corner, or standing in a queue, or over a pint of mild and bitter in the George or 'Carbolic'. It concerned morals and often led to fierce rows and fights. Men would reluctantly battle for their wives' injured reputations, but worse women would fight – with shoes, rolling on the ground, hands locked in each other's hair trying to wrench it out at the roots. It was a most horrible sight and fortunately not too commonplace.

ELEPHANT BOYS

12. MEETING THE NEW CROSS BOYS

Gang culture was consistent across London. Most areas had their teams, mobs or boys. It's interesting how names applied to gangs: the Walworth Road Team, the Angel Mob, the Kray Firm and the Elephant Boys. Close to us was a sprawling anomalous crowd known as the New Cross Boys, who were held mostly in contempt by the formidable south London gangs at the Brick, Elephant and Brixton. It has to be said they were more fun than their celebrated rivals. Often two hundred or more strong, they would stroll the Canal Bridge area near where the Old Kent Road meets New Cross Road and close to the Millwall football ground.

They inhabited youth clubs around Ilderton Road, plagued the Den at Millwall matches, could be seen in large numbers at New Cross dog track and outside losing their money at crown and anchor and find the lady. Their patch was from Canal Bridge, round the back of the Old Kent Road, through New Cross to Deptford and across Peckham. They knew the local villains and liked to be seen talking to the likes of the Rosa brothers, Johnny and Harry Carter, Dicky Frett and Ronnie Roff, who cut a large figure in his splendidly tailored full-length overcoat.

Ronnie Roff was short-sighted and wore those thick lenses which magnified his eyes, so perhaps he didn't always know who he was talking to. He was a local tough from Albany Road, on the corner of which stands the Thomas à Becket pub. There used to be a boxing ring upstairs, there, where Henry Cooper and his brother Jim once trained. Ronnie and older brother Mickey were enemies of the Richardson brothers. Charlie once was accused of putting a couple of pistol shots in the direction of their council flat over some disagreement concerning some other party. Charlie was up and coming as south London's top man, often getting called upon to administer such admonishments. He was charged with that shooting and acquitted. Johnny Nash, a hardnut from north London was not so lucky: when he was brought into the police station Mickey Roff leaped out of a chair and steamed into him before the police could stop him. Nash lost some blood, gained some respect and was found guilty. He received a two-year sentence.

It could all get confusing. The Roffs fought the Richardsons, as did the Harris brothers, Johnny and Benny; but the Harris brothers were also at war with the Carters who were cousins of the Roffs. The Nash family, six brothers from Islington, mixed in all this. Later they came to prominence in the period between Spot/Hill and Richardsons/Krays with whom they co-operated until being broken up by the police in the '60s.

I first met the New Cross Boys when Johnny, who was straying from our bunch, persuaded us to go to a youth club somewhere around Canal Bridge. At first I didn't like the flash attitude of this noisy, pretentious crowd – particularly a boy named Alec, who was louder and even more obnoxious than the rest. I was used to the respect shown to people around the Elephant. This fellow didn't know anyone, so he didn't know better and got a bit saucy. I nearly put one on him. Among their leaders was a boy named Johnny Daly, who at that time lived in Pomeroy House, New Cross. Later Daly linked up with actor David Hemmings to form Hemdale Promotions, which put on the Evel Knievel show at Wembley and had some involvement in the Rumble in the Jungle when George Foreman met Muhammad Ali in Zaire. A long way from New Cross.

They could be fun. One night, six of us crammed into a taxi. We disembarked and two of the New Cross Boys took to their heels followed by us after the briefest delay. We learned you always run in the opposite direction of the taxi, giving the cabbie no chance to outrun you. After a spate of this it became impossible for young men to get a taxi around New Cross. I wonder if that's when West End taxi drivers first balked at going south of the river.

A while later we met up with those boys in the New Cross Road.

We had been called to assist someone named Bates (not the boy at the Greg) who was in a quarrel with five lads. As we approached, Bates was stabbed a number of times in his arm and back with a small flick-knife. In the skirmish the knife fell to the ground. I picked it up and pocketed it. The assailants had run off and we went looking for them. When they were spotted they ran away, pursued by some New Cross Boys. We joined in and I easily outpaced our crowd, leaving them some way behind. I was after the last of their bunch, who was lagging behind his mates. He disappeared into the grounds of New Cross Hospital and I pulled up to regain my breath. Fortunately for me I had run myself out. When the New Cross Boys caught up with me they excitedly discussed the big silver revolver that one of the five had pointed at them. I then knew how I had so easily outpaced them.

Trips to the seaside were popular. On one occasion the New Cross Boys descended on Southend. This preceded the visits by mods and rockers, but probably set the scene for later events. The trip is memorable for several reasons. The first is that about twenty of us had fish-and-chip meals in a restaurant on the front and then all got up together and walked out while the panic stricken proprietor tried to get his bills paid. The knack here was not to be last out. The poor devil had no chance of getting paid as the last five or six of us forced our way out together.

The gang reassembled in the Kursaal and was about fifty strong. Pure chance produced another gang of about the same strength who were there for the same sort of mischief. It didn't take long for a fight to start. It was in the cafeteria under the great dome and quickly developed into one of those furniture affairs with an interesting culmination when our lads grabbed trays from the pile on the self-service counter and skimmed them across the hall after a retreating enemy. I can still picture dozens of trays flashing through the arcade leading to the main exit, accompanied by clangs and crashes and the cries of anguish and roars of success as they crashed into our fleeing rivals. By this time the police were about and we split up again into smaller groups.

There was a carousel in the park behind the Kursaal and some of our lads – who had been involved in a skirmish with some fairground people earlier in the day when they were near the beach – came face-to-face with them again at the roundabout. Their leader was a big fellow, tattooed and very nasty looking, with a

ELEPHANT BOYS

bicycle chain that he was swinging menacingly in the face of our small outnumbered group. None of them really fancied their chances against this tough character and the matter was resolved when we came up and Johnny Roberts grabbed him from behind and held on for grim death while Ginger Simmonds pummelled this hardnut until he finally sank down. The rest of their mob was so surprised they never did a thing and we walked away unharmed. Later in the day some of the lads came upon this fellow who offered to go down on the beach and fight any one of them, 'straight, street or knives'. There were no takers.

Of the numerous gang fights that stand out are the battle at Goose Green and the devastation of the New Cross House. Goose Green is near Peckham and there was a good deal of rivalry between their local gangs and the New Cross Boys. A liberty had been taken when some juveniles from New Cross had been badly roughed up by some Peckham Boys. A return visit by some of the New Cross Boys had ended in a rout as they fled what turned out to be a very underestimated tough gang.

An expeditionary force set out from the Elephant and Castle to put matters right. This was an assortment of Elephant Boys and co-opted teams from New Cross and Clapham. We were two hundred strong and searched the area, eventually splitting into smaller groups in the vicinity of Goose Green. With us were some of the youngsters who had been beaten. One of our smaller groups walked into about forty youths and were surrounded by them. The leader of this unknown gang got very tough with our scouts, but the tables were turned when the bulk of our gang surrounded them. It could hardly be called a gang fight as we outnumbered them five to one. Command of our mixed group had been assumed by Waggy, a renowned villain from Clapham. He grabbed a lead cosh from the rival leader who, after slapping some of our lads with it, had stuffed it into his trouser belt and covered it with his jacket when the main gang appeared. Waggy taught him a lesson by repeatedly slapping him in the face with his own cosh and taunting him about his bravery when he outnumbered our smaller group. This fellow just turned to jelly and was lucky not to be badly beaten. After grovelling, he was allowed to leave with his gang, who were not the ones we were looking for. We never found them.

This may have been the same Waggy who was the nephew of

celebrated robber Frannie Daniels – an associate of Billy Hill, and better known as Frannie The Spaniel – and who was later out of the country when police came to question him over the shooting of Scotch Jack Buggy, whose body was found washed up on a Sussex beach. Charges were never brought against Waggy, but Frannie was eventually acquitted of Buggy's murder.

The New Cross House affair was amazing. Fifteen or twenty of us were there for a drink. It was not our regular pub and soon we fell out with the regulars. A fight started which was better than the best saloon brawl in a Hollywood western. Chairs, tables, bottles and glasses were thrown about. A heavy tape recorder was pulled from a shelf and dropped from a height to crash through the top of a grand piano. The whole drinks display, including a huge mirror behind the bar, was shattered by bottles and furniture and the inside of the pub was completely destroyed. Unfortunately knives were in evidence and some minor wounds were inflicted. It is very easy to get carried away in such circumstances. I had in my pocket the flick-knife which I had picked up from the ground after the previous scuffle in which the boy Bates had been stabbed. As we were leaving the pub I found the knife in my hand and even though my memory is cloudy I am told by my friends that I challenged some of the onlookers to a knife fight. Vaguely I remember someone screaming at me, 'You'll get five years, you'll get five years.' At that I hurled the knife, which stuck in the pub door, before being dragged away by my friends. Such are the dangers of carrying a knife.

The New Cross Boys were pretty much a disaster. There was a flea-pit cinema called the Rialto near the Blue Anchor market area of Bermondsey. It was part of what they regarded as their territory, although it really was the pits. I heard that one boy, edging along a row towards a vacant seat in the dark, stepped into a pile of shit deposited by a previous occupant. On one occasion one of them flicked a live cigarette end into the air to land many rows in front: it landed on a man's raincoat which was folded on his lap. He lost his rag and offered to take them all on. It was an offer the chastened lads declined.

On another occasion they were actually driven out of the Rialto after they picked on a couple of lads, only to find several rows of them stand up. In the pandemonium to get out an usher tried to

stop them leaving. As he stood with arms outstretched, Alec threw an ice lolly from the back which lodged on the bridge of the fellow's glasses. Henceforth he was known as the unicorn.

A better cinema was the Astoria at Canal Bridge. It was one of those marvellous art deco palaces which sadly have now disappeared. The Astoria and nearby pubs were a popular gathering area. There was also a number of small cafés which provided late-night meeting-places. The gang had its 'camp followers'. Girls would hang on to the gang for the fun it brought. It also brought about 'line-ups' round the back of the Astoria, which was one of the group's more interesting innovations. Maybe they couldn't fight, but they had their accomplishments.

New Cross itself was popular for the New Cross House before we made ourselves unwelcome. I first met Ginger Simmonds here when I happened on to a running battle near Deptford Broadway. Simmonds overtook a lad who had run by me and dropped him at my feet. I didn't even know a fight was going on. It was on this occasion I met up again with Charlie Don and watched him down some fellow with a rain of punches. Ginger and Charlie both were 'punchers'. Ginger Simmonds was the only real fighter the New Cross Boys had, with the possible exception of Mickey Hulbert. Charlie Don was just making a guest appearance. He was an Elephant Boy with West End connections.

Ginger Simmonds was a red-haired, florid-faced brawler. He was strictly New Cross, but on occasion paid a visit to the Elephant. Near Christmas a bunch of us engaged in a snowball fight outside the Trocadero cinema. Into the mêlée stepped Eddie Richardson. I had tossed a snowball at him as he came along; naturally he joined in. Suddenly, Ginger, who didn't know Eddie, grabbed him and shoved a snowball down his neck. I couldn't believe it. Neither could Eddie. He cracked Ginger on the chin and put him down. Ginger got up and whacked Eddie back and they started into each other.

Eddie's packamac wrapped itself around the two of them as they slid and gyrated on the slippery surface. Eddie stepped back to remove his mac. Somehow it was explained to Ginger just who it was he'd picked on and as they prepared to resume Ginger cried, 'Let's not fight, we're both from the Elephant.' Eddie replied that he was from Camberwell and launched another attack. To give Ginger his due, he stood up well until the fight was stopped. I think Eddie was surprised by some hard punching. The following night Eddie was talking of the

ELEPHANT BOYS

fight and blamed his packamac for the lack of a finish. I thought he was a bit ungenerous on that occasion, but I never said so.

Johnny had got to know all of the New Cross crowd and was also responsible for introducing us to Charlie Don. Johnny was gregarious by nature, but had an opinion of his fighting prowess that was not shared by the rest of us. He had been a good friend of mine, but lately was not entirely trustworthy as a buddy. He talked a big fight, but he was not known for having had a one-to-one stand-up scrap. Somehow he had even managed to avoid his initiation fight. Johnny performed his best when we were all there and a general free-for-all was going on. We became fed up with his constant bragging and on the occasion that he brought us into conflict with another group of boys (due to his always looking for trouble) it was decided to let him get on with it and fight one of theirs to settle the matter. They put up Billy Sims who had a few amateur bouts behind him. When they were finished Johnny's face was swollen to twice its size and his bragging was cured.

At times the New Cross Boys would descend on the West End. They were not into jazz, but knew numerous eating-houses in and around Soho where we enjoyed many a spaghetti Neapolitan in late-night restaurants. As cinemas were very popular, a visit to one or more of the West End variety was a good night out. Leicester Square had the Empire, Warners, the Leicester Square Odeon and Leicester Square Theatre, all showing the latest films. Right on the corner of Piccadilly Circus stood the London Pavilion,while other comfortable cinemas were located in Haymarket, Lower Regent Street, Shaftesbury Avenue and Tottenham Court Road. Believe it, or not, it was possible to sit in silence and enjoy a film without the constant crackle and rustle of sweet-wrappers, the chomping of teeth and the fidgeting and chattering which today destroy the pleasures of a comfortable night out.

There's no doubt that the New Cross Boys were more fun than their more notorious cousins from the Elephant, but their pretentions could be wearisome. My last visit to them had me intervening in a quarrel outside the Marquis of Granby at New Cross. For my pains I received, from behind, a full quart bottle of brown ale smashed over my head. I had to be rescued by my own mates, who ran along from the New Cross Inn. The New Cross Boys had all vanished. I still have the zigzag scar to remind me.

ELEPHANT BOYS

13. UP WEST

The West End is a short journey from the Elephant and Castle. The Bakerloo line serves Charing Cross and Piccadilly Circus; alternatively there are numerous buses to the livelier West End streets. We had started early in our teens with an initial interest in the 'penny arcades' in the Strand when that was an interesting thoroughfare. As youngsters we only visited the seaside once a year for a holiday, if we were lucky, and the slot machines in the Strand's amusement parlours provided an interesting pastime. They even had 'What the Butler Saw' machines with flimsily clad females flashed on to the screen for the briefest time. No matter how much you put in you never saw any more.

Kiosks in these arcades sold American cigarettes. Our favourites, even at such a young age, were Pall Mall and Chesterfield, which looked chic as they were longer than English cigarettes and hung nicely from the corner of the mouth. In the Strand, near Covent Garden, was the Black and White Milk Bar which became a favourite visit for a coffee and a doughnut. Other entertainment included an occasional fun visit to the cartoon theatre in Waterloo Station. Tom and Jerry and the incredible Sylvester the cat, with his sadistic and furtive attempts to gobble up Tweetie Pie, were novel to us and provided noisy amusement.

As we grew older, eating-houses in Soho streets became popular – particularly one in Beak Street which specialised in spaghetti dishes and was packed by the lads most Saturday late nights. Daly's Bar provided salt beef sandwiches, the trendy titbit for sophisticated westenders. Hamburgers were only just emerging at

ELEPHANT BOYS

that time, although the hot dog had already been imported along with expresso and cona coffee.

West End cinemas were much plusher than those in south London and we visited them quite regularly. On one occasion there was a long queue outside the Warner in Leicester Square. We were at the back. With wonderful inspiration Dave Parker, who was wearing a handmade black barathea double-breasted suit, stepped to the front of the queue and directed them to one side, at the same time waving us through. It was a magic moment. Even the staff thought he was someone in charge and issued us tickets.

Then there was the Lyceum ballroom. Sometimes on Saturday nights, which was very formal, I remember Billy Tennant's band filling in on one occasion for Oscar Rabin and applying strict rules on dancing. Only waltzes and quicksteps and the like were allowed. Tennant refused to play to jiving or any form of casual dress. After one visit they never saw us again until Oscar returned with his lively jazz style.

Sunday at the Lyceum was great. Jiving was the in-form of dancing – as opposed to the despised raucous, limb-mangling, jitterbugging performed to traditional jazz in the unwholesome abysses of the un-cool. The afternoon jazz club and evening sessions in the Lyceum were often taken in on the same day, and not just for the music. Gangs from many areas met in uneasy peace. The Elephant Boys were the toughest and occupied the area to the right of the bandstand. There were contingents from east London. One led by Curly King was a huge gang of smartly tailored lads who masqueraded as villains and crowded into the space to the left of the bandstand. Any time trouble erupted they were most agile in cramming through the doors to get out: they were good fun, but couldn't fight to save their lives.

I read with interest lately the memoirs of Kray firm member Albert Donoghue: a reference to Curly King described him as 'King of the Teddy Boys'. It's true that Curly wore the velvet collar and Edwardian-style suits fashionable at the time, but even he didn't wear the cheap lurid clothes of the authentic Teddy boys. Albert says he 'leaned' on Curly, who had been bullying some old boy. This reminded me that the Press once labelled Tony Reuter 'King of the Teddy Boys' just to make a good story. I wonder what would have happened if Albert had chastised the wrong 'king'. Tony was the sort who would swallow you whole and spit out the pips, if he was having one of his charitable days. Curly was a joke, but, as I say, good fun.

Fights were not very numerous in the Lyceum. Isolated incidents were often between local lads and American servicemen who tried to act out Humphrey Bogart roles. I remember a good fight in the gallery in which we got involved. Chairs were showered down on a bunch of American servicemen who were trapped in the front row of the gallery. The only way out for two of them was over the top, a terrifying drop on to the edge of the dance-floor. Both were badly hurt. To give the Yanks their due, they had a go. In one personal quarrel I was attacked by three Americans after a squabble over a girl. I collected a split lip before receiving help from my friends. I had clung on to a large American lumberjack lookalike and was wrestling with him when Dave punched him in the back of the neck and put us both on the floor. Dave's timing was always good.

Both the Dumb-Dumb Boys, led by Pinkie, and the Hoxton Gang, led by Bobby Ramsey, were regulars at the Lyceum. Eric Morley, the eventual organiser of Miss World contests, was the manager. Bobby Ramsey was employed as a bouncer there and afterwards at the Locarno, Streatham, where he strutted around with a train of hangers-on including a one-time British Cruiser Weight boxing champion. Ramsey was a short, broad-shouldered ex-professional boxer who seemed as wide as he was tall. He mixed with the West End mobs, associating with Billy Hill's gang which claimed to control London's underworld and was constantly struggling with the other contender, Jack Spot. Ramsey had fled South Africa after he and Hill had cut up the local Jo'burg boys with machetes and razors. Like Spot, Hill recruited his heavies from southeast and east London. Ramsey's toughness was not in doubt: he kept things in the Lyceum reasonably quiet.

In one of our sillier moods the Elephant Boys invented a daft game called 'got you at it'. In the relaxed atmosphere of the Lyceum we would rap the back of the neck of one of our colleagues by placing the back of one hand on his neck and smacking it with the other hand. When they spun round snorting for action, a shout of 'Got you at it' cooled the atmosphere and sometimes got a laugh – although it could be practised to a point where tempers frayed. It was a sort of 'chicken'. You could dice with death by picking on a tough guy. I once got Steve Reyburn a real stinging blow and he

nearly put one on me. This gave me a sort of kudos with the boys, although I must confess that Steve liked me and I guessed he would tolerate the insult. He weighed about sixteen stone to my eleven and a half and although he was a good mate he was entirely unpredictable. He turned and as I spluttered out the words I saw the sudden venom in his eyes. Because he was big I'd given him a fair old whack and, though he let it go, we could all see he was smarting.

He had to go one better. Bobby Ramsey was dancing near the edge of the dance-floor. Suddenly, thwack! Ramsey spun round and Steve looked him straight in the eye, 'Got you at it.' In a silent Lyceum, Ramsey swallowed hard: he had a position of importance, his mates were looking on, what would he do? Was it to be a battle of the titans? He glimpsed that wicked look in Steve's eyes. 'All right, Steve, you got me,' said Bobby and he carried on dancing. Steve was a strange one. Because I had upset him and he couldn't quite figure out what to do about it, he upbraided the toughest person he could find. Tough as Ramsey was, I think he made a sound decision. But I was nearly the cause of mayhem that afternoon.

Ramsey damaged his reputation when he beat up some small-timer in the Locarno, Streatham. The boy apparently thought he was tough and for some reason threatened Bobby with a split tonic bottle. Ramsey really gave him a beating. Those who saw it reckon he took a 'right liberty'. Later he ran with the Krays until Ronnie gave him a good hiding. Ramsey had a go at, or had beaten up, a popular East End ex-boxer who was a much lighter weight than the burly Ramsey. Ronnie took umbrage and laid into Ramsey who covered up and took his punishment. He stayed on the scene and could be seen at boxing galas and sporting dinners. But his heavy days were over and finally he faded to obscurity.

Pinkie gave me my worst fright up to that time. He was a hefty, gingery-haired albino with a fearsome reputation. The small gang he led were all deaf and dumb; each one wore a light grey tailored suit and they did the rounds of the jazz clubs and ballrooms. Apparently they picked up the rhythms through vibrations. It was in a packed Flamingo Club in Wardour Street that Dave Parker spotted Pinkie. We were just inside the doorway close to the bar, unable to squeeze into the crowded club. Dave pointed him out to me with a warning not to stare. Naturally I stared. At that, Pinkie started towards me through the crowd. I attempted to shout to Dave but my voice pitched so high it disappeared. So too did Pinkie, straight out the door. I still vividly recall his advance towards me, my moment of panic, and my shameful silence afterwards. Years later Pinkie was being sought for questioning in a shooting. I'm not sure if the murder warrant was served; at that time he was said to be residing in Spain.

Tough as they were, though, the Dumb-Dumbs made a mistake by tackling some of the Elephant Boys in the Lyceum. The ruckus continued outside and a fight started. The Dumb-Dumbs were forced to flee and one of them was overtaken on Waterloo Bridge where he was dangled over the parapet in an attempt to get him to speak.

The Lyceum closed as tastes changed and the magnificent palace with its art deco design was allowed, sadly, to decay. It has now been restored as a theatre and is much the same as it was before. Without the gangs of course.

Barry Reyburn was as solid as an oak. There would be little point in hitting him – it would just bounce off. He was as unpredictable as his brother Steve and, when in one of his mischievous moods, 'a man to leave well alone'. Not everybody had the sense to do that. One such was a relative of the well-known escaper Alfie Hinds. Alfie, accused of breaking open the safe of Maples Furnishing Store in Tottenham Court Road, became a celebrity in the late 1950s through twice escaping from court and prison. His relative chose a different way to make his name. He confronted Barry in a snooker club in Leicester Square. The story went round the Lyceum shortly after it happened.

Barry was playing snooker. His tease and companions were occupying another table, playing doubles. For some reason, jogging of cue arms took place and glances were exchanged – at which, either in ignorance or suicidal courage, the uneducated one decided to push it beyond the point of Barry's patience. Playfulness turned to petulance when Barry broke his cue over his head, laying him out. Outnumbered, he ran from the club pursued by ten or more of the man's friends. Those who saw it said Barry ran around a corner, pulled up, and turned on his pursuers as they came round after him. Bosh, wallop, bosh! According to witnesses, they were

ELEPHANT BOYS

lying all over the place. Those who managed to get in a punch could do nothing: he just got among them and dropped those that didn't run. He was a terror and as tough as they come. Like Steve he would walk away if he couldn't be bothered to fight. Those of us who had seen him in action couldn't believe stories that he hid in the toilet in the Imperial Billiard Hall when two heavies came looking for him. Some say it was the Krays who were growing their reputations at that time. Barry already had his reputation; perhaps he just couldn't be bothered.

At the Elephant, top punchers, as they were known, came from families like the Garretts, Carters, Reyburns, Richardsons, Roffs and Brindles. There were also individuals such as Boy Boy Stanford, Danny Irving, Frankie Fraser and Bonker Hammond. A family from East Lane, the Pastionis, were a tough crowd. Tony was a broad-shouldered swarthy puncher. He was not a gangster, but could he fight. On one occasion we were approaching Camberwell Green on foot from the direction of Walworth Road. We walked into another group of boys not known to us and some jostling and insults were exchanged. Their leader suggested that he and one of ours settled it on behalf of the two groups. We put up Tony. They went behind the Regal cinema in Camberwell Road. In a few minutes Tony came back with this dishevelled bundle in his arms and laid it on the pavement. It was settled.

One of the Pastionis could lift two hefty men above his head, one in each fist. Gino, the eldest, was as strong as a horse. I saw him throw a chair with his teeth from a café in Portland Street to the Mason's Arms around the corner in East Lane. Gripping the chairback in his teeth he hurled it till it stopped bouncing, then picked it up again. It took three throws. Some just liked being tough; others chose to become leading lights in the West End underworld.

The West End gangs have a long, long history. Protection, gambling, prostitution and drinking clubs have been their main activities. Prostitution was governed mainly by foreign imports such as the Messinas. The other rackets had been pioneered by a succession of London gangs. Billy Kimber had a connection with many drinking and gambling clubs, supported by Bert, Wal and Jim McDonald.

For a bookie to set up around London's dog- and horseracing

ELEPHANT BOYS

courses he had to pay a 'rent' for his pitch and a service fee for the bucket and sponge to clean his chalk board between races. For this he received protection. Without protection the boys would turn over his stall and frighten him from his pitch. Protection didn't always work. Billy Kimber, the hardnut from the Elephant (and later the Midlands) considered the London pitches came within his domain and employed some heavies from the Elephant to watch over his interests. They would chiv a bookie who was paying tribute to the encroaching Sabinis. Many bookies paid twice, but it was getting out of hand as other gangs – particularly the White Brothers and the Cortesis – also began to squeeze an affluent source. Darby Sabini sought overall control by persuading the Whites and Jewish heavies to join him. It was then that Kimber got wounded in a shooting scrape when he objected to the new arrangements. Alf White saw the way things were going and added his own personal strength to Darby's.

Darby Sabini pulled many lone operators together to form his racecourse gang. There was even a time when Kimber, Wag and the Sabinis and Cortesis were friends. Darby was a first-class organiser and had a sweet set-up around all the London horseracing courses. A number of villains got their juvenile starts with Darby's outfit, including Italian Albert Dimes, Frankie Fraser, Lennie Garrett and Johnny Carter. Darby was supposed to have gained his reputation by beating up the leader of the then Elephant Gang, a thug named Monkey Bennyworth. My problem here is that I've never come across anyone who ever heard of Monkey.

(Aunt Ada reckoned the confusion was with the Bennewith family who ran an organised auto burglary business. They would steal cars, drive to a warehouse – usually cloth or made-up garments – break in and fill several cars and vans with the proceeds. She remembered Will and Jim Bennewith, but no one called Monkey, which is a horseracing term. Ada said the Bennewiths were all big lads who could look after themselves but were not part of the Elephant gang. They lived at the Borough from where they mounted raids into the City and West End.)

Darby Sabini's strength was in his organisation and his ability to attract hard men to support him and stay with him. This was something Jack Spot failed to realise the importance of at a later date. When Darby retired after internment during the Second World War, his brother Harryboy took over and strengthened his

ELEPHANT BOYS

alliance with Alf White. Alf still commanded a lot of support in Hoxton and Islington. Gradually Alf's sons took over. Led by Harry White, they could not maintain the same loyalties. They were overthrown in 1947 by Jack Spot, Johnny Carter and their henchmen Billy Hill and Jock Russo in a sprawling battle involving scores of combatants. Advising Spot was Wal McDonald, by now in his sixties and a sort of gangster emeritus. It was his last fling. Clubs were smashed and there were some severe beatings. A bad rumpus in Jermyn Street saw one or two ears cut off and a few guns fired, which caused a stir as shooters were fairly rare fifty years ago. The Whites were driven back to their stronghold in King's Cross and the Angel and even there took a pasting.

Harry White told his story to a pal on the *Daily Herald* and was frank enough to admit he was scared of Spot. The article is too sympathetic to Harry, who acquiesced with Spot's badgering of point-to-point bookies and maintained his own business interests at the tracks with Spot's help. It is also a good example of how much the Press detested Spot. Harry was nowhere near as tough as his old man, Alf, and was in danger of being pushed aside by young tearaways. At least Spot allowed him a percentage of earnings; others would have driven him off. He interestingly notes that his dad used to take two pounds a time as a contribution from bookies to help manage the events. I'll bet he did, for it was a nice little earner. Spot pushed it up to seven pounds, no doubt allowing for the ravages of inflation.

For a while Spot and Hill ran dozens of spielers in the West End and took percentages from many others. They were pulling in hundreds of pounds a week and enjoying their reputations as bosses of London's underworld. It was not long before they fell out. Perhaps it was only possible to have one boss. Those of us hanging around the drinking clubs and spielers could see a rift developing: both were showing signs of jealousy, though I have to say that I thought it was more down to Billy Hill, who was being carried away by his belief in the image which the newspapers were building around him.

In a bid for supremacy Hill recruited lieutenants from west, north and east London. Shepherd's Bush and Islington, particularly, provided strong support. Albert Dimes was to throw in with Hill and bring with him the likes of Battles Rossi and Johnny Rice. These were remnants of the Sabini Gang and all had Anglo-

Italian backgrounds. Dimes was Alberto Dimeo. Rice was Ricco.

Dimes had been involved in the 1941 killing of Harry 'Little Hubby' Distleman. This incident followed a brawl in the Old Cue Club in Frith Street, Soho, that had left Distleman's friend Eddie Fletcher needing stitches. Little Hubby, Eddie and others had made a return visit and started to smash the place up – bringing the manager, Antonio Babe Mancini, from the cellar. Babe, another dreg of the Sabini crowd with a history of wounding and general bad behaviour, launched a frenzied attack on Little Hubby and his friends, spotting the walls and ceiling with blood as he slashed away with his dagger. Although he was supported by Dimes and others, most of the damage was actually inflicted by the excitable Babe. He finished it off by plunging his six-inch dagger into the chest of Little Hubby, who proceeded to thresh about in a desperate attempt to reach the street. On doing so he died.

Albert Dimes escaped with a caution for unlawful wounding, although he was returned to the RAF from which he had deserted. It was a time when we were at war with Italy: Babe got the shortest of shrifts at his trial, then took the longest of walks to the gallows. Years later it emerged that Mancini was offered a reduced conviction for manslaughter if he pleaded guilty, but he was so convinced he'd be acquitted of murder that he refused the offer. Whoops!

Jack Spot, real name Sam Comer (some say Comacho), was a Jew. He put it about that he was called Jack Spot because he was always on the spot when there was trouble. The truth is more humdrum. He had a mole on his lower left cheek, which led to his being called 'spotty' as a child. It would not have been a good idea to call him that when fully grown – although he was quite content with Jack or Jack Spot which had the flavour of American gangsterism. In some ways the London gangs mirrored the gangs of New York in the 1920s and '30s which were made up mainly from Italian, Jewish and Irish immigrants (although the Irish never got so much as a toehold in London).

From Whitechapel, east London, Jack had gained his reputation protecting Jewish traders and, according to him, by leading them against Mosley's Blackshirts. Much of his trade he learned from Dodger Mullins. Jack was a big, hefty fellow with a punch like a mule's kick and a dexterity with the razor that was legendary: a stripe down the cheek or under the chin, or from one cheek, under

ELEPHANT BOYS

the chin, and up the other, delivered to order. He invented the practice of striping a razor down the side of a leg and around the buttocks so his victim feared to sit down in case the stitches came open.

Even though he extorted money from his own, they loved Jack. Probably it was because he crushed smaller gangs from West Ham and the Mile End Road and the loners who had a habit of demanding cash from shopkeepers in lieu of a beating. Many traders did not trust the police, or had something to hide, so they turned to Jack. To move into the West End he had recruited a strong army from the Elephant, including such notables as Lennie and Jimmy Garrett, Johnny Carter, Bobby Brindle and Frannie Daniels – a really tough crowd who had outgrown the Elephant and Castle.

With this top team Jack was in a very strong position. He held court in the Beargarden lounge of the Cumberland Hotel in Oxford Street where he became an object of interest for the Press and villains alike. It was the 'thing' to be seen having a cup of coffee with the boss: it oozed Al Capone and infuriated Billy Hill, who had grand plans for himself. Billy also considered himself boss and decided to set up a similar situation in a hotel in Bayswater, the Royal Lancaster, I think. The hotel didn't take kindly to his posturing. He was in the habit of turning up with his well-suited and hatted minders. Bobby Ramsey always preceded him through the entrance; then Billy, often accompanied by Frannie Daniels, would saunter in flanked by bodyguards, two of whom were well-known professional boxers.

Some of us went to visit Billy and were the cause of great consternation for the management. We arrived early one Saturday morning for Billy's expected arrival at 11 a.m. We passed suspicious doormen and headed for the lounge, only to find a couple of dozen others had got there before us but were being prevented from entering. There was a genial uproar as the lads jostled the management and it was quite humorous until somebody chucked a big marble ashtray across the room and caused the men in charge to start yelling 'Phone the police'. The lads then congregated on the step outside where they circled about, refilling any spaces made by the management who were trying to open a pathway. In amongst all this a taxi pulled up and a little American with an enormous hat got out. I shouted 'Here's

Billy!' The poor fellow was surrounded, slapped on the back, his hat pushed over his eyes, hand luggage grabbed and passed up the sloping drive, then somebody touched him up and he was left in a state of complete bewilderment. Then we all strolled into Hyde Park and along the path to Hyde Park Corner before dispersing. Some of us went over to the Cumberland, hoping to see Jack, but he wasn't there and Billy Hill hadn't shown up at the Royal Lancaster either.

Later Jack made a show of free drinks in the bar of the Cumberland for some of the boys. The barman, Alex, named a cocktail Jack Boss. It was a Manhattan made with Scotch whisky and French vermouth (there was a standing joke that anyone ordering a Manhattan had better not expect Italian vermouth when Jack was around).

There was a respite when Hill went to live in his fabulous residence in Tangier, running the occasional yacht-load of contraband – ciggies, not drugs – over to Gib and Spain. He foreran the now well-developed industry of British villains in their sunny lairs. Eventually his yacht, the *Flamingo*, sank in mysterious circumstances.

Jack promoted a policy of paying twenty pounds a week to the wife of any of his team who went to prison in his service. His mistake was in not paying it. When Lennie Garrett received five years for laying out a policemen (with a pair of Stillsons he kept strapped to his wrist for just such a purpose), Jack failed to come up with the dosh. 'My boy, you wasn't working for me was you? I didn't ask you to do a copper did I, you know what I mean.' Jack couldn't have written their contracts too clearly: when Lennie came out, he deserted Spot and brother Jimmy went with him.

The Garretts could operate very well on their own. Frankie Fraser changed sides and became Billy Hill's top man. This left Johnny Carter and Bobby Brindle. Things went from bad to worse for Spot. The Carters and Brindles fell out with each other. This is the way I heard it: Jimmy Brindle had beaten up young Nicky Carter. Johnny got to hear of it before Bobby Brindle had got word. Johnny asked Bobby for a lift home. Bobby obliged, dropping Johnny near his home. Johnny was walking away when he turned and went back to the car. Bobby wound down his window to see what Johnny wanted. Johnny gave Bobby a stripe down his cheek. 'Give that to your brother,' said Johnny. Jimmy Brindle was married to Eva,

ELEPHANT BOYS

Frankie Fraser's sister. Frank then had the needle with the whole Spot outfit and worked on Hill to do them once and for all.

After the *Flamingo* sank in July 1954 Hill decided to put together a team to control all of the West End and the districts of London, right out to the suburbs. Backing him was Billy Howard. Although Spot was enraged, he failed to understand the strength Hill was building around him. Hill put out feelers around the Elephant and a number of 'meets' were made in West End pubs. We all waited our turn. Mine came in late 1954, when I accompanied Johnny Carter and Lennie Garrett, in company with Dave Morbin and a few others.

Hill bought the drinks in the Bath House in Soho's Dean Street, where he had laid on a tasty buffet. *People* crime reporter Duncan Webb sat close by and Carter became suspicious that he was being set up for one of Webb's exposés. Johnny was not impressed by Hill's talk of organisation and he was not convinced that the gangs could act together. To do so they would have to bury too many differences, he said. Lenny Garrett tried to calm him. However, as soon as Hill said that Frank Fraser had come over to him, Carter wanted to fight everybody. He gave Webb a nasty tongue-lashing and we all watched as Lenny, then Billy, tried to steer him away from Webb's table – I say steer, because it was not going to be a good idea for anybody to get hold of him. Hill only had Slip and Sonny Sullivan with him, all too knowing to take on Carter when he was like this.

Carter was adamant that the best way to run London was to put the frighteners on everyone who wouldn't pay. He didn't want the ponces (his word for the fence, safecrackers, pickpockets and con men) that Hill associated with calling the shots. He could see Hill in the background raking in the money while the soldiers did the work and the bird. Carter was at odds with everyone – Fraser, Howard, Frannie Daniels (whom he had recently threatened to put in cement). He thought Spot had the right idea: chiv any bastard that didn't 'come along'. He was openly contemptuous of Hill's 'Mafia connections'. The story going around was that Hill and Dimes had been to Paris to meet with representatives of Meyer Lansky, said to be Tommy Lucchese and Vincent Teresa.

It was an embarrassing episode. Carter stormed out and we followed him. To remain would have looked as though we were backing Hill in a coming battle with Spot. We made gestures to Hill that indicated we had better go. A shrug of the shoulders when Johnny's back was turned said as much. For me it was a toss-up between Johnny and the buffet, but safety prevailed. Lenny Garrett and Dave Morbin went back in. Lenny could act as an individual without any comeback. He was too dangerous for anyone to mess with.

Carter went to the Galahad Club in Charlotte Street and nearly chinned the manager when he objected to his language. I persuaded him into a taxi and went off to buy a spaghetti to replace the tasty buffet I had missed out on. Webb went off to write a 'spectacular' on Billy Hill, the Boss of London's Underworld.

Hill's plans rapidly fell apart. Spot resented Duncan Webb's backing of Billy Hill, so he broke his writing arm as an *aide-mémoire* to who really was the guv'nor. Then Slip Sullivan had his ribs tickled with a two-foot-long carving knife and we all thought Johnny had been busy. It was a great relief when we heard it was entirely domestic: Slip's volatile Irish wife had been responsible for his sudden departure.

Spot and Carter now went looking for Billy Hill. Instead, they found Scotch Jack Buggy – a nasty fellow from Kentish Town, but said to have been born in the United States. In support of Spot and Hill, Buggy had partnered Scarface Jock Russo in the battle to overthrow the Whites. Like Russo, he had connections to Glasgow gangs and tried to grab a piece of the Soho protection rackets; unlike Russo, he was not well enough connected to any London gangs who could protect him. He had to choose which way to go. He did not choose wisely when he decided to cultivate Billy Hill.

Crafty Hill publicly recruited Buggy to go after Jack Spot. When we came on him lurking outside the Galahad Club it was common knowledge that he was out to fill a contract on Jack. I walked right into him. Buggy pulled a revolver from his overcoat pocket and pointed it at my face. Vividly I remember the metallic click as it failed to go off. He fled, but he couldn't outpace me. I brought him down by grabbing the belt at the back of his overcoat. Spot and some others came up and one of them ran a knife down Scotch Jack's face and thighs, the only parts not covered by his heavy overcoat. The road was busy, so we left him there. In time he limped back to Glasgow. He returned some years later, still making a nuisance of himself. It was his body that was found bobbing around in the sea off Seaford, Sussex, after he was shot, some say, on the orders of Albert Dimes.

Hill now made noises about his alliance with the Italian mob from Clerkenwell, claiming to be in charge of the biggest team in London. With that Carter did up Billy Blyth, Hill's emissary to the Italians, and Spot gave Dimes's follower Tommy Warren a good kicking. It was looking increasingly nasty for Hill, who was also being investigated for putting up the Jockey Fields job, where a KLM Dutch Airline's bullion van had been hijacked (relieving the company of £45,000 of untraceable gold). Hill may have put up some money, although word was that it was Billy Howard.

Hill, who had dumped his wife Aggie, decided with Gypsy, his new consort – who frightened me more than he did – to emigrate to Australia. They should have checked first: they would have found that Webb's chronicling of Hill's exploits had made him a celebrity in the Antipodes, so the authorities stamped their passports 'return to sender' and they were back in no time.

By this time Spot was without any realistic support, but he didn't know it and he was tough. I'd been listening to morning rehearsals in the Flamingo jazz club in Wardour Street, after which I decided to walk to a drinking club in Rathbone Place where I knew I could get a drink and probably join in a game of poker. As I was getting there, Jack came out of Charlotte Street. With that big beaming smile, he clapped a huge arm round my shoulder, squeezed my arm with his big fist that had fingers the size of a bunch of Fyffes bananas, and steered me back down Rathbone Place. By now he did not like to go anywhere alone. He wanted to buy me a salt beef sandwich: would I walk with him to Shaftesbury Avenue? I agreed, none too enthusiastically.

I remember every step of that walk. Out of Rathbone Place, across Oxford Street, through Soho Square, Jack nodding to this and that, and me bestowing recognition with a wave of a hand to a loafer here and a toady there. Then into Frith Street. As we were getting there, Spot saw Italian Albert Dimes. Albert had recently declined to pay Jack for use of a bookie's pitch. He'd also given Jack's wife Rita a bit of sauce – not a good idea. Without a word, Jack was across the road. After an exchange of swearing, he put one right on Dimes's chin. Italian Albert went down like a sack of potatoes. As Spot went to give him a few kicks, Johnny Rocca grabbed him around the waist and tried to pull him off. I had to get involved – if I didn't all my respect would have gone with everyone – so I jumped on Rocca and we pranced around like a

ELEPHANT BOYS

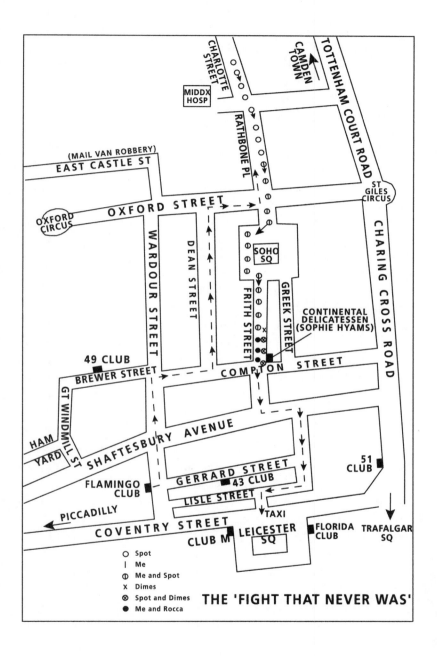

THE 'FIGHT THAT NEVER WAS'

Legend:
- O Spot
- | Me
- ⊕ Me and Spot
- x Dimes
- ⊗ Spot and Dimes
- ● Me and Rocca

couple of old-time dancers, not really wanting to mix it. He kept screaming at me, 'Are you in this? Are you in this?'

Spot dragged Dimes up and whacked him again. Dimes, half stumbling, half being shoved, went through the doorway into the Continental Delicatessen on the corner of Frith and Old Compton Streets. Rocca and me swapped a few blows. He said, 'Turn it up, what's all this about?' I replied, 'I only came here for a salt beef sandwich.'

Inside the shop the proprietor, Sophie Hyams, a game old girl, had grabbed the scales – not the pan, but the heavy cast iron stand – and hit Jack on the head, splitting his scalp open. A knife had come from somewhere and both Spot and Dimes were leaking blood. We watched as Dimes slumped in the doorway and Jack stumbled out of the shop and sat on the pavement. Hands tried to pull him up, but he was too heavy. Then he pulled himself up and crashed through the doorway of an Italian barber's, of all places.

Then it was police, ambulances, the whole works. Rocca and I took a calculating look at the scene and each other, then legged it. A few friends of mine had gathered and they followed me down to Leicester Square, where they put me in a taxi directed to the Borough. Dimes was also put into a taxi although he was badly hurt. Spot was taken away by ambulance to Middlesex Hospital.

When arraigned for making an affray, Spot and Dimes set up a classic defence strategy. The police conveniently reported Jack as saying, 'Why only me? Albert did me and I get knocked off.' Albert was reported as saying, 'Spotty does me up and I get pinched. That can't be fair.' At their trials each blamed the other. No one knows where the knife came from: the delicatessen proprietor was sure it hadn't come from her store. Surely it must have been Dimes's weapon. Spot would have pulled it as he crossed the road, and besides, Dimes had behind him his part in the demise of Little Hubby Distleman. Both Spot and Dimes were acquitted of making an affray.

At this time I was known as Mac and to distinguish me from other Macs I was often referred to as Mac from the Elephant. This could be confusing because Freddie MacDermott was also called Mac from the Elephant – probably the name originated with him. He was not a villain, but had a reputation as a good fighter (some of his prowess was attributed to me, who shamelessly allowed it to boost my reputation). Suddenly the police were looking for a Mac, so I got pulled in and quizzed about my part in all this. Words like conspiracy are floating about. Conspiracy is a lock-up-and-throw-away-the-key job, so I was well pleased with Jack. Not many years later the police would charge the Great Train Robbers with conspiracy to rob the Royal Mail – a ruse to justify those extra-long sentences of thirty years for what was no more than an armed robbery that would usually carry a maximum of fifteen years. Anyway, apart from my 'reputation', the police weren't too interested in me and were satisfied that I wasn't the Mac involved in fixing the evidence for Spot. They gave me a caution and I believe Rocca got the same for his tango with me. He was a bookie, I suppose about fifteen years older than me; I saw him years later and we had a drink together. It was then that I realised fully just how much bigger than me he was.

Spot's wife Rita, Moisha Blueball (so named because of a shrunken appendage), Sonny the Yank and Peter 'Doughnut' MacDonough were done for conspiring to pervert the course of justice. They'd put up some dotty old parson to tell a cock-and-bull story to get Jack off and it had all come unstuck.

In the meantime it was all still happening . . . The Press had labelled it the Race Gang Wars – 'race' in those days referred to courses, not people. Dimes was a well-respected villain, something had to be done, but what about Johnny Carter? Johnny and brother Harry had been busy cutting up Hoppy Stan's and Charlie Knight's gang. They then found time to do Charlie Woodbridge, battered outside the Windsor in Garnies Street, Peckham, just for being a friend of the Brindles.

A few days later Frank Fraser, Dave Rosa and Dicky Dido (Richard Frett), all from the Elephant, and two others (one was probably Billy Blyth), lay in wait for one of their own outside the Tankerville Arms in Goda Street, Lambeth. As Johnny Carter, his wife Sheila and a friend were about to leave, they were rushed by Fraser and his crew. Johnny ran through the pub and out of another door. They caught up with him in the street, where he battled them for two hundred yards while being hacked and slashed. He ran into a building and slammed the door. They broke it down. He escaped into the bathroom. They broke in. Clubbed with a three-foot stopcock and cut with knives and razors, he managed to grab a knife from Frett and drove them out of the bathroom. When they'd gone he collapsed on the stairs. In hospital he collected sixty stitches.

Two days later Harry Carter was attacked by six men in Trundley's Road, Deptford. Harry ran into a fruiterer's and engaged them in a spectacular free-for-all – cucumbers and cabbages against starting handles. Still on his feet at the end of it, he told a passing Pressman, 'If there had been three or four of them I would have done them, but six is a bit too much, even for me. My younger brother Johnny will be returning from Glasgow in a few days and he will sort it out.'

It must have slipped Harry's mind that Johnny was recovering in hospital.

Spot was then returning to his flat in Hyde Park Mansions, off the Edgware Road, with Rita and a friend, when a dozen or so hard men – led by Frankie Fraser and including Hill and Dimes – attacked him with clubs, hammers and razors. He had no chance and received wounds requiring over one hundred stitches, a new record. Rita got a clout when she tried to help Jack.

Huge Press interest was aroused and the police acted swiftly. Johnny and Harry Carter were arrested for carving up Woodbridge. South London brothers Johnny and Benny Harris were picked up for the attack on Harry Carter. Fraser was arrested and charged with attacking Johnny Carter and then with attacking Spot. Carter's wife, who initially identified Frett and Rosa, then could not be sure; and, in a nice twist, the defence lawyer was not allowed to ask Carter if he was a member of a south London gang called the Elephant Boys. Not surprisingly, Frett and Rosa each received seven years for the attack on Johnny Carter. Fraser got seven years for the attack on Spot, but the other charge for attacking Carter was dismissed. Going down for seven with Fraser was 'innocent' Bobby Warren, promoter of up-and-coming street-fighter Lenny McLean. Billy Blyth got five years, while Battles Rossi and Billy Dennis drew four apiece. Dimes and Hill, conveniently, could account for their actions at the time of the attack.

Still it wasn't over. Tommy Falco, Billy Hill's chauffeur, complained that Spot had attacked him outside the Astor Club and slashed his arm. It turned out to be a put-up job. Hill's men had cut their own man in an attempt to put Spot away. A chilling thought for me is that Rocca was generally suspected of having done the cutting. Scarface Jock Russo, who had first agreed to be the victim, had changed his mind and when someone else stepped in he went to the police. Jock was a real hard man from Glasgow who, with

Spot, had played a prominent part in the White Gang's downfall. He was half Scots and half Italian, just like his cousin Albert Dimes.

All this ado didn't prevent Billy Hill and Frannie Daniels from buying up pitch concessions at race meetings. They simply did it through Billy Gilbert – a relative of the old-time villain Freddie Gilbert who, when questioned by a newspaper reporter, said they were 'very nice fellows'.

At this point it was difficult for me to decide what to do. I didn't know if I was in bad with Hill. After a fierce punch-up in the Number 11 Club in Frith Street, between the Italians and some of us who had gone there not looking for trouble, I decided to go to ground. When I emerged I tried as often as possible to be seen in the company of Eddie Richardson: he was growing in reputation in the West End and was being cultivated by Hill and Dimes, who needed to maintain the strength of their team. This team had lost not only Spot and Carter's attackers, but a number of others convicted of robbery, including George Moore (one of Billy Kimber's old team).

Billy Hill was a real West Ender, born at Seven Dials on the Holborn side of Leicester Square – in earlier years reminiscent of Fagin's habitat, and a stone's throw from Soho. He had the reputation of being London's premier gangster in the mid-1950s. He was a great self-propagandist who manipulated the Press very well. They liked him, whereas Spot was hated, especially as he beat up Hill's newspaper friend, *People* crime reporter Duncan Webb (who was as bent as any of the villains he wrote about). Spot had been fined fifty pounds for breaking Webb's arm, which he thought was value for money. Webb took solace in marrying Cynthia Hume, ex-wife of Donald Hume, a notorious murderer of the time.

Billy liked to spread stories about himself. Before the Great Train Robbery in 1963, the big raid had been the 1952 Eastcastle Street robbery. A Post Office mail van was tricked into stopping in the West End street, two cars filled with robbers swooped in and blocked its escape, the four crew were attacked and the van hijacked. When the van was found, it was minus £290,000, another new record. Billy allowed it to be broadcast that he was the mastermind. Curiously, the police accepted his story, but there is no record of them actually taking him seriously. When Bill was buying the drinks in his New Cabinet Club in Gerrard Street, people would eagerly listen. He was a shrewd, calculating thief; but I don't think the Eastcastle Street job was his.

The dispute between Billy Hill, as 'Boss of Britain's Underworld' (a title taken from a book ghosted for him by Duncan Webb) and Jack Spot, as 'King of Soho', became a wrangle between two villains rapidly getting past their best. They fought and re-fought their battles in the pages of the Sunday papers. Spot had his life story written by Hank Jansen as *Jack Spot – Man of a Thousand Cuts*. (The only copy I know of this is in Dublin's Trinity Library.) As a piece of history it was on a par with Webb's book about Billy Hill. Jansen was better known as a prolific writer of cheap-thrill detective books. Spot and Hill still await serious biographers.

Spot, after his slashing by Fraser and company, became a target for every villain out to make a name for himself. His clubs were broken up and his protection business melted away. Declared bankrupt, he never regained a prominent position in the underworld. Warned that an attempt by a 'Broadmoor inmate' to kill him or have him killed was serious, he took off. Heading first to Dublin, he then attempted to settle in Quebec, Canada, from where he was deported in September 1957. That was the end. He slipped into obscurity, told his story to whoever would listen and lives, sad and alone, bemoaning his lot. Meanwhile Billy Hill and his lawyer, Marrinan, suffered a prolonged bout of phone tapping and police surveillance which finally curtailed Billy's business activities. He died in 1984.

For Johnny Carter it was all downhill too. He and brother Harry were attacked in a pub in the Old Kent Road. Outside, Harry had his leg broken and Johnny had to jump into the canal to escape. Scores were being settled and he got done a few more times before he, too, faded away. His best days were well behind him. At one time he was raking in money from bookies in New Cross dog stadium, extorting protection from clubs in south London and the West End, and receiving pay as a heavy for Jack Spot. I remember him well from the Smithson incident and I can understand why it took so many to do him when he was at his best. The last occasion I saw him was at a restaurant in Greenwich. Part way through a meal with friends, we were interrupted by an argument between two men at a nearby table. A fight developed which was more like a choreographed ballet as they pranced about, tipping over tables and generally smashing the crockery. As they left, Johnny arrived and stood silhouetted in the doorway: he had on an almighty stetson perched over his scarred face. It was an obvious message to the proprietor that this is what happens if you haven't got protection. Thankfully he didn't see me. Like Wyatt Earp, he died with his boots off, no doubt still wanting to fight everybody.

My own career as a gangster had taken an abrupt turn when I met my wife-to-be, Gillian, at William Jones Clifton in 1958. Up to that point I had constantly been involved in battles against an assortment of gangs. Coincidentally, we were at that time still at war with the Angel gang, and the very place where I sometimes met my girlfriend was at the Angel. She lived in Canonbury, Islington.

For company, I carried a heavy brass imitation Luger which I had obtained from Brian Howliss (I'd fought him along with Billy Mitchell some years before). The gun was believed to have been fashioned by a German prisoner in the Second World War and had somehow got into the hands of Brian's Dad. When Brian showed it off around the square, I just told him I was having it, and I did. It was a yellowy colour, but quite realistic from a few yards away – although if it was shoved in front of someone's face it would have been recognised as a fake and would have to have been simply a cosh.

After a year of all this, I decided I preferred to be at peace with my neighbours and make a commitment to my future life. So in a symbolic gesture, I hurled the Luger over the railings of Islington's New River Walk into the narrow stream. It was more than a weight off my mind. The thing weighed a ton, tucked into my trousers under my shirt. It was cold, too.

ELEPHANT BOYS

14. THE SOUTH LONDON FIRM

Hill gradually gave way to the Richardsons. Later the Krays came into the picture. It has to be said that all the time the Richardsons were in the West End the Krays were never more than visitors from their own manor in the East End. There are those who say there never was any strife between the Richardsons and the Krays. This is not so. A number of incidents occurred in the 1960s and were set to continue.

The Richardsons had the position of strength: they were better organised and more intelligent than the Kray firm. Eddie, backed by Albert Dimes, had established Atlantic Machines, installing one-armed bandits into clubs, shops and gambling haunts. The Krays were envious, but kept their distance. They had thought of themselves as next in line for power in the West End and were unaware of Eddie Richardson's depth of presence.

They decided to find out and made a probe into the family business in New Church Road, Camberwell. They asked a team of four, led by one of their henchmen, south Londoner and future Great Train Robber Charlie Wilson, to survey the premises of Peckford Scrap Metals and 'talk to the boys'. They questioned Roy Hall; then, convinced he was just a labourer, moved from the office to the yard, at which it is said Eddie appeared with a carboy of acid and a purposeful expression on his face. This encouraged the four interlopers to make a rapid retreat. It was the only occasion any of the Kray firm and their associates are known to have forayed into the yard.

Soon after that, Frankie Fraser was made a partner in Atlantic Machines – a shrewd move by the Richardsons. Not only was Frankie a south Londoner, but he had earned a reputation in the 1950s as London's premier hard man. He was the sort who would attack a buzz-saw if he had a mind to. Completely fearless, volatile and dangerous, he was never put off by the reputations of others and was not afraid to have back-up to make sure he won. Not a big man in build – he had the disadvantage of being only five feet six inches tall – he was nevertheless quite capable of taking on much larger opponents. To bring down Johnny Carter, he brought in the likes of Dave Rosa and Dicky Frett, both extremely dangerous and vicious men. Even though Carter gave them a good fight, he collected sixty-plus stitches.

For Spot, a dozen or more of them waited in the shadows and gave him no chance. Even though he was without friends Spot was still a dangerous man. Frankie allowed him no possibility of flight. This ruthless streak made him palatable to the Krays. They invited him for talks, yet he decided to team up with the Richardsons: proof that he always went with the strength.

Much of the strife had involved bookies cutting each other up. More trouble was to come. The advent of betting shops, in 1960, brought the street bookies from their street corners and darkened rooms into the legitimate world. New industries sprang up – one of which was protection for betting shops and one-armed bandits installed in betting shops and clubs. Within the latter Eddie Richardson developed his flourishing business of supplying fruit machines. He didn't need to charge protection: the fact they were Eddie's machines was sufficient to deter would-be safeguarders.

A favourite watering-hole of the Richardsons was the Astor Club, in Grosvenor Square, where they could mix with celebrities and artful wheeler-dealers who knew every means of double-dealing and business chicanery ever invented. It was here that Kray man Eric Mason's friends attacked Glaswegian Jimmy Boyle and his pals, knocking one of them out – apparently not realising they were guests of the Richardsons. Eric's reward was a good hiding, then a ride to a run-down building where he was given more of the same and had his hand pinned to his head with an axe. After his re-education Eric was tidied up and dropped off at hospital and told not to be a naughty boy again, a chastisement fully accepted by the Kray firm.

It was in the Astor that George Myers, better known as George Cornell, called Ronnie Kray a fat poof. Later he set about Ronnie in an East End pub, right on Ronnie's doorstep, and gave him a good walloping. Ronnie brooded and after the Richardsons were banged up he shot Cornell to death in the Blind Beggar pub in the Mile End Road. I knew Cornell, he was one hardnut, and it is typical of him to be on Kray territory. I think he was such an embarrassment to Ronnie that he just had to go.

Long firm fraud, not invented by Charlie Richardson, but certainly perfected by him, became big business. It was brilliantly simple. Go to suppliers, order and pay for goods – usually toiletries, which are easily shifted – to set up a trading relationship. Then order the big one on credit and disappear; flog the goods through hundreds of small shops dealing in general goods and pocket the money. Wide boys will always find something to latch on to. The police, pushed by public and politicians, launched periodical blitzes on gangs. They worked their way through the Spot and Hill–Dimes gangs, only to be faced with the Nashes, Richardsons, Krays and several other clever outfits. The Richardsons were the brightest. The Krays and Nashes let their feuds become too public, although to give the police credit they eventually got them all. The Richardsons were really stitched up by the police, but that's part of the game.

If you have been brought up on bomb sites and scratched out a life, inevitably you become sharp-witted. Add to that an ability to fight and your emergence as a leader is assured. I knew Eddie Richardson when he was a stonecleaner. I was in the car behind him when he turned his Mark 2 Jaguar over at the foot of Shooter's Hill and helped lift it so he could get his leg free. In his company I learned how to push a lighter refill cylinder up the exhaust pipe of a car and how to let down tyres by dropping a piece of grit into the valve cap and screwing it back on (when the cap was removed the grit fell out and the reason for the flat was assumed to be a puncture; horribly, we would do more than one tyre, for maximum inconvenience).

When our wages had been exhausted by a Friday night's binge of merriment and gambling, we earned ten bob for a Saturday morning's work shovelling coal into sacks at an Old Kent Road depot. Eddie, Terry Kelly and others would always finish before me, then fill my spare sacks so I got my full whack. You learn to

ELEPHANT BOYS

appreciate mates like that. I'm convinced he saved my life on at least one occasion. My fondest memory of him is when we both were hard up and he broke in half his last cigarette to share with me, as I often did with him. He could be extremely good natured and great fun to be with.

Sharp-witted is no exaggeration. The Heathrow Airport scam is a good example. Car park attendants at the airport had devised a system of altering times stamped on parking tickets. So many were involved, and so much was taken out of the car parks, that they were earning between them half as much as the car parks authority: £1,000 a week went into the pockets of the cunning collectors. But someone talked, as always happens, and someone was listening, said to have been a Brindle, and where goes a Brindle there is a Richardson nearby. Soon Eddie called upon the talkative one for a donation. It took some threats and a few right-handers, but there was little choice other than to hand over half the earnings. This was typical of Eddie, climbing through a window of opportunity.

By now the police were looking hard at the Richardson operation. Eddie had been charged in Southport, Lancashire, with sticking a glass in the face of a club manager as encouragement to buy his machines. Eddie and Frank Fraser had also whacked a few bouncers as part of their business endeavours. Witnesses had come to court too terrified to give evidence and Eddie walked. Questions were asked in the House, while the Richardson portfolio at Scotland Yard expanded a few more pages. All this failed to inhibit the expansion of trade for Atlantic Machines. They were signing up clubs all over the country.

Stories of torture at Peckford's yard were circulating. Charlie had been holding court over his empire, which now stretched from his Park Lane offices to South Africa. There was a touch of megalomania about Charlie. Those who offended him were brought to the yard for chastisement, beatings, tooth-pulling, feet nailed to the floor, that sort of thing. Occasionally private parts were connected up to a dynamo which, when the handle was turned, sent a small current to those sensitive areas. For good measure it could be administered in a bath of cold water, but Charlie always cleaned everybody up afterwards – he was fastidious about this.

In later years a Kray firm member said he feared only Frank

Fraser. If that is true, he must never have taken the full measure of the Richardson team. Charlie and Eddie were ferocious fighters. I saw Eddie after he and Charlie had fought each other, and I've seen Eddie after numerous fights, but this was the worst I'd seen him look, with his puffed and bruised face. Apparently Charlie looked much the same. Backing them was Fraser, who had a chilling reputation. Then there was ex-docker Cornell, a brute of a person, scared of no one and an expert in the long firm business. The team also included Jimmy Moody and others with fearsome reputations. And of course they had on call everyone from the Elephant.

The fluidity of the Elephant Gang meant that they sometimes fought among themselves. The Richardsons had beaten up the Rosas, who had beaten up a Brindle. At the request of Billy Hill on behalf of Frankie Fraser (at that time sojourning in one of Her Majesty's hotels and unable to personally exact vengeance), Charlie, Eddie and some others walked into the Reform Club at the Elephant and Castle, where they smashed and battered the Rosas unconscious. It was a savage beating designed to give a serious message: don't mess with Fraser and the Brindles or they'll get you. The same Rosas had backed Fraser in his war with Johnny Carter and Jack Spot – it could all get a bit confusing – but the Rosas were quick to let it be known that their services were available to the Richardsons when required. Other families, such as the Callahans and Hendersons, were also on tap. However, it was a Henderson who inadvertently brought a premature end to the Richardson organisation. It came in typical Eddie Richardson style.

The place was Mr Smith and the Witchdoctor, a club occupying the premises of the old Savoy ballroom at Catford, south London. The club was splendid compared to the many seedy drinking clubs and spielers usually found south of the river. The owners also owned the night-club in Southport where Eddie had been accused of smashing a glass in the manager's face. Perhaps because of this, they thought he was the right man to protect the Catford club against undesirables. The opulence of the club attracted every bad man in south London who was used to after-hours drinking and expected the same service in Smiths.

An ugly atmosphere was developing in a good-class gaff. Second-rate teams were making patrons and management uncomfortable, police presence was out of the question, yet something had to be done. Eddie would certainly have considered the club within his

ELEPHANT BOYS

compass, although he would have seen it like the Astor – something upmarket that would attract showbiz people and the gentry. Gangsters like mixing in showbiz society, just as many performers and politicians like to be seen in the company of celebrated villains. Lord Boothby, Tom Driberg and Stanley Baker are the well-known examples, but there were so many. The Astor, in Grosvenor Square, was a full mix of the good, the bad and the downright ugly. I believe it was Eddie's intention to preserve Smith's appeal and that his services weren't so much sought as offered gratis.

One of the teams making a spectacle of themselves by their uncouth behaviour was Billy Haward's boys from Abbey Wood. They were a tough bunch, well known around Deptford and Lewisham. The insalubrious drinking and gambling holes in that locality attracted the low-life who couldn't yet make it in the brighter lights. Haward had pretentions. He had his own dive, minded a number of other spielers and was also looking to branch out. In his team was Peter Hennessey, one of a notorious south London family with a long history of violence and thievery. Peter had just come out of prison after serving six years of a ten stretch for burglary. Big and rough with a decidedly unpleasant disposition, he was hopelessly out of touch with current reality; but being eager to impress his associates with his prowess, he had become a loud-mouthed braggart. In the relaxed atmosphere of Smiths the primitive behaviour of Haward's team could not be tolerated. The management could do little to stop it, for such action would have been very risky. It has been suggested that the Richardsons were minding the club and that Haward's mob had deliberately (or in error) demanded protection money, causing Eddie to intervene. But I never heard it that way. More likely it was a word in Eddie's ear from the management, an offer of free drinks, and a hint of sanctuary, which would have been both sensible and appealing.

Trouble was clearly expected, at least by the Hawards. Billy had a sawn-off shotgun stuffed inside his jacket. Dickie Hart, an insidious hanger-on with the Krays and lately with Haward, had a .45 automatic. Others had knives and coshes. Word was being flashed around the neighbourhood that trouble was afoot and phones were hot with calls for reinforcements for both teams.

When drinking time expired, Hennessey decided he wanted

ELEPHANT BOYS

more and began to slag off the barmaid. Eddie told him 'No more', the evening was over. A prolific stream of abuse from the ignorant Hennessey was directed at Eddie. Such an affront was a shock to someone who accepted deference from others as entirely natural. The teams were evenly balanced: Eddie, Frank Fraser, Jimmy Moody, Harry Rawlins and Billy Staynton versus Haward, Hennessey, Hart, Billy Gardner and Henry Botton. It could have been off straight away but Eddie, riled by Hennessey's invective, invited him on to the dance-floor one-to-one. Hennessey accepted and jackets came off.

Within seconds Eddie had hammered Peter to the floor and was bent over him, banging in a few more punches. Haward tried to pull his sawn-off, which got caught up in his coat. Moody took a thick glass bar away from Botton and smashed it over Billy Haward's head, knocking him out. Hart panicked and fired his big calibre automatic, hitting Rawlins in the shoulder. In the following mêlée Hart shot Fraser in the leg and Botton fired one barrel of Haward's shotgun, peppering Eddie Richardson in the buttocks. Somehow Hart caught a bullet from his own gun and, near to death, staggered out into Farley Road. Friends of the Richardsons, who were arriving, received the balance of the shotgun by whoever was wielding it at that time. Pellets spattered about the roadway and lodged in clothing and footwear. New arrivals joined in the fighting, which had now spilled into the road outside. Over twenty people were embroiled in one big free-for-all. The dying Hart took a few kicks and gasped his last through a stoved-in face. Fraser, whose leg was broken, was helped over a garden wall and he lay in the shrubbery until later discovered by a policeman who trod on him. Moody, and another, bundled Eddie and the badly bleeding Rawlins into a car and dropped them off at hospital. Haward staggered from the scene, his gashed head pumping blood. Hennessey and Gardner crawled away into the night. Gardner had tried to calm things, but was forced into the fight when the guns came out to stop Haward's crowd getting a hiding.

Hart died soon after arriving in hospital and Fraser was charged with his murder. Although acquitted, he and Eddie received five years apiece for affray. Botton also received five and Haward, because of the gun, got eight years. Botton had pointed up Fraser for Hart's killing and liked to brag about it; he was a nasty piece of work and I had a quarrel with him when he came out. Years later

he was blasted to death on his own doorstep in a feud with other south London gangsters. Amazingly, Peter Hennessey was not charged, even though it was his mouthing-off which caused Eddie to straighten him. Hennessey went from bad to worse, finally slagging off some of the south London 'wild bunch' at a boxing dinner in a Kensington hotel; when it was all over he had multiple stab wounds and was finally quiet. Jimmy Moody was shot to death in the Royal Hotel pub in Hackney in 1993 by parties unknown, in a feud that is still going on. Billy Haward has recently gone back inside for an unorthodox bank withdrawal.

But before all that came the torture trial.

Eddie Richardson and Frank Fraser were brought from prison to join Charlie Richardson in the dock at the Old Bailey. There they faced numerous accusations of violence and extortion against a background of criminality and intrigue. Charlie's dealings in South African gold-mining had been 'exploded' in the newspapers after one of his men, Johnny Bradbury, had been tried for the murder of South African gold magnate Thomas Waldeck. It appears Waldeck attempted to con Charlie and the suggestion was that Bradbury shot Waldeck as a reprisal. Faced with death, Bradbury had denied the killing and put up a smokescreen, claiming fear of London gangsters who were holding mock trials and torturing their victims and who had forced him to drive the killer to Waldeck's home. In spite of this, Bradbury was found guilty of murder and sentenced to hang.

To escape the rope Bradbury began shouting the odds about Charlie Richardson and his empire of long firm fraud and violent enforcement of his will. At the same time the Heathrow Airport scam and the Smiths fight were filling newspaper columns. It was 'kingdom come' for the Press, especially once Eddie and Frank had been arrested and George Cornell had been gunned down in the Blind Beggar by a rival gang. (Everyone knew it was Ronnie Kray, but at that time no one would say. Even Alby Woods, another of Charlie's friends who had been sitting next to George when he was shot, 'could not identify' the killer.) Police raids brought in Charlie soon after he arrived back in Britain, leaving Bradbury to his fate. He was reprieved some time later.

Dozens of others were rounded up. The Press, recalling with relish the days of the Spot–Hill troubles, gave the trial the full treatment. Stories of witness-tampering during Eddie's trial for the

Smiths fight were printed, with the finger pointing towards Charlie. Evidence of Charlie torturing swindlers and thieves who had crossed him was 'trotted' out by some of the most questionable of witnesses – including one who had given dodgy evidence at Jack Spot's trial. Teeth-pulling, toe-breaking and being nailed to the floor complemented tales of severe beatings where men were said to have swollen to twice their size after Cornell, Moody, Eddie, Fraser and Charlie had punished them. The *tour de force* was the 'torture box', said to be an old army field telephone with a handle which, when cranked, caused an electric current to travel along wires attached to the private parts of Charlie's victims (who were sometimes doused in cold water for maximum efficiency).

All this was vehemently denied by the Richardsons, but they had no chance. Charlie received twenty-five years; Eddie, Fraser and Roy Hall got ten; Tom Clark collected eight. Moody, however, was acquitted. Charlie received another five concurrently for his attempts to nobble the Smiths jury.

After fourteen years Charlie got fed up and walked out of open prison to stroll around London completely ignored by the police. Eventually he was recognised by a young WPC and taken back until his release in 1984. Eddie's story is sadder. After his release he was sentenced in 1990 to twenty-five years for conspiring to import a large cargo of cocaine. I was working on a suburban newspaper when they ran the story of his conviction. The photo they published was so far removed from the Eddie I knew, it broke me up for a while. The editor couldn't understand why I was upset: he could only see the black-and-white story, but life is more than that.

Frank Fraser has achieved celebrity status. Although in the 1950s he was known amongst villains and their retinue as 'the man', his public reputation was obscured by those stories about Spot and Hill. Finally he's been recognised as the artful, daring hardnut we all knew. He continues to be someone you should treat with prudent deference. Although he's retired, he still managed to get shot in the face near the old Clerkenwell haunts where only the ghosts of the Sabinis, Cortesis and Albert Dimes recollect the old days. Darby Sabini died in 1950 and Albert Dimes in 1972.

No doubt the Richardson empire deserved to fall. Underworld conglomerates like theirs are certain to fail, for they are outside the law and so it's just a matter of time before they go down. Long-term criminal organisations cannot succeed, and to operate

ELEPHANT BOYS

in the short-to-medium term they must have the acquiescence and collusion of the police and others in high places. But even then they have no final protection when their activities become public. The law protects the establishment. Largely this includes those running any sort of business until they put a foot publicly wrong.

To bring some perspective: it is the law that allows a crook to set up as a double-glazing salesman, go to a home, charge eight thousand pounds up front, bash out the old windows, ill fit a cheap replacement and leave without finishing the job. When the swindled demand their money back, the crooks declare bankruptcy and open up down the road under a different name to do the same to somebody else. It is the law that allows this, and laws are made by governments. I have met some of the riffraff who have been nailed to the floor. Do this to one or two crooked politicians and businessmen and see the effect it will have on standards in public life in our country.

Was there ever a Don of Soho? The Messinas, who ran prostitutes, had Eugenio. He resembled the archetypical godfather and even suffered exile in the traditional style of American mafiosi. He was strictly a purveyor of flesh, some of it high class, much of it through white slavery of girls abducted or set up by his brothers Carmelo, Alfredo, Attilio and Salvatore. They were Italian immigrants and contemporaries of the Sabinis and Cortesis – all of whom dismissed them as pimps.

The hard men of the London manors and Soho did have their Don. Billy Howard (not to be confused with Billy Haward) had the respect and obedience of the underworld. Importantly, he had an 'in' with the police. He settled grievances and had a hand in everything. He even leaned on the Krays for a percentage of their club earnings. Billy owned a share in several clubs and casinos and headquartered at Winston's night club in Bond Street. He received tribute and provided protection; he knew and corrupted the right people, especially police officers and prison guards. Those who had not paid their contributions received no help. He also doled out good hidings, having reached his position by first of all being a top puncher. In July 1956, as the dust of the race gang wars was settling, Billy Hill tried to live up to his reputation by 'pulling' Billy Howard. It was a serious misjudgement: Billy spanked Hill in front of his friends.

Howard was an Elephant and Castle man with tentacles that reached all around the West End. In many ways he resembled Billy Kimber of old. His is the great untold story of the underworld. Old Dave Morbin, who knew about these things, rated Billy Howard the best.

ELEPHANT BOYS

15. EPILOGUE

Recently I have walked the claustrophobic streets around the back of the Borough. The old Guy's Hospital buildings still stand beside the newer tower block that occupies what once was Great Maze Ponds. Inside, the old building doesn't seem to have changed much. The 'Carbolic' still presides over Newcomen Street, but with no tarry blocks to guard and no doodlebugs to curse. Snowsfields winds its way up to the old Guinness Buildings and Snowsfields School, where children still cavort in the highly-fenced playground. It all seems so small now. I went to peer through the school's fencing, but conscious of the fears associated with lone strangers, I soon moved on.

The debris has gone. So has the rag-and-bone merchant and my Dad's shed. Kipling Park remains. Laxton Street School, where once we rested between homes, has recently been pulled down. Balin House still fronts onto Long Lane. I sneaked a look at the balcony outside No. 60 to see if it would pass my mother's inspection. The flats are run down. The motor car has taken over the 'square', while graffiti vandals have contributed much more to the walls than our chalked arrow finders and occasional sexual remarks. The electricity substation remains, with its ledge still available as a meeting-place. I don't suppose they smoke cigarettes poked into the bowl of a clay pipe as we once did, or get high on Cuban cookies.

Another block of flats occupies what once was the mortuary-cum-water tank. For those who lived there after the war it is easy to recall where once stood Fry's timber store and the bomb-shelter entrances protruding from the rubble. Mermaid Court is there, and

ELEPHANT BOYS

yes, the Blue Eyed Maid. Along the Borough High Street, going towards London Bridge. It is now impossible to see where the entrance to the Deep once stood. What's in the mile of tunnels beneath? Southwark Council told me that the original shelter was in the tunnels of the old King William Street Branch Line which closed before the Second World War. After the war they fell into disrepair and were sealed. Some of the tunnels now comprise part of the ventilation system for the Northern underground line at London Bridge. Some locals I spoke to believe the tunnels are used for storage of government documents and secret material. They say there is a secret entrance from a shop in the Borough High Street.

Across Long Lane is Southall Place, scene of my fight with Billy Mitchell and Brian Howliss. In Crosby Row is Charterhouse Church, which housed the boys' youth club, further along. What was the girls' club is now a crèche.

The Chapmans have gone. So have the Rotherys, the Mitchells and the McDonalds. The ghosts of Freddie Smith, Ruby Sparks and the Boxman would still recognise the old streets around Weston Street, Leathermarket, across Snowsfields to the arches beneath London Bridge and further away at Whites Grounds. You can still buy pie and mash at Manzes in Tower Bridge Road, but no longer watch a sparring match over a whisky American in Toby's. Bankside is now a trendy retreat for City finance wizards and tourists visiting Shakespeare's Globe Theatre or wobbling their way to the Tate Modern over the new Millennium Bridge. The Anchor pub still remains, while the old Clink prison site (which gave its name to world-wide slang) is now a macabre museum. The Borough Market's existence is threatened and a proposed wine metropolis is set to dominate the area. Further on, in the sheds beneath the arches of Waterloo Sation, Buster Edwards ended it all – unable to come to terms with selling flowers for a living.

The Elephant has changed. What Hitler's bombs could not achieve Southwark Council did with ramshackle efficiency. They pulled everything down, erected random blocks of flats and built a grotesque shopping centre with a pink – yes, pink – elephant and castle. It *is* the original, but true to the taste of the area it is hideous. Gone are the Trocadero, the coffee-stall (even the road on whose corner it stood), the George and the Imperial Billiard Hall, closed in 1956 after one last fine for being run as an illegal gaming house.

You can no longer make a date beneath the Guinness clock. A silver-coloured box stands by the circus, as if to challenge its symmetry. The place has no soul: only East Lane is left to remind me of what it once was like. Its final fling was in 1954 when the short space between the circus to Elephant Road was jammed with screaming Teddy boys trying to get into the Trocadero to see Bill Haley and his Comets in *Rock Around the Clock*. Youth culture changed with rock and roll when subtle shades of modern jazz and the crooning of Sinatra and Ella took back-stage to noisy twanging guitars. As talent turned down, the volume went up. Perhaps the décor came to match the music.

I turned the corner into a street, off the Walworth Road, and walked into Frankie Fraser. He has recently moved from Islington, back to the stamping grounds of his youth, now living in a snug house with a hidden garden in Walworth. Frankie is looking fit for his seventy-odd years. We reminisced about the Morbins, Richardsons, Reyburns and Garretts. His last knowledge of Lennie Garrett is that he got badly cut up by someone he opened his street door to.

A walk around Clerkenwell and King's Cross is worthwhile. Clerkenwell still retains its village air, with small cafés, pubs old and new and a cosmopolitan atmosphere. It rivals Soho. The Griffin, Yorkshire Grey and Bull are still there and many streets still remain from the 1920s. Great Bath Street is now Topham Street. Alas the Fratalanza is no more.

At King's Cross the railway station dominates the area; perhaps racing men still locate close to the station. The Bell has disappeared. Collier Street, where Alf Solomon shot Billy Kimber, remains, but the houses are all pulled down. Not far away, the Angel is still recognisable. The whole Borough of Islington is becoming more and more trendy. Tony Blairs have replaced Alf Whites.

Soho is disappointing. Streets are dirty and piled with rubbish. Some sleazy porno parlours tout their tawdry messages to the grey-mac brigade; beggars pester locals and tourists alike and bleary-eyed youngsters, zonked out on drugs, haunt the fun arcades along with rent boys and all sorts of weirdos. The call-girls have gone upmarket and moved to King's Cross. The shop still stands on the corner of Frith and Old Compton Streets, but no

ELEPHANT BOYS

spots of blood speckle the pavement. The clubs I knew have gone, but there are plenty of eating-houses and opportunities for a good night out. I just wish they would clean the place up.

Villains are never far from sight, though the large organised gangs disappeared with the Richardsons and Krays. The Admiral Duncan pub, scene of George Sewell's battering by the Elephant Boys, is now a pink palace, the one that recently suffered a bombing tragedy.

FOOTNOTES TO HISTORY

'Beware uncle Wag when he takes his hat off.' Ada's words stayed with me over the years. A hat pushed into the face or slapped around the chops is a lost art. So is spitting in the face of an opponent to give a moment's edge. 'Always have an edge' (a lovely expression from the movie *The Outlaw Josey Wales*) sums up the attitude of the street-fighters. They fought with hats and coats pushed or thrown into the face, followed by a punch, sometimes from behind because they had circled their opponent before the impediment could be snatched away. I once saw a man beaten to his knees with the skilful use of a trilby. These gangsters mostly fought among themselves, sometimes with fists, or with an open razor with two-thirds of the blade taped to stop it slicing too deeply – just enough to produce a nasty wound in the days when surgery was incapable of preventing a livid scar. Many a cloth cap carried a safety razor blade sewn into its peak.

Another trick was a tabloid-sized newspaper, folded again and again until it fitted into the palm of the hand and was as hard as a stone, a go-anywhere weapon. In my day the *Evening Standard* was favourite. These fellows knew how to bust a nose, gouge an eye, squeeze a bollock and break an arm with accomplished ease. They had a ruthless streak. Most people will tell you they are going to hurt you: sometimes it is a bluff, sometimes they are strong enough to carry out their threat. The professional never lets you know until he's on you. That ability to launch an attack without warning gives a vital edge. I love those old westerns where the young tearaway sizes up the old gunfighter and says, 'What's so different about him? He's only got two hands the same as me.' The difference is that the old hand might be slower, but he makes up the difference by not hesitating that split second into the kill.

ELEPHANT BOYS

These old hands knew when to 'fight or give'. They would play percentages. If the odds were against them they 'give' and wait for a better opportunity. There is also an ability to be unpredictable and inscrutable: it's never easy to know when you're stepping over the mark.

I have mentioned certain people in my text where my understanding of them helped form my early view of life. I cannot help noticing the similarities between them and the characters I have written about. It is an obvious danger when writing about past reputations that the truth about their disreputable lives becomes obscured. These added footnotes concern robbers, some of whom thumbed their nose at corrupt society; thieves and con men who had quicksilver brains; and gangsters with an ability to organise the means of obtaining wealth out of any window of opportunity. I ignore sleazy pornographers, rapists, serial killers, drug dealers and muggers which the underworld and I hold in contempt. I hope this round-up will show why some people, although incorrigible criminals, were also 'lovable rogues'.

The James and Younger Brothers

I took my opening quote from a remark made by Bob Younger after his capture following a calamitous raid on a bank in Northfield, Minnesota in 1876. The most celebrated gang in history must be the James/Younger gang comprising Frank and Jesse James and Cole, Jim and Bob Younger. Although they did not invent train robbery, which had been practised a year earlier by the Reno Brothers in Indiana, they certainly perfected it and can be credited with the first bank robberies. Their technique was simple: ride into town, fire off a lot of guns, cause panic, loot bank, ride out. It worked for many years. Then the gang raided Northfield, way outside their normal territory. They had ten years' successful looting behind them, so perhaps it was bravado that caused them and three others to raid so far from home. The odd three were killed; all three Youngers were badly shot up and captured; and the James boys limped back home to Missouri, where six years later Jesse was murdered for a reward. Frank James and Cole Younger lived out very full lives, finishing on the lecture circuit telling how it was done while lamenting their misguided ways. Despite killings, none of them ever considered they had ever done anything seriously wrong.

Wyatt Earp

This cunning devil was as much con man as frontier peace officer. He developed his reputation by pretending to be associated with many famous outlaws and lawmen of the time. He claimed to have arrested the notorious English gunfighter Ben Thompson following a shoot-out in which a sheriff had been killed; also to have chased Clay Allison out of Dodge City and arrested the notorious Bill Anderson. The Anderson he spoke of was not the terrible Bloody Bill of Civil War days, but some minor horse-thief, and records show that he never arrested Thompson or chastised Allison – both of whom were extremely dangerous men.

Earp was clever at weaving his life story around events that took place 'somewhere else'. He was not Marshal of Dodge City, but one of a number of assistant marshals, and it was probably the assistants who did the fighting. He was arrested for conducting an early confidence scam where a 'gold-brick' was sold in a quick deal to passengers passing through Dodge City on the train. One 'wife' of his was a prostitute and another committed suicide.

He told the story of the Gunfight at the OK Corral many times, refining it to a bullet-by-bullet ballet in the book that was ghosted for him. The notion that anyone in a gunfight could count the seconds and the bullets is bizarre. The truth about the gunfight is that chief of police Virgil Earp deputised his brothers Wyatt and Morgan, and the boozy dentist Doc Holliday, to arrest members of an outlaw clan generally called the Clantons. In the attempt the two McLowery brothers and Billy Clanton were shot to death, Virgil and Morgan were wounded and what was left of the Clantons ran away. The morose gunman John Ringo – often placed at the fight – was enjoying a day off.

Events following the fight show Wyatt was a dangerous man frustrated by his lack of fame. It galled him that others had been written about while he was about to be forgotten. He therefore embroidered a mix of fact and fiction which he peddled to newspapers, magazines and, in his last days, Hollywood. Whatever is said of him, he will not now be forgotten. Alas neither will his fictional Buntline Special, with its ridiculously long barrel, dreamed up by fiction writers.

John Dillinger and Baby Face Nelson

Dillinger's crime spree lasted just fourteen months. In his youth he had been gaoled for his part in a store robbery and received a very stiff sentence for this first offence. In gaol he met professional thieves like Homer Van Meter, Charles Makley and Harry Pierpont. When released he arranged for nine prisoners to crash out of gaol. Before they escaped Dillinger was captured and some of the escapees returned the favour by busting him out of gaol. However, they shot the sheriff.

After capture with his first gang, Dillinger escaped from Crown Point Jail and teamed up with Van Meter, Red Hamilton, Baby Face Nelson and Wag's old friend Tommy Carroll to continue a crime spree which made headlines all over the world. It was the age of the Tommy gun and the high-powered car and no sophisticated security systems.

After a fight, when they were surrounded by the FBI at a roadhouse in the wilds of Wisconsin and escaped in a blazing gun battle, they were hunted down. Carroll was shot dead by detectives Steffen and Walker on 7 June 1934 in Waterloo, Iowa. It was said he reached for a gun – in exchange for which he received five bullets. Under a blanket on the back seat of his parked car was either the whole or the remainder of his arsenal. Also despatched in 1934 was Dillinger after betrayal by Anna Sage, the so-called Woman in Red. He was slain while leaving a cinema in Chicago. One month later Homer Van Meter was set up for the cops to kill and retrieve his stuffed money-belt. Before the year was out Baby Face Nelson was fatally wounded while killing two FBI agents.

Verne Miller and Pretty Boy Floyd

Verne Miller was the real name of Vince Moore, who fired a shot at Wag after being given a going-over after insulting Neva Gerber. Miller worked for Al Capone, but also hired himself out to gangs who wanted a professional gunman for bank raids. In 1933 he and two others – possibly Pretty Boy Floyd and Adam Richetti – killed one FBI agent and three police officers in the attempted rescue of one of Miller's bank-robbing friends who was also killed in the ambush. The event became known as the Kansas City Massacre and, more than any other single act, was responsible for the arming of the FBI and an improvement in their powers of pursuit and capture. J. Edgar Hoover used these circumstances to build the FBI

into almost his own personal secret service capable of frightening even Presidents.

Floyd, probably the most prolific of bank robbers, was gunned down in 1934. Richetti went to the electric chair and Miller was found dead by the side of a highway, thought to have been the victim of a gang war or a punishment squad for bringing so much heat on the underworld.

Bonnie Parker and Clyde Barrow

These Texas scumbags robbed country stores and gas stations, murdering without provocation. In numerous shoot-outs they killed a dozen or so police officers and civilians and became the target of a huge manhunt. After a string of narrow escapes, they were traced to a farm in Louisiana by a mixture of FBI, Texas Rangers and local police officers – one of these, Frank Hamer, had been the nemesis of many old-time Texas bandits. A fusillade of shots perforated the duo's automobile and the nasty pair were so well riddled that it was impossible for later biographers to claim that they had escaped to Mexico (the supposed route of so many notorious gangsters).

Owen Madden

OK, I'm cheating a little bit when I say Madden was England's contribution to American organised crime, but he was born in Liverpool of Irish parents. His record, as the leader of a New York street gang who worked his way up to a syndicate chieftain through killings and extortion, is second to none. New York in the 1920s and '30s had many such gangs. Also nurtured in that environment was Bugsy Siegal – who with Mickey Cohen would subjugate Jack Dragna and the California Mafia – and Dutch Schulz who, unlike Madden, couldn't change with the times. Schulz bucked the syndicate and went to an early grave. Madden oiled the wheels of the syndicate and passed control to Lucky Luciano, retiring to Arkansas where he lived as gangster emeritus until his death in 1965. Jimmy Spenser worked for Madden in his early days: Wag always believed one of the reasons Spenser hurriedly departed New York was that he'd been involved in one of Madden's killings.

Murray Humphreys

Although he was born in America, Humphreys never forgot his Welsh connections. His parents retained British citizenship for many years and maintained contacts back home. The Kimber connection is unclear, mostly because so little is known of Billy Kimber. Humphreys was an early convert to the rackets. He had worked for Big Jim Colosimo, mainly in houses of gambling and prostitution. Unlike Colosimo, he was willing to change with the times and he easily transferred his loyalties to Colosimo's successor, Johnny Torrio. By the time Torrio brought Al Capone from New York as his strongarm man, Humphreys was well placed as the brains within the outfit. He owned and controlled many enterprises and was sufficiently important to be listed by the Chicago Crime Commission as one of the city's most prominent racketeers. He survived years of investigation, only being imprisoned in later life for tax evasion. He succumbed to a heart attack (which didn't prevent stories of murder and suicide) in 1965.

It is one measure of a person's notoriety that their manner of death is often contested in some way. There is no doubt that Humphreys would have been well placed to find Kimber a route back to England. It is intriguing to think that Wag may have used the same route.

Nick Licata

I always thought of Licata as a Los Angeles gang boss, but he seems to have originated in the cities of Chicago and Detroit. He appears in Mafia folklore as an associate of Jack Dragna (rather than a rival) and is always depicted as being in Los Angeles much later than when Bert and Wag worked for him. Wag's stories to Ada add something to the history of the time. My feeling is that Wag had a fondness for Dragna and a loathing for Licata.

It is possible that Licata was implicated in Bert's death. He left for Chicago for a long stay immediately after the murder. In view of what happened to Bert's killer, he may well have been wise. It is also interesting to note that Wag stopped off in Chicago on his way back home and hurriedly left when tipped off that he was in some sort of danger. Could he possibly have sought Murray Humphreys' help in locating Licata?

ELEPHANT BOYS

Soapy Smith

Jefferson Randall Smith had practised all manner of confidence tricks on the American mainland. He was expert at selling fake gold bars and he had a special scam where he hid dollar bills in bars of soap to entice buyers in the mining camps to buy an unappreciated cleaning agent. Soapy, as he became known, had his own men in the crowd who bought the bars and did a jig when they found a dollar inside. (Of course, no one else found one.) He transferred his operations to ships carrying prospectors to the Alaskan goldfields, then on to land at Skagway where he systematically relieved Klondikers of their purses and sometimes their lives. He controlled the town, appointing his own police officers and judges, and stealing as he pleased. Eventually a vigilante organisation set out to clean up Smith's outfit. Undaunted, he decided to fight them. In the final showdown Soapy and the vigilante leader, Frank Reid, shot each other to death on the Skagway dockside.

William Howe and Abe Hummel

Howe and Hummel were the original shyster lawyers. Located in New York, they brought about the acquittal of murderers and racketeers through the brilliant flamboyant oratory of the times and prolific use of bribes. Thieves came to them for protection and guidance; politicians feared their ability to manipulate the legal system; many also feared exposure for favours done. New York had more corrupt officials than any city at any time. Howe and Hummel became wealthy on retainers. They became so powerful and threatening that it took framing, disbarring and gagging to get rid of them. Abe Hummel fled to England and tried unsuccessfully to corrupt the British legal system. He died in London in 1926.

Robin Hood and Dick Turpin

We can dismiss Robin Hood quickly: he exists only in fantasy on only the flimsiest evidence of reality. Along with King Arthur and Odysseus he belongs to the myths. Because we would like to believe he existed, he will endure.

Turpin is different, he is both myth and reality. I suppose he is east London's contribution to this survey of the disreputable. Born in Essex, he was part of a gang of robbers and murderers who were mostly exterminated for the high rewards put on them. Turpin escaped to become a persistent highwayman. His image is inextricably linked with the tricorn hat and cloak and his ride to York on Black Bess – all debatable, probably untrue. He was the most hunted man of his time and scored spectacular successes on the road. His reputation was such that he changed the habits of travellers in and out of London. While sojourning in York, under the name John Palmer, he was arrested for poaching. Letters that he wrote led to his true identity and he regained the celebrity status which persists to this day, even though he was hanged in 1739.

Jonathan Wild

When looking for historic London underworld bosses it is not easy to find distinct characters in the fog of British criminal history. Wild is a perfect example of the cunning all-round bad man. He was a receiver of stolen goods, a bounty hunter, robber chief, extortionist, blackmailer and murderer who served both sides of the law – often collecting rewards for rivals he sent to the gallows. With more than a touch of megalomania, he exhibited the empire of larcenists and murderers he had put together and strutted the streets of London with his band of ruffians, demanding respect and tribute in goods and money. It couldn't last: Wild was arraigned for multiple offences and publicly hanged at Tyburn Tree, close to Marble Arch, west London, in 1725. Dickens most probably had him in mind when he dreamed up the villainous Fagin.

Sidney Street Siege

While the saga of Stinie Morrison was being acted out an event happened which caught the public's imagination and took the spotlight off Stinie for a while. Variously called the Houndsditch murders and the Siege of Sidney Street, it came about in December 1910 when three policemen were shot down during an attempt to arrest some burglars. In January 1911 the gang of thieves was traced to a tenement block at 100 Sidney Street in London's East End, from where they opened fire wounding another policeman. A massive force of armed police cleared people from the buildings while exchanging shots with the besieged gunmen. The gangsters could not be dislodged.

Sensing an early moment for greatness, Home Secretary Winston Churchill sent in soldiers and made a highly publicised personal visit to the scene. To the Press, what was a local gang of thieves

ELEPHANT BOYS

suddenly became insidious anarchists led by one Peter the Painter. During more exchanges of gunfire the building caught fire and the gunmen were prevented from leaving the building by a fusillade of shots when they tried to fight their way out. Two bodies were found in the fire-gutted building, both of local gangsters of uncertain backgrounds. This allowed Churchill to further the story of anarchism, so as to rebut accusations of glory hunting. Peter the Painter never was caught: even today it's not known if he really existed. Stories of the siege, anarchism and Stinie Morrison are often intermixed, but with no connection ever proved.

Charles Peace

His was the name every child knew as a London crook, with a reputation second only to Jack the Ripper. The difference is that Peace was a thief so skilful in the art of disguise that he moved freely around London despite being the subject of the largest manhunt of the time. I remember my Dad telling me stories of Peace casing a joint while disguised as a musician playing a violin in the street. Although he fits well into south London folklore, Peace was actually from Sheffield and fled to London when suspected of murder. He settled in Evelina Road, Peckham, south London (later Billy Howard country) from where, he committed a series of burglaries using an extensive home-made thieves' toolkit. Arrested after shooting a policeman during a struggle to detain him, he was seriously injured when he jumped from a train returning him for trial for a murder in Sheffield. Peace was hanged in 1879.

Chicago May (Mary Sharpe)

Mary was a Dublin lass who intimidated, blackmailed and grafted her way through life. After a start in Ireland she transferred her unwholesome talents to the USA, where she became Chicago May Churchill – wife of Dal Churchill, a train and bank robber who overstrained his talents and was left dangling from a telegraph pole by a frisky posse.

May developed a career of prostitution, excelling in the badger game (where unwary clients were blackmailed after photographs were taken, usually along with their wallets) to make her name a byword for nastiness. Some of this was in partnership with Dal's replacement, Eddie Guerin. Driven out of Chicago, then New York,

ELEPHANT BOYS

May touted her trade around Europe's major cities. She paused only to help Eddie to rob the American Express Company's Paris office of a quarter of a million dollars: a tidy sum not far into the twentieth century.

Eddie went to Devil's Island. May did slightly better and alighted in London, where she carried on her evil ways. When Eddie tired of the climate in the Americas he joined her, but also had a little dalliance with her young friend, which nearly proved fatal. May and her debauched bodyguard, Cubby Jackson, shot Eddie outside a Bloomsbury hotel. May's looks and disposition were not improved by a fifteen-year sentence for attempted murder.

Messina Brothers

Not my kind of gangsters, these sleazy imports built up a significant vice empire in Mayfair, London, in the 1930s. They were born in Egypt of Italian parents. During the war years they continued developing their brothels by bringing girls from abroad to add to the home-grown variety who were already serving American GIs. Supposedly hunted by police because they had not registered for service in the armed forces, the brothers always managed to evade capture. There was some suggestion that money was changing hands. They survived through the 1940s and grudgingly earn a place here because they did do battle with other gangs engaged in the same enterprise.

Eugenio was gaoled for slashing the tips of two fingers off Carmelo Vassalo, the leader of a gang of Maltese pimps who tried to recruit some Messina girls. In 1951 they were the subject of a major exposure by *People* crime reporter Duncan Webb. This led to brothers Eugenio, Attilio, Carmelo, Salvatore and Alfredo being gaoled or driven out of the country. It has to be said they exploited a weakness of other gangs who looked down on prostitution as something only foreigners got involved in. The size of the Messina empire caught everyone by surprise. They turned Mayfair – one of the West End's most prestigious addresses – into a tawdry flesh market. One story Jack Spot told in his Cumberland sit-ins was of charging the brothers for protection after roughing up the good-looking procurer Attilio, who couldn't risk having his face carved.

Donald Hume

An interesting fact about *People* reporter Duncan Webb is that he

ELEPHANT BOYS

married Cynthia, the ex-wife of murderer Donald Hume. Hume had killed Warren Street dealer and car-thief Stan Setty (to avoid paying for cars provided for sale on the black market), cut up his body and dumped it from an aeroplane over the Essex marshes. The bits of Setty recovered were not enough to convict him of murder, although Hume admitted to the crime in later years when he was free from prosecution. It took the Swiss to gaol him for murder after he shot a taxi driver while escaping from a bank robbery. Deported to England, he died insane.

Webb's nose for a good story made the *People* the best crime newspaper. What is less known about him is that he also liked the company of crooks, failing to tell on his favourites such as Billy Hill.

Nash Gang

The Pen Club did for the Nashes what Mr Smith and the Witchdoctor was to do for the Richardsons. The club was located in Duval Street, Whitechapel: one of the seediest streets in the East End and adjacent to the patch where Jack the Ripper had slaughtered five women.

Managing the club was Fay Sadler, who was Tommy Smithson's girlfriend at the time I knocked Tommy out in the Forty-seven Club; she played host to the badmen of their time, including the Nash brothers from Islington, who are said to have had an interest in the club. They were into blackmail and extortion – backed up by their boxing skills and a team of similarly qualified hard men.

On the night of 6 February 1960, Jimmy Nash and two of his minders set about Selwyn Cooney. At that time Cooney was manager of Billy Hill's New Cabinet Club, but he was playing an away game at the Pen. A few days earlier he had given Ronnie Nash a black eye in a quarrel over a motoring incident; his come-uppance was to be floored by a rain of punches and kicks from Jimmy and his mates. The sound of breaking furniture brought club bouncer, Billy Ambrose, upstairs to enquire what all the fuss was about. He was answered with a bullet in the stomach. Seconds later Cooney was shot in the head. Ambrose survived, Cooney did not. He was found sprawled across the pavement in Duval Street.

Jimmy stood trial for murder. That trial was abandoned, due to a spot of attempted jury nobbling, but he stood trial a second time. Even Jimmy could not conceal his surprise at the not-guilty verdict; alas he did have to put up with five years for causing grievous bodily harm to a dead man.

The affray brought the whole Nash operation into close scrutiny and it emerged that they had stepped into the void left after Billy Hill's retirement. An interesting suggestion was that Selwyn Cooney had also been vying to be the new 'Boss of Britain's Underworld'. Whatever the truth, the Nash gang faded with startling alacrity, leaving the way clear for their pals the Richardsons and Krays.

To round off, I must mention two real spinechillers who belonged to my Dad's childhood, but were often used to curdle our blood when Dad wanted to put the wind up us.

Jack the Ripper

In 1888, the year after my Dad was born, Jack the Ripper struck in a series of five grisly murders in the streets around Whitechapel in London's East End. In those same streets the forebears of Alf Solomon and Jack Spot were putting down their London roots. The quantity of the killings is small compared to latter-day serial killers, yet he's most likely the best-known multiple murderer. So many theories abound about the Ripper, which only go to prove that nobody knows who he really was. He is a figure to frighten naughty kids – like the 'bogeyman' who will 'get you'. Just as my Dad was warned against late-night adventures, he used the same tales to chill the blood of his children who could easily believe the Ripper was still out there in the darkness.

Neill Cream

This other chiller haunted the streets around Waterloo in 1891, a weird quack doctor who coasted the low dives of north Lambeth. Dressed in top hat and cloak, he dished out powders and pills to young ladies plying their trade. The potions, containing strychnine, brought about at least four agonising deaths – two in Stamford Street, just around the corner from Broadwall, where William and Phoebe McDonald once lived. Though born in Scotland, Cream had been reared in Canada and had a string of poisonings behind him in Canada and the USA before bringing his ministry to England. For me he has all the credentials for Jack the Ripper; alas he is said to have been in prison in Illinois at the time of the Ripper murders. He dangled from a British rope in 1892.

ELEPHANT BOYS